D1497171

MEMORIES
OF TIMES PAST

Memories
of Times Past

Stories and Photos Recalling Life
in the Early 20th Century.

Marta Hiatt

Northern Star Press, Publishers
http://www.NorthernStarPress.com

Northern Star Press, Publishers
http://www.NorthernStarPress.com

Copyright 2008 Marta Hiatt
NorthernStarPress@earthlink.net

Library of Congress Cataloging-in-Publication Data
Hiatt, Marta,
Memories of Times Past/Marta Hiatt
Includes bibliographical references and index
ISBN 978-0-9620929-4-7
History. 2. Americana. 3. Twentieth Century. Title.
Library of Congress Control number: 2007942025
Printed in the United States of America
First Printing, 2008

Book design by www.KareenRoss.com

*A Nostalgic Collection of Personal Stories and
Photographs Recalling the Way Life Was in
the Early Part of the Twentieth Century*

PRAISE FOR MEMORIES OF TIMES PAST

"*Memories of Times Past will appeal to both a younger audience who will sometimes be amazed at the way things were, and older people whose own memories will be stimulated by reading these interesting stories, and viewing the photographs about the past. It's a great book!*"
—**Art Linkletter, star of TV and radio.**

"*I had no idea I was old enough to recognize and relish so much of the past that Marta Hiatt recreated in this lovely, charming, worthwhile read. Those who take my advice and read it will thank her for this relief from our troubled present.*"
—**Ed Asner, Actor**

"*One cannot dip into this book without staying awhile. - You'll be surprised at what you recall.*"
—**Betty White,** *author, actress, star of "The Golden Girls."*

"*Reading the stories in this book took me back to a pre-teen time— I'm in New England listening to Jack Benny on the radio. At the exact same time Johnny Carson was in Iowa, listening to t he same program. Little did we know we were schooling ourselves for the great adventure called 'The Tonight Show!'*"
—**Ed McMahon,** *Television personality, comedian and author.*

"*Illustrated with a wealth of vintage black & white photographs, "Memories of Times Past," is a journey of nostalgia touching upon the highlights of modern American history. ...The snippets of revelation about how daily American life used to be are driven home with firsthand testimonies of ordinary people who lived in those times. This is a virtual American history museum in book form.*"
—**Midwest Book Review, Orgeon, WI.**

OTHER BOOKS BY MARTA HIATT

Mind Magic, Techniques for Transforming Your Life,
Llewellyn Worldwide Inc., 2001 (*www.martahiatt.com*)

Inspirational Quotations from the Concept-Therapy Philosophy
Northern Star Press, 2008

Northern Star Press
http://www.NorthernStarPress.com
NorthernStarPress@earthlink.net

ABOUT THE AUTHOR

Marta Hiatt, Ph.D., MFT, has a doctorate in Psychology and is a retired psychotherapist who had a private practice in San Jose, California for 25 years. She is also author of "Mind Magic, Techniques for Transforming Your Life," and "Inspirational Quotations From the Concept-Therapy Philosophy." Dr. Hiatt was on the faculty of the Continuing Education Department of the University of Santa Clara, and taught seminars in self-development in the San Francisco Bay Area for many years.

You can contact Dr. Hiatt at
NorthernStarPress@earthlink.net

DISCLAIMER

The author has made every effort prior to publication to identify copyright holders and secure their permission to print copyrighted photographs. If notified, the author will be pleased to rectify any omission of acknowledgement at the earliest opportunity.

ACKNOWLEDGEMENTS

I am very grateful to all the people who contributed their stories and photographs to this book: friends, family, acquaintances and even strangers. Learning the way they lived in the past has been both educational and fascinating. I especially wish to thank the many people whose old photographs were published in "Reminisce Magazine, the Magazine of the Good Old Days," who gave me permission to publish their photos in this book.

I am also appreciative to be living in the age of the Internet and the World Wide Web. Without this huge resource, the research involved in producing this book would have taken many years.

To my family:
Lorraine, Adrian and Linda

CONTENTS

PREFACE

On my sixty-fourth birthday I sat in the warm sunshine in my Southern California garden, full of flowers still blooming in December, sipped my Colombian coffee, and contemplated the extraordinary historical changes since I was born in 1935. As I reflected on some of the incredible events that have occurred, I thought it would be interesting to review a small part of history through the personal stories of people who were eye-witnesses to the dramatic changes in American life in the 1900s, particularly those born in the first half of the century. For four years I wrote letters, sent emails, and endlessly quizzed friends, family, and even strangers I met in the grocery store or on a plane. Compiled here are their personal remembrances of the enormous changes that have occurred in their lifetimes; a trip down memory lane for the older generation and, perhaps, some surprising insights into the way life was, for those who are younger.

This book is a nostalgic journey back to a time of Model-T Fords, stay-at-home-moms, vinyl long-playing records, atom-bomb shelters, strict rules of etiquette, radio days and manual typewriters.

People who lived in the twentieth century witnessed more change in their daily lives than anyone who ever lived throughout history. This past century had enormous impact on the evolution of mankind, especially in the technological advances that have improved and simplified our lives, while at the same time making them more stressful and complex, requiring great coping abilities.

The greatest technological changes were in the communication revolution, from the first wireless telegraph message in 1901, to fax machines, modems, Palm Pilots, e-mail and the Internet. At the beginning of the century, electricity was a luxury, transportation was still largely by railroad or horse and buggy and, if you were fortunate enough to have a telephone, it did you little good, since few of your neighbors had one. The first airplane flight was launched in 1903 and, sixty years later, mankind was traveling in outer space and walking on the moon! Radios didn't begin to proliferate until the 1920s but, by the last half of the century, we had televisions hooked up to the World Wide Web beaming satellite photos of events around the world the moment they were happening. For people born in the early 1900s, the changes have been staggering!

In his inaugural speech accepting re-election as president in 1996, William Jefferson Clinton said:

What a century it has been! America became the world's mightiest industrial power; saved the world from tyranny in two world wars and a long cold war and, time and again, reached across the globe to millions who longed for the blessings of liberty...

Indeed...what an amazing century it was! I hope you enjoy this trip down memory lane or, for those born in the latter half of the twentieth century, learn how different life was for your parents and grandparents.

Marta Hiatt,
Long Beach, California

CHAPTER ONE

Lifestyle:

from Uptight Conformity to "Let it all Hang Out"

At the end of the twentieth century, people who were born in the first half, (and even some of those who were not), longed for the "good old days," especially of the forties and fifties. The decades immediately after World War II were ones of great prosperity where a life-long marriage, respectful and well-behaved children, and the legendary "home with a white picket fence," were the prevailing values. But those who look back in longing for the supposed serenity of the past often overlook its difficulties. Every age has its hardships, but also its particular improvements. Everyday living was much harsher in the early part of the century than it is now, and physical labor was a part of most people's daily life.

At the beginning of the century, only fourteen percent of homes had a bathtub, and only eight percent had a telephone. Most women washed their hair only once a month, and used borax or egg yolks for shampoo. Many generations lived in the same house, or on the same street, as their relatives. If someone decided to leave home they usually rented a room, or a flat in a boarding house, because apartment buildings were basically unknown. Sometimes these homes served meals as part of the rental agreement because the housewife was home all day and could easily cook for two or three more.

I lived on a farm when I was a boy in the thirties, and one thing I especially didn't like about it was there wasn't any bathroom. That meant we didn't have a bathtub, so every Saturday night my mom would heat buckets of water on the wooden stove, and fill up this huge tin tub. It took forever to get that ugly thing full of water. Then each of the six kids had to take turns getting into it and getting bathed. Of course the water never got changed, so you didn't want to be the last one in! On the other hand, we didn't have the consciousness about hygiene that people have now and, being kids, how dirty the water was didn't make much difference to us. What was more important, was how cold it was by that time.

We had an outhouse in the field behind the house, so you sure didn't want to have to go to the toilet after dark when there were all kinds of noises and little critters out there. Maybe even snakes! If we had to go in the middle of the night, we always kept a potty under the bed that we'd use. For toilet paper we kept the old Sears, Roebuck catalogs in there and tissue-wrappers from crates of fruit that mom used for canning. That was pretty primitive. I'm amazed we didn't always have constant rashes. -- Billy Joe Simpson, barber, born 1940, Atlanta, GA.

Today's technological advances mean people in northern states no longer have to awaken shivering in a frigid home where the pipes may have frozen overnight, and the coal-burning furnace didn't warm the house until you had washed and were eating breakfast. Until the mid '50s, coal was the most predominant heating fuel, except in gas-rich areas of Texas and Oklahoma, which were heated with natural gas. And it was very dirty. Every chimney spewed thick, black, sooty smoke all winter, and some of it made its way into the house. Firing was an hourly chore, trudging up and down dark basement stairs. Some homes had hot-water heat from room radiators which were much cleaner burning. Now the simple matter of turning up the thermostat makes the house toasty warm before your morning coffee is ready. Or, you can put the thermostat on auto and prewarm the house before you even get out of bed. This kind of luxury, which we take for granted, was unheard of until almost the middle of the century.

It was my job to help dad carry out the ashes from the furnace once a week in a big tin tub, and leave them on the sidewalk in front of the house for the coal man to empty into his truck and haul away. It was a dirty, messy job, but it wasn't as bad as the job the poor guy had who delivered the coal. If you forgot to leave the basement window open for the coal to be poured into, he just left it on the ground and you had to shovel it into the basement yourself, and then shovel it into the furnace. What a hassle that was! – Ray Harting, retired, born 1929, Trenton, OH.

In spite of modern conveniences, the double-income family today has a different set of hardships. The kids are often packed into a bus that may take them miles to an integrated school, while their parents sit in traffic for a long and tedious commute to the office. Their latch-key children won't come home to mom preparing milk and homemade cookies for them, and then go outside and play with the neighbors' kids. Instead they will probably return to an empty house, get their own snack, and glue their eyeballs to the TV. Their parents will arrive home late, hungry and exhausted, and often prepare a quick frozen dinner, or maybe phone for a pizza, while they all sack out on the couch watching television; too tired to do much else. The time saved with modern appliances is often spent on the road commuting .

Caro, Michigan, 1917

Caro, 1946

The 1917 picture above, of the small town of Caro, in the thumb of Michigan, shows the original Hotel Montague on the left, which burned down and was rebuilt of brick. Beyond it is the old fire hall with a bell tower to ring numbers. Each area of town was assigned a number, and by listening to that number everyone knew where the fire was. For example, 36 would be 3 rings followed by 6 rings. In 1946 the town was fully decorated for Christmas to welcome home the returning World War II veterans. – Charles Beyette, Cass, MI.

Please Entertain Me

The social interaction of playing card and board games has been replaced by the isolation of watching television. Before TV, when couples invited friends over for dinner, having nothing else to do after the meal they often sat down to a game of bridge, or Monopoly, or even poker. Housewives with a little extra time often invited neighborhood women to a game of bridge every Wednesday afternoon. But friends seldom get together to play card games anymore, instead, after dinner they often retire to the living room to watch a video rented from the local Blockbuster. Occasionally, a fad such as Trivial Pursuit comes along, and for a time people gather around the table and enjoy interacting with each other.

We no longer have to go outside to interact with the world because we can now do it on our home computer, or TV, or state-of-the-art audio and video entertainment centers, where we can pre-tape the shows we like to watch, and even skip through the commercials if we want. Then we can wrap ourselves in a blanket and curl up on the couch, safely ensconced in our little cocoons, protected and isolated from the big bad world outside our dead-bolted door with the "Beware of Dog" sign in the security-alarmed window. For those of us from an older generation, the carefree and safe days of our youth are forever gone; for us, our children and our grandchildren.

Mildred Courtney (2nd from right) and neighborhood ladies playing bridge in 1950, in Missouri

People today often wonder what we "old-timers" did to occupy ourselves in the evenings when we didn't have television. They seem to think our lives were boring then. Actually, what I think is boring is how people live now — being vicariously entertained by those mindless sitcoms, instead of using their own imaginations and inventing things to do. Society is dumbing down because we don't even read books anymore; in fact, a lot of people don't even read a newspaper, and they have very little idea of what's happening in the world.

In our family we always ate meals together; mother and my sisters and I prepared them, and we cleaned up afterward too. Dad and my brothers retired to the living room where dad usually read the paper, and the boys played a game together, usually on the floor. When dad wasn't reading the paper he was often in his workshop in the basement fixing something. When we kids did our homework there might be some mellow music playing on the radio, with very few commercials, but there was no background noise from the TV to interfere with our concentration. Sometimes my mom played the piano after supper and we all stood around it and sang. I loved those times, and they're some of fondest memories of my childhood.

The author's parents in 1932, both operatic singers

We read books and even had conversations! We were creative; we played board games together as a family, and we invented games. On Sunday evenings we all sat around the table and listened to the radio together, programs like   "The Lone Ranger," "Jack Benny," "Fred Allen," "George and Gracie Burns" and "The Shadow Knows."

Of course everyone had chores to do, and we didn't expect to get paid for them. If my brother wanted to play baseball with the boys at the park he had to mow the lawn first, or maybe wash the storm windows before he'd help dad put them up tomorrow. We girls would help mom prepare supper, which might involve peeling a big pot of potatoes, or a big bunch of carrots, or shuck a bowl of peas. After supper we'd wash the dishes, and maybe fold the laundry.

On Sundays we would all pile into our new silver Pontiac convertible and actually go for a ride! We didn't have freeways, only highways, just two lanes, sometimes not even paved, and there were few cars on them because not many people could afford one. In the summer we would all go to the beach—it wasn't even crowded, and the water was clean. Or, we would go to the community pool at the YMCA. On festive occasions we would visit our grandparents where we kids read comic books and played board games. The adults sat around the huge oblong dining room table which encompassed almost the entire room, and ate grandma's delicious food, which she'd spent all day preparing, and talked to each other. Sometimes they argued about politics, but at least they interacted and exchanged ideas. I really enjoyed our visits to grandma's. – Lorraine D'Angelo, born 1936, Toronto.

Grandma D'Angelo loading the table with food in 1940

Enjoying the Outdoors

What did we do when we were kids in the '40s? After school and during the summer, we found all kinds of ways to amuse ourselves outside, because we had no other choice. We didn't have Nintendo or any kind of video games or Internet chat rooms, so we found some creative ways to entertain ourselves. We played with marbles and jacks and, if we had a ball, we could play handball against a wall, or we would find a stick, or even mom's broom, and use it for a bat. We would draw squares on the sidewalk with chalk and play hopscotch, or get a jumprope and skip double-Dutch, or sometimes even just play tag. It's amazing what you can do when you have a lot of imagination and very little money. The neighborhood was always full of kids out on the streets who would come around and join our games. And they were always welcome; the more kids, the more fun we had. Often we'd leave home in the morning during the summer and play all day with our friends, coming back in time for supper. Of course our parents couldn't reach us all day because we didn't have cell phones or pagers then, but no one was worried about us. Life was safe.

I remember when we were really small we lived in a house that had a huge yard stuffed with full, overhanging trees that created arbors and caves and neat places to hide, so we could amuse ourselves for hours out there; just me and my two siblings. Another happy memory I have of that house was that, in the Fall, my dad used to burn the leaves in a huge barrel, and I loved the smell of that. You can't do that anymore because of the air pollution, but we had so few people and cars in those days that it wasn't a problem.

When we got a little older we had roller skates to skate around the neighborhood challenging each other to go faster. But we didn't have the fancy "in-line" blades of today; sometimes it was just a pair of steel wheels welded onto a metal slab that we latched to the soles of our shoes, with a key to tighten them. And the shoes weren't expensive $150 Reeboks or Nikes, they were just a pair of plain shoes with leather soles that quickly wore out.

In the wintertime we found lots of things to do: the usual snow-ball fights, and building a snowman, and there was a park at the end of our street that had tennis courts that were turned into a skating rink in the winter, so we spent most of our evenings ice skating there. When we were lucky enough to get our dad to take us for a drive out to the country, we'd throw our sleds into the trunk of the car and spend the day sledding down the hills. And there was no charge either for a full day of fun. It's no wonder we weren't chubby like a lot of kids today—we got so much exercise. We really did things together as a family, and those are the happiest moments of my childhood. –Adrian Brutus, born 1939, Charlevoix, MI.

Sweet Sixteen

When we were teenagers in the forties we weren't afraid of criminals, or child molesters or drive-by shootings; we were more afraid of our parents, or our friends' parents, if we did something wrong. And if mom found out, she would often say: "Just wait till your father gets home." That usually meant a spanking. We didn't do drugs because there weren't any and only bad men on skid row did evil things like that. The most trouble we got into was getting hold of a few cigarettes, usually snitched from mom's purse, and smoking them out by the back fence where we couldn't be seen from the windows of the house. It wasn't fun because we choked and coughed the entire time, but we wanted to be sophisticated like Humphrey Bogart and Ingrid Bergman.

In the evenings during the summer, when we were teenagers, we would sit out on the front porch and watch for our friends to come by and chat, or maybe even play a game. Now in the West there aren't any porches anymore so kids can't do that. In my day we usually hung out at the local coffee shop where they'd let us sit for hours just drinking mugs of black coffee and maybe having a muffin or some toast - white bread of course because that's all there was. Restaurants and kids' homes were our gathering places because we didn't have cars, so we didn't drive up and down the street endlessly cruising like they do now, and there were no shopping malls to hang out at. Most parents preferred to have their teenagers invite other kids to their house so they could keep an eye on them. By the fifties a few of the boys had cars and they made parents frantic if their daughters weren't home on time. Because there wasn't any birth control available to unmarried people, the back seat of the car was the most frequent place that girls got pregnant.

Things are so different now. Kids come home from school and there's no one there, and they have nothing to do except watch TV or hang out at the shopping mall with their friends and maybe even get high, or find some kind of trouble to get into. They sure don't organize games to play together, that wouldn't be cool. – Jordan Harbor, executive, born 1942 in Buffalo, NY.

My sister Barbara (left) and I loved listening to our old 78-rpm
records in the '50s at our home in New Kensington, PA. Note the pull-out
record player and fold-out radio behind us. - Gloria Pomykala

Blue Laws

At the beginning of the twentieth century most people worked six or even seven days a week. The five-day work week was instituted in 1935 so that people could have more rest and relaxation. Four years later, in 1938, the forty-hour work week was established. When women began to work outside the home during World War II, Saturdays were needed to do chores, because Sunday was reserved as the Lord's day. As recently as the 1970s many cities had laws on the books commonly known as "blue laws," which were designed to preserve the sanctity of Sunday, the Sabbath day, and encourage people to attend church. Shopping and laundry were not to be done on Sundays, and most cities closed down completely. This was a great inconvenience to many people who couldn't buy a loaf of bread, go to the Laundromat, browse in a bookstore or library, or go to the bank until Monday morning. Extra food had to be on hand in case guests dropped in for dinner unexpectedly, because the housewife couldn't run to the store for two more pork chops. Children had better not develop a cold or a bad cough on Saturday because mom couldn't get any cough medicine until 11 a.m. Monday morning. People who had to work on Saturdays were particularly inconvenienced by these restrictive laws because they didn't have a day to run errands. Although Jews observed the Sabbath on Saturday, they were outvoted by the Christians, and thus they had two days in which they couldn't do chores or shop. Some young entrepreneurs took advantage of this and earned pocket money by offering to run errands for the neighborhood Jews.

Gradually, shopping malls began to appear, often skirting the highway at the edge of town, where they were not governed by the rules of the city. National Department Stores opened the first mall in a suburb of Saint Louis. They were open on Sundays and did much of their business on that day. Increasingly, the practice of strolling down Main Street to shop was replaced by walking for blocks through strip malls.

Because the blue laws were really designed less for giving people an opportunity to go to church, and more for merchants who didn't want to pay their staff seven days a week, the competition from shopping malls, and public demand, finally won out. As more and more women joined the work force, the need for Sunday shopping became a necessity, and blue laws were either changed or ignored, much to the chagrin of devout Christians.

I think Laundromats sprang up in the early '50s. I rented a room in someone's house at that time and I remember they wouldn't let me use their washing machine, which was down in the basement, so I had to carry my laundry in a big brown grocery bag for three blocks, and pay a dime to wash it. Of course I didn't have a car, and we didn't have plastic bags either. Mini-markets started to open around then and, years later, 7-11's, because a lot of people worked nights and weekends and couldn't get groceries, especially on Sunday when everything was closed. – Tracy Pickering, born 1936, Detroit, MI.

The first TV dinners arrived in 1952, packaged to look like a TV screen, and had to be heated in the oven because there were no microwaves. Price for a turkey dinner with mashed potatoes and peas: $1.29.

In November,1996, the City Council of Oakland, California decided to purge some old laws from the books that were no longer applicable. This included a law against washing your underwear on Sunday!

The Great World War: Bombs, Bogart and Butter

America was in shock on that "day of infamy," December 7, 1941, when Japanese fighter planes wreaked havoc on the military base at Pearl Harbor. The U.S. was no longer safe. We declared war, but it was four long years before America could claim victory.

The war years were a time of parties and glamour, where men wore tuxedos to the theater, and women twisted their hair into a French roll and wore full-length satin and velvet dresses. Ballroom dancing was in fashion, and Vogue magazine featured evening gowns appropriate for showing off on the dance floor. People tried to counter the anxiety and distress of the war by living for the moment, and many a marriage was quickly arranged between men and women overseas, or on their way.

The war popularized cocktail lounges and restaurants with jukeboxes where, for a nickel, one could listen to "The White Cliffs of Dover" or "You'd be so Nice to Come Home To." Cocktail parties became fashionable in the forties where, instead of being invited to a sit-down dinner party, large groups of people stood around drinking martinis, smoking, and trying to be charming. People came and went at no set time, and bounced around from person to person. It was usually very superficial.

Courtesy Library of Congress

I remember my parents used to have 'spaghetti and poker parties' every Saturday night during World War II. We had a nanny then who shooed us kids off to bed, but we used to sneak out of our rooms and watch them from the top of the banister. A lot of middle-class families had maids or nannies in those days to help the housewife with her chores, and the usual three or four kids.

Tables were set up in the living room with about six people at each table playing poker, and my mom was one of the best players. There were lots of cocktails and cigarettes on the tables, because almost everyone smoked and drank back then. The popular "Warsaw Concerto" was constantly playing on the phonograph, but of course someone had to get up at the end of the record and put the needle back to the beginning of it so they could hear it again.

In case there was an air-raid warning, my folks pulled the heavy blue-velvet drapes tight, and they even pinned together the little cracks where the drapes met. No light was supposed to be seen outside the house. These warnings happened frequently and were very scary, but not nearly as frightening as it was for people living in Britain or France where it was followed by real bombs. – Betty Roberts, waitress, born 1938, Toledo, OH.

World War II also brought restrictions: sugar, soap, milk and steaks were hard to get. Many states introduced rationing for commodities which were in short supply, and gave people a certain number of coupons, based on the number of people in their family. Gasoline was rationed in 1942, but that wasn't much of a hardship because few people had a car. The garishness of the nineteenth century was replaced by the simplicity imposed by the war's restrictions, and the new word in decorating was "modern," which meant no ornate frills like they had in the past.

Courtesy Library of Congress

We got coupons for meat during the war, and of course there were never enough for a family of six. My mom managed to get some nylon stockings where she worked, and she'd take a couple of pairs down to the butcher and he'd give her a few steaks in exchange. We had chicken every Sunday, but it was only one chicken divided up between mom and dad and four little kids. I'm amazed my mom made it go around. I supplemented by eating lots of bread and peanut butter later in the evening. Milk was rationed too; in fact the first summer job I had as a teenager was counting the milk coupons collected by Acme Farmers Dairy. Once your coupons were used up, that was it for the week, so needless to say we didn't drink too much of it. — Sara Humphrey, former history teacher, born 1934, Toronto.

A Shopper Uses Stamps From Her Rationing Book During WWII

When nylon stockings first appeared, women rushed to the stores to get them. Before that we had silk stockings for those who could afford them. In 1945 nylons were $4 a pair, out of the financial reach of most women, so we wore rayon or cotton ones which were thick and ugly, but they weren't nearly as bad as the horrible Lyle ones I had to wear to school back in the thirties. Because nylons were in short supply, if we got a run we would sew it up with matching thread with as tiny and neat a stitch as we could make. Eventually, when they had two or three prominent stitched runs, we

had to throw them out. They also had a dark seam down the back and that was a big pest because you were forever tugging at it trying to keep it in a straight line down your legs. I don't know what the point of that was. We had only begun wearing them when the war broke out, and we had to give them up for cotton stockings because nylon was needed for parachutes. —Angela Corelli, homemaker, born 1920 in Detroit, MI.

Woolen and cotton fabrics became very scarce because they were needed for the military, and polyester had not yet been invented to take their place. Leather was also needed for boots and coats, so civilians were issued coupons to buy shoes, some of which were soled in cardboard-like materials.

To help out with the war effort, in 1943, our elementary school class in Owosso, Michigan was asked to knit afghan squares for wounded veterans. (I'm in the front row, right.) - Richard Mathewson, Norman, OK

I remember my kids wanting to ride tricycles or be pulled in a wagon, but we couldn't buy them anymore because metal was so scarce. My son kept patching up his old bicycle because there was no hope of getting a new one. Even roller skates were nowhere to be seen because they required metal to make. The kids' toys were mostly made of wood. Towards the end of the war, you couldn't buy any meat anywhere, and we ate a lot of fish and macaroni and cheese. It was a hardship, but nobody complained because we knew we had to do it to win the war.   —Joan Trent, Toronto, Canada.

Because their men were abroad fighting World War II, the forties saw numerous women going to work in factories to help build ships, planes, weapons and tanks. These women were nicknamed "Rosie the Riveter" in newsreels and magazines. When the war ended, they were fired from their jobs and expected to go back to the home and serve their husbands and children. Before the mid-sixties, women could be fired, or refused to be promoted, simply because they were female, with no other reason given. Many young women were not hired on the excuse that they would get married, have babies, and quit their jobs, which often did happen.

President Roosevelt announcing the draft in September, 1940 in anticipation of the U.S. fighting Germany and Japan.

After both of the world wars there was a great emphasis on the family, and people were encouraged to put all their energy into having a happy marriage and bringing up their children. In the first half of the twentieth century the majority of children were born to fathers who were the breadwinners, and mothers who were homemakers. Until mid-century, the typical family consisted of a father who was a full-time, year-round worker until death or retirement, the mother was a full-time homemaker without a paid job, and all the children were born from their union, almost always, after marriage.

When I was in school in the '40s the teacher asked us whether we thought males or females had a harder time in life. Being a male, I naturally thought it was us, although I wasn't under the delusion that women just sat around all day eating bon bons and reading "True Confessions." I knew how hard my mom worked and I wouldn't want to trade places with her. But it really frightened me to think that I was going to have to work every single day until I retired, except for two weeks in the summer, to support a wife and maybe three or four children, all by myself. And, at the end you get a gold watch and drop dead within five years. It seemed like a tremendous responsibility and a long, bleak, hardworking future. Frankly, I didn't know if I was going to be up to it. – Bill Henderson, former salesman, born 1936, Niagara Falls, NY.

The postwar period was one of unlimited optimism and prosperity that began about 1945 and ended in the early seventies. It was a time of shag carpets, avocado-colored appliances, car fins, cocktail parties, T-bone steaks and dry martinis. We danced to the melodious sounds of Benny Goodman and Tommy Dorsey, and Bergman, Bogie and Bacall competed with Hepburn and Tracy for our $3 movie fare. Americans achieved a greater level of creature comfort than any nation has ever known before. In addition to a plethora of consumer goods, we enjoyed a greater level of personal freedom than any country in the world.

Sgt. Bill Hoffman (front row right), and soldiers of G Company, 2nd Battalion, in the 50th Infantry Regiment of the 82nd Airborne, in full gear (World War II vintage equipment) before boarding a jump plane at Ft. Bragg, North Carolina.

Taking Cover

Americans faced a nuclear scare in 1961 when President Kennedy confronted the Russians over the Berlin Wall. Kennedy urged families to build their own bomb shelters, and those who could afford it, did so. The government was asked to identify public spaces that could be used for group shelters, and to stock them with food and water that would last for two weeks. *Life* magazine ran a special section on how to build your own shelter, and optimistically proclaimed that ninety-seven percent of the people could be saved if they were in a shelter when a nuclear bomb dropped. "Fallout shelter fever" hit America in a big way, much to the delight of stores that sold the right materials. In one decade, over 500 bomb shelters were built by American families.

My folks couldn't afford to build a shelter, but we did stock the basement with enough food to last us kids and my parents for two weeks. We already knew how to "rough it" because we loved to go camping, and we had sleeping bags, a Coleman stove and a portable toilet, so we thought we'd be okay if we had to live down there for awhile. There wasn't any electricity, but we had flashlights, battery-powered lamps and a portable radio. Mom put up some curtains to divide it up and give us some privacy.

Some people couldn't be bothered building a shelter, either because they didn't believe it would give adequate protection, or they didn't want to live in a radioactive world that had been devastated by atomic bombs.

The big question we worried about was our friends, neighbors and relatives. We didn't have room to stock more food than our family of five needed for two weeks, so what would we do if a neighbor came to us asking to be let in? And what about complete strangers? It was quite an ethical dilemma and some people even wondered if it would be right to shoot someone who tried to force his way into their shelter. My mom thought it would be morally wrong to turn anyone away, but my dad thought that was ridiculous, it would be every man for himself. – Scott Ranchon, retired airline pilot, born 1935, Portland, OR.

Courtesy Los Angeles Times

Strife in Black and White

In 1955 "Ozzie and Harriet," an extremely popular weekly television program about an incredibly harmonious, loving and happy family that never fought, or discussed sex, race or politics, best personified America's cherished fantasy of domestic bliss. In spite of this serene portrayal of daily life, all Americans were not content.

On the first day of December, 1955, Rosa Parks, a thirty-nine-year-old black woman, boarded a bus in Montgomery, Alabama. Tired and weary from a long day at work, she sat down in the front section, where Negroes were prohibited. A white man approached and told her to give him her seat. Ms. Parks refused. The driver stopped the bus and called police, who handcuffed and arrested her. The ensuing trial resulted in the boycott of the public bus system by hundreds of Negroes, protesting having to sit in the back. The home of the boycott leader, Rev. Martin Luther King, Jr., was bombed. This incident led to the Supreme Court's ruling a year later that segregation on transportation was illegal. The civil right's movement was born, and changed the course of history.

Rosa Parks Being Fingerprinted.
Courtesy Gene Herrick, Associated Press.

In 1948 California became the first state to declare miscegenation laws were unconstitutional, and the U.S. Supreme Court declared laws against mixed-race marriage unconstitutional in 1967.

In 1958 when I was seventeen I dated a black man who was a chiropractor. It didn't matter to my father that he was an educated, polite, well-dressed, professional person, dad threw a hissy fit! Even though I really liked the man and hated my father's bigotry, it just wasn't worth it to continue seeing Daniel and have to deal with the storm at home. Besides that, everywhere we went people stared at us, and you could see the hostility on their faces. And an ironic thing about it was Daniel's family didn't seem very happy about him dating a white girl, although they didn't actually say anything; but the atmosphere was pretty cold when I met his family. – Marsha Mason, administrative assistant, born 1941, Trenton, NJ.

I am Woman, Hear Me Roar

Jean Wicks in 1943

Carried on the tide of patriotic fervor sweeping the country at the outset of World War II, I enlisted in the U.S. Navy in 1941. I was part of the first class assigned to the newly formed WAVES (Women Accepted for Volunteer Emergency Service.) After basic training in Cedar Falls, Iowa, I served as an Aviation Machinist Mate, Third Class, at another base. I fell in love with a sailor from Tacoma, Washington. Since married couples on base were forbidden, we married without permission and kept it secret. We served together on that base for quite some time and were never found out. – Jean Wicks, Omaha, WA.

The greatest cultural change of the century was the woman's movement, which was resurrected in the late sixties, and freed millions of females from dependency on their husbands, sending them en masse into the workplace, and in search of higher education. Feminism radically and inalterably changed the role of women from being subservient to men and generally considered inferior, to the introduction of women into management and formerly male-only jobs, with demands for equal pay. This was greatly resisted by some males who wanted their wives to have dinner on the table in the evening and a clean ironed shirt awaiting them in the morning, and had no plans for helping to change the baby's diapers. Women's entrance into the workplace meant shared housework, a notion foreign to most men, and considered beneath them.

Even though the women's movement was ferociously protested by some men, and also some dependent women who were frightened they would lose their protective status, it swept across North America and much of the Western world, and changed women's status forever. Although feminism was initially promoted as freedom from drudgery for women, and an opportunity for self-actualization, after the inflation of the 1970s, women contributing a second paycheck to the family became a necessity.

Protesting Feminism in Pennsylvania

When I married Paul in 1952 I was twenty-one and had worked as a secretary since I was eighteen. I had two years of high school, and some secretarial training, and that was enough in those days to get a good job. Not many females had completed high school, and it wasn't required as long as you could type. I fully expected to keep on working until we had children but, as soon as we got home from our honeymoon, Paul told me to quit my job Monday morning. He was eight years older than I, and he had a good job which could provide for both of us financially. I asked him why and he just said that standard phrase of the day: "No wife of mine is going to work." That was all that needed to be said because you were supposed to obey your husband in those days. It really scared me because I knew that meant I'd be totally dependent on him and, if I wanted a dollar for something, I'd have to go to him and ask for it. I just wasn't the type to be that helpless so I pleaded with him to let me work part-time. He finally said okay, provided I kept the house clean and had supper ready when he got home from work.

Paul had a car that he drove to his office, and I had one too, but he prevailed upon me to sell it when we got married. Since it was a big old gas guzzling Buick that I'd bought second-hand, I agreed. After I sold it, he wouldn't let me drive his car, so I had to carry the groceries home eight blocks from the store, even in the winter in sub-freezing weather. On Saturdays Paul would go out all day exploring hardware stores, boat docks and other places he liked to hang around. In the meantime I was supposed to clean our two-story house from top to bottom and, when he got home, he actually gave it the white glove treatment and complained if he found any dust. For years I never protested his treating me in such a demeaning way because I was doing my best to be a good wife; after all, that was a woman's highest calling in the fifties. It's hard for me to believe now that I submitted to this type of treatment, but that was a different world then and your husband was king.

I went back to school in the seventies and got a degree in accounting, and then I divorced Paul because I was fed up with waiting on him. He was devastated and couldn't understand what went wrong because, as he told the marriage counselor, "he loved me and was perfectly happy with our marriage and thought I was too." When she asked him what he loved about me, he said I was a great cook, kept the house clean, and took good care of him. I thought I detected a flicker of disgust on the therapist's face, but I could have imagined it. – Joanne Anderson, accountant, born 1931, Dover, MN.

Before the '60s, after a woman graduated from high school, her traditional and most accepted role was to get married, stay at home, raise a family, and be economically dependent on her husband. If she decided not to marry, for most women the only jobs open to them were teacher, nurse, secretary, clerk or waitress. She was often refused admission into college, and so-called "male" jobs were openly denied her. Until 1975 newspapers carried "Help Wanted" ads divided by gender. A woman could get a job selling dresses or lingerie, but she couldn't sell washing machines or vacuum cleaners. A large-ticket item, or anything remotely mechanical, was reserved for men to sell. Even by the end of the century, very few car lots had female salespersons.

Fifty years ago there were almost no female office managers, company presidents, architects, airline pilots, police officers, politicians, lawyers, judges, psychologists or doctors (and many people—especially men—would not go to the few that were practicing.) Supreme Court Justice, Sandra Day O'Connor graduated Magna Cum Laude from Stanford University in California in 1950, but she discovered that no law firm in California would hire her and only one offered her a position—as a legal secretary.

When I was in high school I announced to my mom one day that I wanted to go to college and be a journalist. I was an A student in high school, and I always liked to write. Being a journalist in those days meant being a writer because we didn't have TV and video cameras to tell a story, so it was written up for the newspaper. My mother's reply is still burned into my memory: "Don't be silly, girls don't go to college, they get married and have babies. If anyone in this family goes to college, it'll be your brother, but we wouldn't waste the money on a girl." Unfortunately, that was a typical attitude at the time. – Marta D'Angelo, writer, born 1934, Toronto

The D'Angelo sisters in 1942 shyly posing for the camera

By the end of the century, women had made incredible progress, but had not achieved equality with men. They still earned only seventy-four cents for each dollar that men earned. Women hold less than five percent of senior management positions, and less than ten percent of our nation's senators and governors are female.

Women moving into the workplace in large numbers created a new industry: day care centers. Although many women had to go out to work because most families could no longer survive on one income, the wisdom of having children reared by strangers was questionable. Some social critics believe the loss of stay-at-home mothers has contributed greatly to teenage crime, rampant drug use, gangs, an epidemic of young, single mothers and, in short, the decline of civilization. They may be right.

Plastic Money

Two other great cultural changes of the latter half of the century were shopping malls and the advent of credit cards, which threw many consumers into debt. Instead of going to a single large department store, such as Macy's or Gump's, people could now wander around inside for blocks, protected from the elements, dazzled by the endless display of goods and the numerous stores. And they didn't need even a dollar in their wallet to purchase something, they just pulled out a little piece of plastic. ATM machines on almost every block in big cities now make it very easy to access money, provided you have some in your bank account. In 1998 Americans conducted over twenty billion transactions at these machines.

I remember when I worked as a secretary in the financial district of Manhattan in the early fifties. The other girls and I were always shopping for new clothes because it was really important in those days to be well-dressed when you worked in an office. Because there was no such thing as credit cards, most department stores would put items on lay-away for you. I used to go to the May Company and put a deposit down on a blouse or skirt, and then make a payment every time I got paid. Then, when the item was finally paid off, it was mine. That meant we couldn't have what we wanted sometimes for several weeks, so we had to learn to delay gratification. But it also meant we didn't buy things we couldn't afford, and we didn't get ourselves into debt over our head. After I got a credit card, all that changed, and I really didn't know how to control myself, and I barely escaped bankruptcy. I've got a lot of clothes and furniture now, but I've also got a lot of debt. Sometimes I think the old way was better. —Marilyn Eddelson, born 1941, New York.

To Love, Honor, but Not Obey

Marriage ceremonies have changed greatly from the solemn, dignified "holy unions" of the past. Usually the words were changed from "man and wife" to "husband and wife," and the word "obey" was eliminated for the woman. Marriages no longer have to take place in a church or city hall, and some have been held in some very irreverent places, such as underwater in wet suits; flying in a hot air balloon and riding on a cable car in San Francisco. One of the more bizarre took place in Japan in 1996 in a corporate bathroom designed by the husband.

Terri Essex of Missouri said she'd always wanted to try sky diving, and finally got around to it on her wedding day in October, 1996, when she leaped from a plane 10,000 feet above the wedding party. The bride's father, Danny Payne, had suggested combining their nuptials with his annual fly-in barbecue. The groom, safely waiting on the ground, said he was more nervous about her landing okay, than getting married.

Divorce: Till Problems Do Us Part

Only twenty-six percent of American households consist of married couples with children, according to a 1999 University of Chicago survey; a steep drop from the forty-five percent in the early 1970s. Divorces in the United States have been continuously rising since the '60s. Divorce is no longer a stigma, as it was in the first half of the century when a person felt shamed and a failure if they admitted to being divorced. Even acknowledging the divorce of one's parents was embarrassing.

In 1997 the U.S. had the highest rate of divorce in the world, and they are usually easy to obtain, although there recently has been some talk in Congress of making them more difficult. Perhaps it is marriage that should be made more difficult.

California was the first to enact "no-fault" divorce, which is now called "Dissolution of Marriage" and, unless there's a dispute about money or child custody, requires nothing more than a statement that the couple has "irreconcilable differences." Although this is an improvement over the days when a spouse couldn't get out of a bad marriage when the other spouse wouldn't agree to a divorce, for the most part, for many people, "they lived happily ever after," is forever gone.

When my husband wanted to get a divorce in 1952 because he wanted to marry his mistress, I refused to give it to him. I was Catholic and didn't believe in divorce, and the only grounds for it then were insanity or adultery. Later mental cruelty was added to that. It's incredible to believe today that you couldn't divorce a spouse even if they were beating you on a daily basis, or came home drunk every night, but that's the way it was. A person was condemned to stay married if their spouse refused to divorce them. Of course you could move out, but you could never remarry and, if a woman left home she could be charged with desertion, and risk losing her children, and never get any alimony, which she needed because she didn't have any job skills.

My husband finally put enough pressure on me that I agreed to give him a civil divorce, but in the eyes of the church I was still married to him.

Then I had to have proof that he was an adulterer, which wasn't hard to do because he already had the girl. He paid a private detective to burst into a hotel room they had rented, and take pictures of them in bed, which he gave to me, and I took them to court, and got the divorce. On the papers it named my husband as an adulterer. I figured that was pretty embarrassing for him because it was a public record.

Then I went to a department store, told them I was divorced, and tried to open a credit account so I could buy some new furniture. They refused to give me an account in my own name. Women weren't considered credit-worthy because most of them didn't work outside the home, always had to use their husband's name on accounts, and had no established credit. It was really a joke because the only reason he had good credit was because of me. I handled the money throughout our marriage and paid the bills on time, and he wasn't capable of saving a penny. Laws were passed in the seventies changing this and forbidding businesses to refuse credit to women. We've come a long way baby. – Riva Everett, sales clerk, born 1941.

Janice and Joe Price in 1952

In June, 1951, I was an eighteen-year-old WAC private who had just finished basic training. I was terrified of anyone with any kind of rank, for fear I'd forget to salute or show proper respect. One day I was in the pool and had just come out of a dive. I had my hands extended and accidentally punched the jaw of a good-looking soldier, who yelled: "You knocked out my teeth!" I envisioned ending up in the stockade, especially when I found out he was a corporal. But the teeth I knocked out were attached to a small partial, which was easily replaced. Ten weeks later, Joe Price and I were dating. We were married February 13, 1952, and are still married. – Janice Wasden Price, Seattle, WA.

CHAPTER TWO

Sex and Social Mores:

From Victorian Prudishness
to Personal Vibrators

*In olden days a glimpse of stocking, was looked upon as
something shocking, now, heaven knows, anything goes.*
– From "Anything Goes," by Cole Porter

*Photo of a model, taken in 1945 by D'Angelo Studio,
considered risqué at the time.*

Foreshadowing Ray Bradbury's *Fahrenheit 451*, in 1918 the U.S. Post Office burned installments of James Joyce's *Ulysses*, because it was considered immoral. Jane Heap and Margaret Anderson were charged with obscenity for publishing an excerpt from it in "The Little Review," and were fined $50 each. A year later swimmer Annette Kellerman was arrested for indecent exposure while trying to popularize a one-piece swimsuit worn with tights rather than bloomers. In 1923 the State of Tennessee forbade sex education in schools because of fear discussing the subject might influence students to engage in sex. Henry Miller's semifictional memoir, *Tropic of Cancer*, was published in Paris in 1934, but the stories of the expatriate's libidinous adventures were banned in the U.S. As late as 1959 the United States Postmaster General banned from the mails D.H. Lawrence's *Lady Chatterley's Lover*, on grounds of obscenity.

During the prudish fifties, movie producer Howard Hughes shocked the nation's conscience by seductively posing Jane Russell leaning against a haystack to advertise his movie "The Outlaw." Jane's large breasts were prominently displayed in a tight-fitting blouse. The picture caused quite a stir and was deemed indecent.

KRISTAL BELL

New York, 1963

In 1962 Helen Gurley Brown's book *Sex and the Single Girl,* provoked an outraged reaction from more puritanical folk. Before the cultural transformation of the sixties, single girls were not supposed to be having sex, or at least not admitting it. Two years later Carol Doda created a stir and started a fad in certain nightclubs, by dancing topless in San Francisco's Condor Club. By the end of the century "Sex in the City" was a popular TV sitcom. In a hundred years we have come from a Victorian prudishness that believed only harlots would display their ankles, to thong bathing suits and underwear, a thin cloth string that, in the back, covers only the dividing line between one's buttocks. In the last years of the century, a now infamous White House intern, seduced a president by flashing hers.

Although it was shown in many theatres around the country, in 1973 a New York Criminal Court judge ruled the motion picture "Deep Throat," "indisputably and irredeemably obscene." It was the first time a hard-core porno movie was shown in regular theaters. With the exception of "Behind the Green Door," subsequent films were never quite as explicit, but these two movies opened the door for visible sexuality to be shown on the local screen.

My boyfriend and I went to see "Deep Throat" even though I had heard that people were actually having sex in the movie. Frankly, I didn't believe it; I was sure that wouldn't be allowed in a downtown theater for everyone to see; you had to go to an 'adult theater' to see that sort of thing. Man, was I shocked when they openly displayed penises and pussies, and actually had what was obviously 'real sex' in living color on the huge screen! It was actually somewhat disgusting and I was embarrassed to be sitting beside Mike while this was going on. I don't think I'm a prude, but this movie made me feel dirty and I wouldn't even let Mike kiss me goodnight after witnessing such raw sexuality. I guess that was the precursor to more explicit sex being displayed on TV and in the movies, but what we see now is actually tame compared to "Deep Throat." – Tammy Gratiz, age 50-something, hostess, Buffalo, NY.

Courtesy Los Angeles Times

By 1980 Dr. Ruth was on national television extolling the virtues of sexual pleasure, and giving graphic instruction on how one could increase it, with a partner or by yourself. *The Joy of Sex*, containing explicit drawings of sexual positions, became a best-seller, and variations of it, such as *The Joy of Gay Sex,* soon followed. Most video rental stores now have an "X-rated" section for pornography, and adult bookstores, which also sell vibrators and other sex toys, now abound in big cities, no longer hidden in back alleys on skid row. The burlesque show, prevalent at the beginning of the century, is now an adult theater, and the performance is more explicit.

The Morals Police

In 1930 the Motion Picture Producers and Distributors of America announced the adoption of the "Motion Picture Code" which was designed to clean up the movie business. The Code forbade the use of words such as "damn, hell, S.O.B, Jesus Christ, (used as a swearword), virgin, seduce, pregnant, bitch, bastard, chippy, broad and pansy." Abortion could be covertly referred to, but the word itself was never to be mentioned. An exception to "The Code" was made when Rhett Butler was allowed to tell Scarlett: "Frankly, my dear, I don't give a damn." Even that benign remark shocked some people at the time.

In 1934 the Roman Catholic Church announced the formation of the Legion of Decency to fight for purer motion pictures, and promised to boycott films it found offensive. Each week churches gave parishioners a copy of what was called "The X List," and good Catholics kept away from movies on the list of the damned.

My mother was a devout Catholic and she did everything the Church dictated. I remember when I was a kid there was a movie called "The Moon Is Blue." I think that was the title. Anyway, we were forbidden to see it because it was on the Church's "X list." The reason it made the list was because the heroine told her date she was still a virgin. Such intimate revelations weren't allowed then; after all, every unmarried female was supposed to be a virgin, so it was unnecessary to verbalize it, especially to a date. Those years were so puritanical even married people couldn't be shown in bed together in movies, they had to be side-by-side in twin beds, usually with a nightstand separating them. And they could never kiss in bed, unless they were dying and it was obvious they weren't about to have sex. A woman had to wear a full slip in a movie, she could never appear in a half-slip and bra. A bare-midriff was shocking! Movie stars kissed with their mouths shut on the screen, you never saw anyone shoving their tongue down someone else's throat like they do now. That's hard to believe today with couples practically fucking each other on TV and actually simulating it in the movies, that people were so incredibly prudish in the early part of the century. Frankly, the old way seemed much more romantic. – Josephine Blondell, born 1934, San Diego, CA.

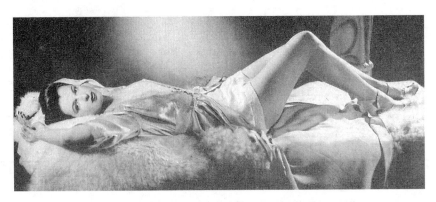

Glamour, 1945 style. Photo by D'Angelo Studios, Toronto

My Irish Catholic mother wouldn't let us buy, or even listen to, a popular record of the day because the song had a line that said something about "Give me five minutes more, only five minutes more, Don't you know that Sunday morning you can sleep in?" That was a sacrilege in her eyes — you didn't sleep in on Sundays, you got up and went to Mass. – Dan Jarzomb, handyman. born 1933, Indianapolis, IN.

The first indication that sex was coming out of the closet came in the forties when sex researcher Alfred Kinsey published *The Kinsey Report*, a statistical codifying of sexual relations in the United States, which challenged many myths about sexual behavior in American society. It stunned the nation; people could not believe that real people engaged in such conduct, especially oral and anal sex and, furthermore, were willing to admit it to a complete stranger. Kinsey also found that American's behavior didn't match their professed attitudes—fifty percent had premarital sex. This stunning book was followed in the sixties by the publication of Masters and Johnson's extensive research in *Human Sexuality*, which scandalized people once again. They found that half of all U.S. marriages were plagued by some kind of sexual dysfunction.

When I graduated from high school in 1954 I decided to move out, primarily because I wanted to bring girls home, and maybe talk them into staying overnight with me, and that was impossible in my parent's house. Unmarried people didn't live together in the fifties, that was considered sinful and shameful. In 1955 I rented an upstairs flat in a family's home for nine dollars a week. It had a little kitchenette, but the bathroom was down the hall, shared by other tenants. I never went downstairs except to go in and out the front door, and give them the rent. Of course we didn't have TV then, so you didn't share the living room with your landlord and watch a television program together. The homeowner said I couldn't have a woman stay overnight in my room, but I managed to sneak one in sometimes when he and his wife went to bed, but I had to get her out before morning. – Mario Angelino, bartender, born 1935, Toronto.

The end of World War II, combined with a resurgence of feminism, hastened the collapse of Victorian values, and advertisers quickly found that romance and sexual titillation increased product sales. When television first came out, sexy women in scanty clothing were selling everything from cars to booze to cigarettes. When the feminists protested that women were being treated as objects, the sex kittens were replaced by professional-looking women in business suits selling cars and other products.

Letting Go of Victorian Primness

Mrs. Duhaney, the neighborhood snoop and keeper of morals

The first airline stewardesses were hired in 1930 and were all registered nurses who wore uniforms that came below the knee. Although they served meals and fetched blankets, their primary responsibility was the safety of the passengers should anyone become sick. By the forties stewardesses were no longer nurses, but were invariably young and beautiful, and were fired if they got married, were over thirty-five, got pregnant, or gained weight. There were quarterly weigh-ins, and they had to wear a girdle on the plane. Their sexuality was promoted in ads such as Continental's: "We Really Move Our Tails For You." After the Civil Rights Act of 1964 men were allowed to be stewards, and the title was changed to flight attendants.

Many appellations were changed in the '70s to reflect women entering the workplace. Mailmen became postal carriers, firemen became firefighters, policemen became police officers, workmans' compensation became workers' compensation. Writers and newspapers began using gender neutral terms, and even churches began using more inclusive language; some progressive ones even dared to suggest that God the Father be changed to our "Father-Mother God."

Anna Mae Craig-Stregger

I worked as a stewardess in 1943, back when that job was considered one of the most glamorous ones a young woman could have. After growing up in Gary, Indiana and attending Purdue

University for a year, I decided I wanted to do something for the war effort, so I applied for a job with TWA. Our uniforms consisted of a sky-blue skirt and jacket with a navy camisole and overseas-style hat. Nylons were so scarce, I'd cry if I got a run. I recall my roommate coming home from a flight and taking her nylons off—just in time for me to put them on! Our shoes were plain brown oxfords; ugly but practical during turbulence.

Flights were longer then, more turbulent and less predictable, but they were much more exciting. Our aircraft was the trusty DC-3, and our crew of three consisted of pilot, copilot and me, the hostess. The passengers were mostly military personnel, who had priority with the airlines. We often had to bump civilian passengers to accommodate them.

In those days of smaller planes and fewer passengers, stewardesses could give more personalized service than they do now. I would visit with passengers, and they sometimes showed their appreciation with letters of commendation. Those years were truly some of the best of my life. I flew the first delegates to the United Nations and occasionally saw celebrities like Howard Hughes. Though bad weather often stranded us in dull places, having a long layover in an exciting big city made up for it.

One stormy night, a tall, handsome naval officer boarded my flight. From then on, my flying days were numbered. A few months later, I married that good-looking Navy pilot. – Anna Mae Craig-Stregger, Saratoga, CA.

Overnight Rendevous

The first building in the world to do business as a motel was the Milestone Mo-Tel in San Luis Obispo, California, which opened in 1925. The architect, A.S. Heineman, coined the word motel, by combining the words hotel and motor. He chose this location because it was the mid-point in the two-day automobile journey between Los Angeles and San Francisco. It ushered in a new era for drivers still in the throes of first love with their newly minted "Model Ts."

In the fifties roadside motels sprang up everywhere and made it easier for unmarried couples to get a room for the night. Most of the time they would register as "Mr. and Mrs. Smith," or the woman would slink down under the dashboard while the man went in and rented a single room for himself. But that was risky because sometimes the night clerk would come out and watch you go into your room to make sure you didn't have someone with you.

When I lived in Detroit during the early fifties I had a girlfriend willing to sleep with me, if we could find a place to do it. She lived with her parents, and I rented a flat in someone's house, and they didn't allow overnight visitors, so we had to get a hotel room. She told her parents she was going to stay at her girlfriend's house overnight. Before we went downtown to rent the room we filled two suitcases with newspapers because no hotel would let you rent a room for the night if you didn't have a suitcase and look like you were traveling. I signed the register "Mr. and Mrs. Robert Thompson," and the clerk accepted it, but all the while my heart was beating rapidly because I was so afraid he was going to ask for some proof that we were married because we looked so young.

One time when we were traveling by car through Georgia, we stopped at a Bed and Breakfast and the woman actually refused to let us sleep in the same room unless we could show our marriage license, so we had to get two rooms. – Robert Kelsoe, office manager, born 1935, Atlanta, GA.

Full-Frontal Nudity

Playboy magazine, whose trademark was photographs of nude and semi-nude women, was first published in December, 1952, featuring Marilyn Monroe on the cover, and photos of her sans clothing inside. There were strident objections that it was immoral, and speculation that this was the end of civilized society. By publishing high-quality articles on social issues of the day, written by well-known personalities, "Playboy" kept up a show of respectability, and gave men who read it an excuse other than sheer voyeurism.

Hugh Hefner, the publisher, built "The Playboy Mansion," which threw lavish decadent parties, and opened his chain of now defunct Playboy cocktail lounges, featuring the famous "bunnies." *Playboy* was followed a few years later by *Hustler* magazine which made no pretense at anything other than the sensual enjoyment of erotica. In 1996 the U.S. Army, concerned about sexism, announced they would no longer allow servicemen to purchase *Playboy* and *Hustler* magazines on the base.

In the eighties the tables were turned and women began openly demonstrating an interest in men's bodies. Talk shows such as "Donahue" began featuring men like the "Chippendale Dancers," a group of males with "buns of steel," who bumped and gyrated to rock music and the screams of delighted females. Some nightclubs opened which were dedicated to women and featured gorgeous hunks who displayed as much of their masculinity as the law would allow, while enthusiastic women ran up to the stage and tucked money into their G-strings.

As a female-oriented contrast to *Playboy*. the May, 1996 issue of *Cosmopolitan,* featured these articles: "Hunks in Trunks: Twenty-five pages of Buff Bods in Bathing Suits." Plus: "The Planet's Most Eligible Heartthrobs, ten Gorgeous Real-life Bachelors for You." Even more flagrant, the cover of *Cosmopolitan's* July, 1998 issue promised: "Multiple Orgasms, Cosmos' Come-Again Guide to Help You Climax Over and Over. Read This, Grab Him, and Head to Bed." *Glamour* magazine's February, 1999 issue featured a cover story on "Sex and Size: How to Maximize Your Pleasure Match." Until the seventies, such headlines would have been considered lascivious and offensive, and might even lead to a law suit. Today it is hardly noticed.

The sixties introduced the phenomenon of "swingers," who voluntarily traded partners at parties, or engaged in group sex. Therapists often had to deal with the fallout from this arrangement, which seemed to suit the male half of the partnership far better than the woman, who often felt coerced into either going along with the game or being left out altogether. A big damper was put on this activity when AIDS became epidemic in the eighties and nineties.

Stores and catalogs began openly selling vibrators, so-called "marital aides," S/M equipment and leather for the dominatrix. Books on how to have better, more frequent, longer-lasting orgasms were openly displayed in mainstream bookstores. Sex therapists hung out their shingles and advertised in major newspapers. Breast augmentation and penile implants became common. Frederick's of Hollywood opened their stores in family-style shopping malls, featuring sexy lingerie and crotchless panties. This was followed by a proliferation of Victoria's Secret stores, an upscale version of seductive-looking boudoir attire.

The Great Debate: Vaginal vs. Clitoral Orgasm

In 1905 Sigmund Freud's "Three Essays on Sexuality," misinformed people for generations about the nature of the female orgasm. Freud declared that a "mature" woman (married of course), would transfer her sexual feelings from the clitoris to the vagina, thus causing women for decades to think there was something wrong with them if this didn't magically happen when they reached adulthood. The women's movement of the seventies, bolstered by the research of Masters and Johnson, proclaimed one of society's best kept secrets, that most women did not have vaginal orgasms, but that the clitoris was the center of sensation, and the equivalent of the male penis. Some men resisted this idea as outrageous, declared it false and a feminist plot to undermine the masculinity of the male. But many women felt the truth was revealed at last; they weren't abnormal, and they didn't have to fake it anymore. "Sensitive, new age" men began paying more attention to pleasuring their partners.

I had taken some psychology in college, and knew that Freud thought women who couldn't have vaginal orgasms were "sexually immature," so I decided I must still be stuck in my Oedipal Complex stage because I couldn't achieve it. I resolved when I had enough money I'd see a psychiatrist and try to work out my unconscious conflict about my father. But in the back of my mind, it didn't quite add up because I knew I could give myself an orgasm through clitoral stimulation, and I knew how to do it quite well. But society said that was wrong because a man was supposed to give it to you through penetration. No wonder so many women faked it!

In 1972 it was a great revelation to me when I read Shere Hite's book "The Hite Report" and realized there was nothing wrong with me because I didn't have vaginal orgasms. I had always believed, and had been told by a few of my lovers who knew my 'dirty little secret,' that I was abnormal. One guy told me the real reason was because I was a latent lesbian. And there were other men who said it didn't matter because women didn't have to have orgasms. Our grandmothers often felt that way too: sex was not a pleasure, but a duty that you had to perform. – Valerie, retired high school teacher, born 1940.

A romantic kiss at a 1920s wedding

When I was in high school, back in the late thirties, the concept of female orgasms was totally alien to me. I never expected the girls I had sex with, or later on my wife, to have or even want an orgasm, and nobody I knew thought this was important to women. Even the women I was with never mentioned it, including my former wife, and I'm sure they didn't have one, but they never said anything, and I never asked them. The guys I knew didn't know anything about satisfying a female sexually, and weren't sure that's what she wanted anyway. And of course, we were too inhibited in those days to discuss such a delicate subject, even with our wives. – Ron Hernandez, age 74, retired railway engineer, Edmonton, Alberta, Canada.

"Come Here Often? What's Your Sign?"

Singles' bars were the hip place in the seventies to pick up guys and gals, but the women who frequented them often felt like they were a piece of meat on display. The personal columns in newspapers became a new way for singles to meet each other, and it was also a way for hookers to find a new audience. Prostitution was legalized in Nevada, and "Escort Services," and massage parlors, which were often a front for prostitution, were advertised in the yellow pages of most big-city phone books.

After the feminist movement, women became more assertive, and it was now acceptable for them to call men for dates and ask them to dance at nightclubs. Women also had to accept the downside of their new freedom; they were expected to contribute to the bill when taken out on a date, and the man no longer had to open the door for them. Some women missed the old conventions, and others haughtily refused them, causing many men to be confused about how to behave in the presence of the new woman. About the same time, impotency became more prevalent in men, and it was suspected in some quarters that there was a connection to women's new found sexual assertiveness.

I divorced my husband in 1975 after fifteen years of marriage, and had to enter the world of dating again. When I went on my first date I was terrified because I knew things had really changed, and I wasn't sure how to behave. But for the first time in my life, I became aware of how the old standards really infantilized women, and gave us the feeling we were incapable of doing anything. My date was from the old school so, when we arrived at the restaurant, I had to sit in the car until he came around to my side and opened the door, which seemed strange because I opened the door of my own car every day without any problem. As we went inside he opened the front door for me, and helped me off with my jacket when we got to the table. Then he pulled out my chair and assisted me to sit down. It was almost like I was disabled. The waitress came and he ordered some wine for us without consulting with me. We both smoked and of course he lit mine. When we got the menu he asked me what I wanted so that, when the waitress returned, he could order for me. Even though I was forty-nine years old, he referred to me and my friends as "girls." I wondered how he'd like it if I called him a boy. By this time I was actually feeling like a little girl.

He paid for everything of course and, when the meal was over, he pulled out my chair, helped me on with my coat, opened the restaurant and car doors for me. Although I know he was trying to

be courteous, it made me feel like a helpless child, incapable of doing anything for myself, not even able to order my own dinner. The only thing he didn't do was cut up my steak. For the first time I understood what the feminists were complaining about when they said men put us on a pedestal. You can't do much from up there.
– Anita Morrison, financial manager, born 1941, Boston, MA.

Quote from the January, 1953 issue of *Better Homes and Gardens:*
If a woman is brainy, she can earn her own living.
But, if she's sensible, she'll let some good man earn it for her.

Mind Your Manners

In 1922 Emily Post wrote her famous best-seller: *Etiquette,* which became the Bible of the socially conscious, and the bane of the socially uncertain. People lived by it for at least four decades, until the hippie revolution of the sixties ridiculed its rigid dictates and threw the book away. But, have we swung from one extreme to another? People today bemoan the loss of civility, and envy the harmony of the fifties' families portrayed in sitcoms such as "The Adventures of Ozzie and Harriet," and "The Brady Bunch."

The courtesy and consideration of others that was prevalent in the early part of the century, was offset by the overemphasis on the correct etiquette for every situation, and the societal disapproval that accompanied failure to display it. Conformity to society's mores was the prevailing mindset, and those who were rebellious and refused to fit into traditional notions of how to behave, were shunned and condemned. People lived in fear of the negative judgment of others should they commit some social faux pas, and shame and guilt governed their behavior. The anxiety about "what will the neighbors think?" caused people to conceal much of themselves, and repress their spontaneity.

The best society is not a fellowship of the wealthy, nor does it seek to exclude those who are not of exalted birth; but it is an association of gentle-folk, of which good form in speech, charm of manner, knowledge of the social amenities, and instinctive consideration for the feelings of others, are the credentials by which society the world over recognizes its chosen members. – Emily Post

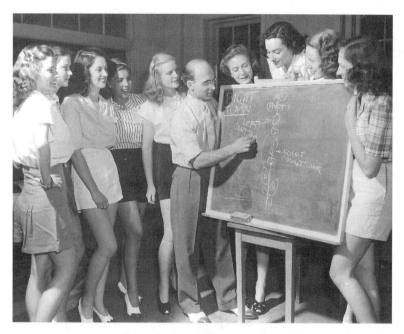

This is a photo of my dad, Andre D'Angelo, who had a School of Charm in 1945 in Toronto. He's outlining the proper way for young ladies to walk. They would practice correct posture by walking with a book on their heads. Lorraine D'Angelo

When we were growing up in the forties my parents sent my sister to "finishing school," where she took lessons in etiquette and elocution. Charm schools for ladies were common in those days. I remember my sister used to go around the house with a book on her head practicing how to walk like a lady. She had to sit down very carefully and make sure she kept her skirt down and crossed her legs demurely at the ankles. Terry was very dramatic and wanted to be a movie star like Bette Davis. She had a silk scarf that she used to flick at you with a haughty look as she flitted around the house. Personally, I thought the whole thing was phony and nauseating, but apparently she thought this nonsense would make her more marriageable. —Joey Perelli, photographer, born 1941.

Children are to Be Seen and Not Heard

In the early part of the century parents had absolute control over their children—there wasn't any Child Protective Agency then—and they sometimes utilized this power with brutal means when their children didn't comply. Child abuse, through harsh punishments such as whippings with twigs and belts, was commonplace, and accepted by society. "Spare the rod and spoil the child," was the rule of the day. The most obstinate of children could be sent to reform school or juvenile hall where the punishment was far more severe.

Ads From The Old Days

WHEW! There must have been a collective sigh of relief from children once this 1950 ad ran, and Mom and Dad installed easy-to-care-for Formica countertops.

he hair brush, razor strap, and switch don't get much of a work-out in homes that have Formica surfaces. Formica shrugs off fruit acids, alcohol, boiling water—and even the most elaborate childish messes. Just wipe with a damp cloth. The super-smooth colorful Formica surface is sparkling clean again. Formica's beautiful color patterns and rich wood grains never need painting or refinishing.

This 1950 ad in Family Circle magazine shows the attitude toward children in the early part of the century: If they're bad, the ad suggests, they can be automatically spanked with either, "a hair brush, razor strap or switch."

Our family did a lot of bickering, and my dad, like many fathers in those days, believed in smacking us around if we did something wrong. That was common back then, and considered acceptable. But the thing I remember about my childhood that was positive was that we always ate supper together. My dad had a bakery business in the forties, and my mom worked in the store with him, but she was home when school got out. When dad got home, each of us three girls had a chore to do to help get supper ready. My brother didn't have to do anything of course because he was a male, and preparing meals was woman's work. Even though my parents were very strict, when we would eat supper together everyone would talk about their day, and what was happening at school, and it made me feel like they really cared about us and were interested in what we were doing. And we got to know things about our parents too, which made us closer to them. It gave us a certain cohesiveness as a family unit, and gave me a real feeling of belonging. When I look back I would say that those family meals were probably the thing that contributed most to my sense of security in the world. And I think the way families are now, seldom eating together, or everybody eating while watching TV, and not really talking to each other, has probably contributed more to the breakdown of society than anything else. – Patricia Acera, homemaker, born 1934 in Charlevoix, MI.

Family Dinner - Good Housekeeping Magazine, 1934

When I was fourteen and going through my puberty years, I started acting out. Before then I'd always been an 'A' student, but I suddenly discovered that boys were more interesting than school. My girlfriend and I started skipping classes and hanging around the local coffee shop. My parents found out and grounded me for that, so I snuck out the bedroom window at night to meet my friends. They found out about that too, and I got a whipping. There were a series of things that set them off; I got caught smoking, and my grades began to fall and they threatened me with reform school.

One night my girlfriend and I got together with a bunch of teenagers who got some booze from a bootlegger, and we had a party at one of their houses because their parents weren't home. The neighbors called the cops and we all got put in the paddy wagon and hauled off to jail where they put us all in a big holding room. When my parents came to pick me up they were furious and my mom whacked me across the face right in front of the cops. The next day I was packed off to reform school for the rest of the summer. It was a horrible place where I had to work in a laundry room in 110-degree heat for eight hours a day. That was the worst thing that ever happened to me. – Barbara, sixty-something, interior designer.

Before Freud popularized psychoanalysis, people didn't seem to make a connection between the way they'd raised their kids and they way they turned out. A child who became a juvenile delinquent brought shame upon the family, and was labeled a bad seed. Sometimes it would be blamed on someone back in the family history that the child was like; maybe great grandpa who was a horse thief. A lot of parents tried to motivate their kids by calling them names like lazy, stupid, worthless, selfish, and that old favorite: "you'll never amount to a hill of beans."

If a family were unfortunate enough to have an unmarried daughter who became pregnant, she was quickly shunted off to a home for unwed mothers or sent to live with Aunt Emily in Iowa, less she disgrace her parents. Sometimes when the boy involved was accused of getting her pregnant, he would get some of his pals to swear they had sex with her too, so she was branded a slut and "got what she deserved" by having to bear a child to full term and then go through the heartbreak of giving it up. If a woman were working when she got pregnant she was automatically fired, even if she were married. It would be considered disgusting to see an obviously pregnant woman working in an office.

Controlling Her Own Body

One of the greatest cultural changes of this century was triggered in 1960 when the FDA approved "The Pill," whose side-effect was the sexual revolution. Women were no longer a slave to pregnancy, and family planning began in earnest. This was the beginning of sexual freedom for women, although it wasn't until the late sixties that the social stigma was removed from unmarried women who had sex. The condom, diaphragm and I.U.D were available in the fifties but, until the sexual revolution of the 1960s, with the exception of men in the military, single people were denied access to contraceptive devices. They weren't supposed to be having sex and, if they did and she got pregnant, then she should pay the consequences for being so immoral. She was a tramp, but he was just "sowing his wild oats."

Marga and Andre's Wedding in 1932 in Toronto

In 1973 the U.S. Supreme Court ignited a firestorm that has divided America to this day when Roe vs. Wade became law, thereby enabling women to legally obtain surgical abortions. Like The Pill, it gave women an option other than having a baby they didn't want, or couldn't care for, or carrying it for nine months and then having to give it away. No issue in U.S. history has been so divisive as this one, and it turned some anti-abortionists into criminals, perpetrating violence, even murder, in the name of their religious beliefs.

In 1996 Planned Parenthood began large-scale testing of a combination of two FDA approved drugs that have been known to successfully induce abortions in the first eight weeks of pregnancy. After years of fires, bombs and threats to doctors and clinics that performed abortions, an already legal and widely available drug may now guarantee any woman a safe, legitimate, easily accessible medical alternative to surgical abortion. It's the Pro-Life movement's worst nightmare.

Now I am a Woman

Menstruation and menopause were words that were largely taboo until after the sexual revolution of the sixties. Women said things like "I've got the curse" or "It's that time of the month," "My friend came today" or, more crudely, "I'm on the rag." Both menopause and menstruation were treated as though they were diseases, and young girls were advised not to exercise or take part in sports when they had their period. Some were even told to take sponge baths rather than a tub bath during that time.

In the first few decades of the century menstruating women wore rags or cotton cloths. Sanitary Napkins were invented by nurses during World War I using surgical bandages. In 1920 Kimberly-Clark, the makers of Kleenex™, marketed a disposable napkin called Kotex™, which was attached to a woman's panties by safety pins. Later elasticized belts were invented that hooked to the pads. They didn't work very well because they never stayed in place and were very uncomfortable. Additionally, women were always terrified that the outline of the belt could be seen through their skirts, and people would know that they were having their period. For shame! In the early 1970s there was a revolution in feminine hygiene when a sanitary pad was invented that had an adhesive strip that stuck to the lining of a woman's panties, and the ugly belts were happily thrown away. In 1930 tampons were introduced, but were thought to be used only by women who were no longer virgins, so unmarried women usually didn't use them.

In the past, women did their best to hide sanitary napkins in their carts when they went shopping by piling other groceries on top of them, and some insisted their husbands buy them because they were too embarrassed. Because they were too shy to ask a clerk for help, stores were encouraged to place the napkins in a convenient place so a woman wouldn't have to mention the word. Some girls dreaded getting a male checkout clerk when they had a box of Kotex in their cart, and would wait for a female if they could.

"How Shall I Tell My Daughter"
Modess Booklet, 1954

When I turned thirteen my mother handed me a booklet put out by the makers of Kotex and told me to read it. It described the wonders of menstruation in glowing terms; in fact I think the title was "Now I am a Woman." I remember it had cartoon sketches of a young girl happily announcing to her mother that she had started her period, and that this meant she was now entering the world of the big people, and was a young adult. It was designed to alleviate the fright many girls experienced when they suddenly started bleeding, whose mothers had been too embarrassed to talk to them in advance about what was going to happen to them. The booklet also told you to buy Kotex pads. When I got older and talked to other women about how they learned they were going to menstruate, many said their parents never mentioned it to them, and some found out only by going to the school nurse in a panic when they started to bleed. One mother simply took her daughter into her closet and pointed at the box of Kotex. "One of these days you're going to need these," she said, "so that's where they are." – Lisa Mahoney, former telephone operator, born 1931.

A U.S. Congressman declared in the seventies that women were unfit to be legislators because menstruation made them emotionally unstable during that time of the month. Naturally, this sexist remark caused an uproar among feminists.

Living in Sin

Living together, which used to be considered shameful, and was called by the pejorative term "shacking up," became widespread after the hippie revolution in the sixties. It was considered immoral, and was even illegal in many states. Landlords could, and often did, refuse to rent to unmarried couples, and it was impossible for them to get a loan from the bank or buy a house together. Today, because living together is common, most states have decriminalized private, consensual acts between adults, even same-sex couples. Domestic Partners' Registries, which were enacted by some states in the nineties, officially recognized the rights of gay couples, or cohabitating, unmarried heterosexuals over age sixty-two.

Hey Man, Don't be so Uptight!

Rebellion against society's rigid, moralistic attitudes began in the fifties with the "Beat" generation, a term first used in print in a 1952 article by John Clellon Holmes in the *New York Times* magazine. The Beatniks were mostly celebrated for their contributions to literature and art, and a few of them were the brightest minds of a generation, such as Jack Kerouac, Allen Ginsberg, Neal Cassady, William Burroughs, Michael McClure, and artist Jay Defoe. The original Beatniks were a "Who's Who" of the fifties literati, and they hung out in an Italian neighborhood of San Francisco called North Beach, where poets such as Ginsberg often gathered at the City Lights Bookstore on Broadway. They were restless, disaffected, rebellious young people who rejected the authoritarian, patriarchal society, and the lemming-like conformity of men in gray suits commuting daily from the suburbs to the city, carrying the corporate symbol, a briefcase. They turned their back on convention and embraced sexual freedom, bebop and Zen. In Ginsberg's words, the Beatniks considered themselves "subterranean." By not conforming to society's values, they felt they could do what they liked and defy authority. The price they paid was the poverty that came from rejecting a traditional job.

The Times They Are A-Changin'

The Beats, followed by the hippies and flower children of the sixties, launched the sexual revolution, and propelled society almost overnight from prudishness to sexual freedom. Their headstrong, fun-loving openness to ecstasy, whether natural or induced by LSD or magic-mushrooms, unshackled uptight society from its Victorian restraints. T-shirts tie-dyed with psychedelic colors, long, colorful dresses accompanied by love beads and draped with a poncho, became the distinguishing garments.

But there was one great difference between the Beatniks and the hippies: the latter introduced recreational drugs to their generation, and thereby to all the generations that followed. Signs promoting drugs, such as "Better Living Through Chemistry," began appearing in San Francisco's Haight-Ashbury district. The words of their guru, Timothy Leary, "Tune In, Turn On and Drop Out," became the motto of disillusioned young people, looking for a different way from their parents to experience the world. By popularizing and making acceptable "tripping out" on drugs, they changed the lives of millions of adolescents, sometimes destroying them.

"Hippies" at Somerset, England in 1963

As a side-dish, they also provided society with new words that became a part of our vocabulary, such as keen, hip, a happening, far-out, groovy, good vibrations and bad karma. People didn't have problems anymore, they had "hang-ups," and that was a bummer. These colorful expressions were replaced in the nineties with the ubiquitous, repetitive and finally meaningless: "Have a nice day," uttered in robot fashion by every salesperson with whom one does business, sometimes more than once.

Flowers in Her Hair

The hippies changed our culture dramatically, some things for the good, such as encouraging equal rights for everyone; but they also contributed to the gradual disintegration of civility and the prevailing social mores. Feelings of shame and concerns about "what will the neighbors' think?" which formerly had controlled people's behavior, became an old-fashioned concept. The hippies helped free people from the puritanical restrictions of the past; to a degree previously unimaginable, they were now free to be whomever they wanted to be, unrestrained by society's dictates, with the exception of the corporate world, where shirts and ties, and the old standards of civility still prevailed.

1960s Anti-VietNam War Banner

The changes of the early sixties that were admirable were the civil rights' sit-ins that led to improvements for minorities; the promotion of altruistic ideals; tolerance of other lifestyles, and the revival of the movement to give women equal rights. But, by the end of the sixties, these idealistic goals began to be replaced by hedonism, rampant drug use, sexual promiscuity, self-centeredness, pessimism about the future, and the belief that government and big business were incompetent and corrupt. "Don't trust anyone over thirty" became the byword of a generation. These polarized young people radically expressed themselves in Chicago in 1968 at the Democratic Convention when hippies and yippies warred with police.

Free Sex Isn't Always Free

A loud cheer went up from the male contingent when the sexual revolution of the sixties began. The new freedom was certainly advantageous for them, but it was questionable whether women, who were now subject to increasing pressure to have sex with their dates and boyfriends, benefited from this permissive atmosphere. For men, the benefits were abundantly clear. The social mandate of the first part of the century that a man should first marry a woman he intended to bed, or at the very least, declare his love for her, was now considered old-fashioned.

I have my own apartment now so no one can tell me who I can have stay over. I remember when I was a teenager, before I got married, it was really difficult to get a girl to have sex with you in the fifties and early sixties. But, after the hippie movement began, the flower children were really easy; promiscuous I guess you'd call it, in the name of sexual freedom. Personally, at the time I thought it was groovy. In the seventies and eighties after I got divorced, I used to meet women at the singles' bars and it wasn't hard to get them into bed on the first date because they knew if they didn't put out the next one would. The age of AIDS and genital herpes changed all that and people are a lot more cautious now about who they're going to have sex with. I suppose sexually transmitted diseases are nature's backlash because of people having so many different partners. It seems nature doesn't like excesses.

Now I meet women on the Internet, or answer ads in the "Personal" section of the newspaper. It's much better because I can find out first if they're intelligent enough to write a sentence. Another popular place for singles to meet are the fitness gyms; they're a showplace for people with good bodies who are attracted to each other. I've also tried joining the dating clubs because you can see the person on a video tape and hear what they have to say about themselves. I've even been tempted to call the psychic hot-line a few times, which is the fad of the nineties I guess, when I've met someone new and want to check her out with my favorite psychic.
– Larry Jameson, stockbroker, born 1951, New Jersey.

Kim and Gill on their first date in 1962, Long Island

Your Place or Mine?

The rejection of conventional morality emancipated men from their traditional responsibilities of taking care of women financially. "Liberated" women began rejecting alimony from ex-husbands as being too financially restrictive for the males, and fostering dependency for females. This was roundly applauded by men who no longer had to contribute financially to the support of their ex-wives, and a few irresponsible men interpreted that to include no longer having to contribute to their joint offspring.

For women who were suddenly proud of their new, and often indiscriminately practiced, sexual freedom, the result was often unwanted pregnancy, an epidemic of sexually transmitted diseases, and abuse by some men who used them for sex and quickly dropped them for the next conquest, which had now become easy. Often they didn't even have to take her out to dinner. Many men were on a perpetual holiday, and genital herpes became a major health crisis.

"Shotgun weddings" became laughable relics from the past; no longer did parents demand that the man who impregnated their daughter marry her and take financial responsibility for the baby. The fathers often just walked away, usually denying paternity, and the single mother went on welfare, supported by tax dollars. Unwed motherhood, which was considered a disgrace until the sixties, became accepted and epidemic. In the 1990s a backlash against single motherhood occurred because of the financial drain on the economy and society's concern for so many children deprived of a paternal role-model. This led to a dramatic change in the welfare laws. Conservative members of Congress supported the teaching of sexual abstinence in public schools, which didn't seem to work very well in the face of the raging hormones of youth.

Singles bars were hot in the seventies and many people would pick someone up and have sex that same evening. It was accepted behavior and you were still "respected in the morning" because almost everyone was doing this. You might have a different partner every week, sometimes more for the guys I suppose. And nobody used condoms because it was the woman's job to take care of that, and the man just assumed she was on the pill or had an IUD or diaphragm. It was useless to ask a man to put on a condom because they wouldn't do it, it might interfere with their pleasure. Pregnancy? Not his problem: get an abortion.

Having been brought up as a good Catholic girl and taught by the nuns that my body was sacred, I couldn't hop into bed with a man

I'd just met that evening. That meant I didn't get many second dates because the competition was fierce, and there were plenty of women willing to let a guy fuck them on the first date, and he knew it. I remember one time I met this really neat fellow at a party and naturally he tried to put the make on me when he took me home. I said no, telling him I'd like to get to know him better first, and I said no again on the second date. On the third date he informed me that, if I didn't have sex with him that night he'd never see me again because I was too prudish. I wasn't going to be coerced into having sex, so I never saw him again, and it was really disappointing. – Marcie Allen, Realtor, born 1949.

Better Dead than Queer

If a homosexual were to admit his predilection to his parents, he was often thrown out of the house, never to darken their door again. People who were attracted to their own sex were called sinners by the Church, criminals by the law and, until 1969, mentally ill by psychiatrists. The latter was rather strange because Freud himself didn't think homosexuality was an aberration, but merely a deviation from the norm.

One day my mother was snooping through my bedroom drawer on the pretense that she was putting away my laundry, when she found a note that a boy in my high school class had written to me declaring his affection. I realize now it was pretty stupid to have kept that note, but it meant a lot to me. When I got home from school my mom flew into a rage and told me that as soon as I finished high school, which was four months away, I was to immediately find a job and get out. In the meantime, I was told I would have to eat my meals in the kitchen because she wasn't going to have a pervert eat with the family and be a bad influence on my younger brother. When she told my dad about it he shouted that he wasn't going to have a sissy for a son, and he always knew there was something the matter with me because I didn't play sports or like football. He told me to get out as soon as I graduated and never come back. My dad died when I was thirty-five and I never saw him again after I left home. My mother finally came around and realized I obviously didn't choose to be something society disapproved of, so we made up, and now she accepts my boyfriend as a son. – Frank, software designer, born 1954, Portland, OR.

In 1969 at a homosexual bar called Stonewall, in Greenwich Village, New York, instead of going passively into the paddy wagons, for the very first time, a group of gay drag queens fought back when the police attempted to arrest them, which was a routine occurrence. The "Stonewall riots" became the basis for the gay liberation movement. Shortly thereafter, the American Psychiatric Association reviewed their definitive guidebook of mental illnesses, the *Diagnostic and Statistical Manual,* and declared that homosexuality would be deleted from the list. Overnight, millions of gay men and lesbians around the world were no longer officially considered mentally ill, and their attraction to their own sex was now declared an alternative lifestyle. In the nineties, a host of scientific papers was published that indicated sexual preference was not a choice, but was biologically determined. The conservative factions of religion denied this and carried on their campaign to demonize homosexuals and call them abominations before the Lord. Both the women's movement and the growing acceptance of gays and lesbians generated a scathing backlash from religious extremists who believed gays were somehow "destroying family values."

I hear religious people talk all the time about how the "gay lifestyle" is destroying the family and, as a lesbian, I've always wondered what that lifestyle is. My partner and I go to work every day, we clean house, cook dinner, and go to the movies like other people do, and I can't think of a single thing we do that's different from the straight lifestyle, except we have a same-sex lover. I don't consider having sex occasionally, which is a very small part of our lives together, a "lifestyle." As for threatening straight marriages,

I think the guy down the street, who flirts with every married women in our neighborhood, is more of a threat to marriage than we are.
– Emily Nager, travel agent, born 1942, Washington, D.C.

Opening the Closet Door

No national organization existed for gays and lesbians before the '70s because few were willing to endure the hostility and prejudice that would follow such an admission. To realize you were gay before 1970 meant living a life of secrecy, constantly afraid of being found out, with the threat of losing your job, being thrown out of your apartment, possibly beaten up, being rejected by parents and friends, and dim career prospects.

A milestone in the long history of prejudice against gays, took place in 1977 in San Francisco when Harvey Milk, an openly gay man, was elected to the Board of Supervisors. Many people congratulated him, but just as many sent him death threats. Some people had to adjust to the new reality he embodied: that a gay person could live an honest, open life and be successful. Regrettably, Harvey Milk was shot to death, along with San Francisco Mayor Moscone, in 1978, by conservative former board member Dan White. His sentence, as a result of what became known as "The Twinkie Defense," for committing two cold-blooded murders, was only seven years, which sparked a riot in the San Francisco gay community. A year after being paroled, Dan White committed suicide.

March in New York, 1970

In Toronto where I lived during the fifties there was one gay bar downtown on King Street near the financial district, so by the time it opened in the evening everyone had gone home from work, and the streets were deserted. Sometimes we could talk a trusted straight girl into going with us in case the cops busted the place, which often happened, and we could quickly drop the man we were dancing with, and grab her. There might be a few lesbians in there too, but this was rare; the women were more hidden and they didn't cruise the bars looking for other women.

A lot of times the cops just came in and threw all of us into the police wagon, sometimes with force, although they didn't need it because nobody every resisted. Sometimes they called us faggots and pansies and made crude jokes about us. The cops seemed to relish hitting gays; I guess it made them feel more manly. In those days police brutality was common, and you couldn't win a case against them because people always believed the word of the police in court. Anyway we were considered such disgusting perverts that nobody really cared what they did to us. It's hard to believe today that it was actually <u>illegal</u> to be who you were. Remember, we weren't doing anything sexual in these bars, just talking to other men, or daring to dance with one, and for that we were arrested and booked, fingerprinted, and fined, or given jail time. Sometimes our names would even get published in the paper, and then that was the end of our job, and we usually had to move to another city. – Gary, former office manager, born 1942.

In 1954 Christine Jorgensen, born a male, had a sex-change operation and became a female. The world was stunned in disbelief that such a thing was possible, moral, or even desirable.

"Shmoos" featured in "Lil Abner" by Al Capp
© *Capp Enterprises, Inc. 2005 All Rights Reserved*

CHAPTER THREE

Household:

Mothers Don't Wear Aprons Anymore

*My grandma, Theresa Olson Donaldson , cooked everything
from scratch. We lived in Arlington, MA and she used to visit
us every Sunday night to watch Ted Mack's Original Amateur Hour.
She died in 1952 at age 90.   - Pauline Cameron*

The invention of kitchen gadgets and other household appliances designed to make our lives easier was phenomenal in the twentieth century! Science and technology have truly emancipated the household members from much of the drudgery of running the home, although it's debatable whether this has given people more time, because today the time saved is often spent on the road commuting.

The emblem of domesticity and femininity in the early part of the century was the ever-present apron. It symbolized the housewife's secondary role when women were defined by their ability to run a household, and how well they took care of their family. Before the '60s a good wife was one who kept a clean house, was a good cook and could make a great cup of coffee.

Aprons were often hand-made by the housewife and covered her clothing neck to knee. Some resembled a tablecloth, but more creative ones were adorned with fancy embroidery or cutsy symbols such as kittens or flower baskets. Elegant aprons made for serving cocktails to guests were often made of tulle and completely porous, so if you spilled something on it, it went right through to your dress.

Mrs. Harriett DeCelles doing the wash in 1940

Washing clothes was something that was always a big chore, especially if the family were large, as most were in the early part of the century. And there were no local "dry cleaners" to take clothes to, although laundries that washed and ironed men's shirts, mostly run by Chinese, appeared early in the century. There was no need for a woman's laundry, because of course women were expected to clean their own clothes. Until electricity became commonplace, ironing was done by heating the iron on the wood-burning stove until it was hot, and continuing to reheat it until all the ironing was finished. Electric steam irons and wash-and-wear fabrics were inventions that pleased the heart of every woman who had to iron mounds of clothing every week.

My mother liked to listen to soap operas when she did the ironing. In the '30s there were three sources of programs available on our radio: New York, Philadelphia and Chicago. This ensured she had an uninterrupted flow of fifteen-minute serials from the time she finished the breakfast dishes until it was time to make supper, which was signaled by either "The Gospel Hour" or "Singing Sam, the Barbasol Man,". — Dick Hassall, Fowler, CA.

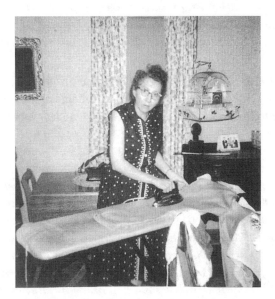

My mother, Edna Falk, spent a lot of time doing laundry in the '50s, says Mary Anne Wyland of Fargo, ND. On the back of this photo mom wrote:"Seems like I never ever got through ironing."

I was born on the South Side of Chicago in 1919. We didn't have a bathtub so my mom would take us kids down to the public bathhouse once a week, where we got our bodies and hair washed. The water was usually cold and it was a lot harder to wash in those days because we didn't have shampoo, just a bar of hard soap that we tried to lather up enough to get the grime out. During the winter my mom would fill a large metal tub with water heated on the stove.

When all the kids were bathed, she'd get into it herself when we'd gone to bed so nobody would see her. People were very modest then, but they weren't as conscious of germs or sanitation, so having a bath once a week seemed just fine, especially to a kid.

Another thing I remember about living in Chicago as a child was that the street lights were gas, and a man in black cloak and a top hat came every night and lit each one of them. Every evening I'd look out the window and wait for him. The lamplights cast a different kind of glow than electric lights; it was magical at dusk and a little romantic. At the same time it was somewhat spooky because of the shadows, but I used to dream about the man I would marry meeting me one night under one of those lights and kissing me ever so tenderly, just like Bogart and Bergman. In the morning the gasman came back and turned them all off, and it was time to face the reality of the day. – Anne Barnett, retired psychotherapist, Berkeley, CA.

As a kid it was my reluctant chore to help mother do the washing every Saturday morning. We had what was considered a modern machine back in the thirties; after all, some housewives were still using wash boards, or they boiled the clothes in a big pot and then hung them out to dry. The "thing" was down in the basement, standing tall on spindley foot-long legs, which meant it wasn't firmly set on the floor, so it would shimmy and shake while it was doing the wash. It wasn't capable of also squeezing the water out of the clothes when they were clean, but it had a set of rollers sitting on top through which we had to take each piece of soaking wet clothing, and pull it through the wringers to squeeze out the water. This had to be done two or three times on each piece. I would turn the rollers with a hand crank while my mother pushed and pulled the clothing through them. Because there were six people in our family, this ordeal usually took most of the day. Of course we didn't have an electric dryer, the sun was it, so we dragged it all outside and hung it up on the line. In the wintertime, we had to hang it on the line in the cellar, and it took forever to dry. What a chore! I hated wash day and would try all kinds of tricks to get out of it, usually to no avail. – June Pannaza, high school teacher, born 1930, Saskatchewan, Ontario, Canada.

"But now — just look at that plate! Like Jack Spratt's platter, it's "licked clean." Since I started cooking my vegetables the Wesson Way, there's never a speck of them wasted. They taste so good now the family enjoys them thoroughly."

My older sister and I had to do the dishes every night, and that was no easy chore in the thirties. We had bar soap then, but no powdered or liquid soap. We had to take the bar of hard brown soap and put it in a little square wire grate that fit around the bar and had a long handle on it. Then we would put the grate in a pan of hot water and swish it back and forth endlessly until it finally made enough suds that we could wash the dishes. When people talk about all our modern gadgets not saving that much time, they obviously didn't know what it was like back then, and how much time it took just to do the nightly dishes. We had five kids and two adults in our family and that meant one pan of water wasn't going to get all those dishes clean, so this chore often took all night. On the other hand we weren't missing our favorite TV show because we didn't have one.

Evenings meant dishes and homework, and Saturday night meant a bath, if you were lucky enough to live in a house that had a bathtub. It was also the night we got our hair washed, shoes shined and clothes inspected for rips to make sure everything was in order for Sunday school. So much activity meant a quick supper which usually consisted of hot dogs smothered with pork and beans. To us kids that was really a treat. No vegetables!

When my parents finally got a dishwasher twenty years later, the whole kitchen had to be redesigned to accommodate it, and the carpenter had to cut a hole in the cabinet to fit it in and hook up the hoses. Of course before we could have a dishwasher our household had to evolve to the point of getting a hot water heater so mom didn't have to heat the water on the stove Now my parents can just put the dishes in there with a little liquid soap, and go watch their favorite TV show. It's really amazing to my generation how convenient it is! And, to top it off, they even got a garbage disposal, something unheard of when I was a kid. Of course, even though they're living in the same house where I was born, it sure has changed over time. One thing I used to hate was that ugly plastic kitchen furniture that was so popular in the 4'0s and '50s. – Lorraine D'Angelo, owner, Lorraine's Bar and Grill, born 1936 .

Two of the things I liked about our kitchen when we remodeled it in 1960 were double sinks and a wooden kitchen table. I think the plastic dinette sets that were so prevalent in the forties were the ugliest things ever invented. Add to that plastic flowers that a lot of people used as a centerpiece, which were great dirt collectors. Thank goodness they were replaced with silk flowers so well-made they can look real. Also plastic lawn Flamingos were a fad in the forties but considered really tacky now. – Anna Monge, hairdresser, born 1941, Toledo, OH.

Turn Up the Heat

Living in the northern states or in Canada was particularly difficult during the winters, which seemed harsher in the early part of the century than they are now. In Buffalo or Grand Rapids or Toronto people would often awaken to overnight snowfalls that completely shut down the city. It was fun for kids because it meant no school that day, or maybe two or three days, and the time could be spent playing in the snow. But for people who had failed to stock enough food, or had medical emergencies, it could be a big problem. Babies were often delivered at home, and a blizzard meant the doctor couldn't make it. But there were usually other woman in the home who knew how to deliver a baby because grandma or the maiden aunt often lived in the same house.

When I was a child in Massachusetts in the thirties, I would awaken some winter mornings to the pleasurable sound of the town's "no school" whistle. A snow day meant a day outside carving out caves and secret hiding places, making forts, and of course, building a snowman. These special days always began by running downstairs to dress behind the warm potbellied stove. We'd have porridge for breakfast, homemade jam, and milk with thick cream on top, which had to be stirred down into the bottle. Then we'd pull on heavy snowsuits which made it awkward to move around, but necessary for a day playing in the cold snow. By the time dusk fell, we were tired, cold, wet and ready to snuggle with a stove-heated blanket. Soaked from head to toe, we'd head rosy-cheeked into the house to be greeted by the smell of a casserole that mother was just taking out of the oven. Our snowsuits were draped over the radiators to dry, the wet wool aroma permeating the house. After the family had eaten together we gathered around the table to listen to Fibber McGee and Molly or Edgar Bergen and Charlie McCarthy, or be excited by some of the brave heroes of the Old West and their adventures. – Annie Montgomery, born 1929, Orlando, FL.

*After considerable threats and promises, our mother, Lois, managed to get
my sister Bettie, 4, and me, 6, cleaned up, dressed and quiet long enough
for this picture to be taken in 1927. We were all fashionably dressed in the
style of the day. The photographer commented on what perfect angels we
were. Little did he know! - William Byerly, California*

**Our house, like many in the earlier part of the century, had a
pot-bellied stove in the living room, and we would cut and haul in
wood all winter long to feed the hungry thing. Of course the fire died
when we went to bed, so in the morning the house would be like an
igloo. Eventually we got a coal-burning furnace down in the
basement, but that had to be stoked with coal every day, and the
ashes shoveled out and hauled outside. It was back-breaking work,
but you didn't dare let it go out or everyone would freeze, or the
pipes might burst. Then, in the fifties I think it was, we had our
house converted to an oil-burning furnace, and that was fantastic. It
was hard to believe all we had to do was turn up the dial on the**

thermostat and the house would quickly be as warm as you wanted it. That led to some arguments because dad was always concerned about saving money and didn't want it to be hot, and mom was always cold.

Another technological breakthrough was when we replaced the fuse box with a circuit breaker. This was down in the basement and the fuses were always blowing out so we had to traipse downstairs with a flashlight and try to identify which fuse it was. And heaven help us if we had forgotten to buy extra fuses! Dad would put a penny in there to replace it temporarily but this was a dangerous thing to do and could start a fire. Circuit breakers, with their automatic shutoff if they were overloaded, were a godsend, and made everyone feel a lot safer. All you had to do was switch the breaker back on. – Ryan Wyrick deli owner, born 1936, Santa Rosa, CA.

The center of activity in our old farmhouse was the kitchen, where this grand old cookstove stood. It was a 1927 Welcome Globe. Our cat loved to curl up under it and keep warm. During the air-raid warnings of World War II we would all sit in the kitchen and the only light was from an orange glow coming from around the draft holes in the stove. That soft light made the warnings a little less scary. My brother is still using this stove in the old farmhouse today, and it's still working fine after 70 years. - Gladys Peters, Berwick, PA.

There are two things I loved most about getting electricity: clock radios, and electric blankets. Upstate New York gets really cold in the winter, it can sometimes even go below freezing and, even if you can get enough blankets on top of you to keep warm, when you first get into bed you always shiver for several minutes until your body heat warms it up. Pre-warming a bed with an electric blanket is my idea of heaven! Another thing I always hated was being rudely and loudly awakened by the ear-piercing sound of an alarm clock, especially at 6:00 a.m. on a cold winter morning. So the invention of clock radios that let me wake up gently to my favorite classical music, and be able to hit the snooze control for an extra ten minutes, was paradise.

You don't have to wind up a digital radio clock either, like we used to do when I was younger. If you forgot to wind the clock and it died during the night then you didn't get up on time, which could jeopardize your job. I remember we used to go around the house before bedtime making sure all the clocks were wound. Later we got pocket watches that only men wore of course, and they had to be wound too. You were out of luck if you didn't have a phone to call the operator and ask her what time it was because there were no radios or TV to tell you. Usually you ran next door and asked your neighbor. Then they evolved to a little wrist watch that you wound yourself, and finally battery watches that you only have to change about once a year. And now I've got a watch that can remember phone numbers and appointments, measure the temperature, give directions, gauge the distance I've walked, receive pager messages, record my voice, swap information with a computer, check my pulse and record my blood pressure. All on a device no bigger than a square inch. It's really astonishing! But the change from analog to digital clocks has meant that some children have never seen the hands of a clock or watch pointing to the actual numbers, and wouldn't know how to read one. —Jack Maruchi, retired contractor, born 1928, Topeka, KS.

I'll have a Cold One

Refrigerators are another appliance that has evolved over time, beginning with the simple box that had a huge block of ice in the top cabinet which gradually melted down into a pan under the ice box. When it was full the melted water had to be carried outside and thrown away, and everybody hated that job! Then the electric refrigerator was invented, but the ice built up on the walls of the freezer and it had to be defrosted each week, a laborious chore that often took hours. Pans of hot water would be placed inside to hasten the meltdown, and save endless chipping with an ice pick. Next came automatic defrosting which freed one from this onerous chore. And now we have huge capacity refrigerators with automatic ice-makers, filters and ready-made cold water. How convenient!

I long for one of those old iceboxes with zinc lining from the 1920s. It dependably chilled my food and provided chipped ice whenever I wanted a glass of ginger ale. But the best part of having an icebox was knowing the man who filled it. Our iceman in Ann Arbor, Michigan, was Mr. Bent, a friendly giant with old-world courtesy. On hot summer days, he was the Pied Piper to all the children in our town. We'd follow him on his route from stop to stop, and he was more than happy to share the little daggers of ice that he chipped from the great frozen blocks he carted throughout our neighborhood.

Mr. Bent knew to a millimeter the size and capacity of each icebox on his route. He chiseled and trimmed until the blocks of ice fit as perfectly as the keystones the Romans dropped into their arches. With his sharp tongs, he'd lug those sculptured blocks up long stairways to recharge the cold in each waiting icebox.

Mr. Bent's team of Belgian horses was the steadiest in town. Though they passed the noisy switchyard every day, not once were those horses spooked by the chuffing engines or banging railroad cars. They clip-clopped along the streets, looking every bit as proud and well-groomed as their master.

In a sense, Mr. Bent was our town crier, for he always knew what was going on. And he was more than glad to pass along the news of the day. —Anne-Marie Nilsen, Ann Arbor, MI.

I remember when we had an ice box and the ice wagon would come and the melting ice would drip out the back of the wagon all the way down the street. To keep the horse from wandering off while the iceman made his deliveries, a heavy iron weight was attached by a long strap and put down on the pavement. It worked much like the anchor on a boat. There was a canvas feed bag into which the horse could put his face, a nose-bag we called it, so the horse could have a snack while it waited. There were also public water troughs all over the city filled with rainwater, where the horses could get a drink. They weren't polluted and nobody ever thought of throwing anything in them, or dirtying them in any way. – Bruce Shenault, former mail carrier, born 1937.

My class is bright
As I could wish—
When Campbell's is
Their noonday dish!
1939

I lived on a farm as a child and, because we didn't have refrigerators, we had our own ice house. In winter my dad would go out on the pond or lake with his ice saw and cut large blocks of ice. These went into the ice house and were insulated by huge amounts of sawdust; enough that they stayed frozen all summer. My parents kept food (maybe a whole side of beef) cool in summer by wrapping it thoroughly and putting it into the sawdust close to the ice blocks. They also used that ice to make ice cream. We kept cows and separated the milk from the cream using a hand-operated cream separator, which was like a centrifuge. The milk went out one spout and the cream the other. The cream was sold and picked up every few days, so we kept it in the ice house in the meantime. We also made our own butter by putting the cream in a churn and taking turns churning it for hours and hours and hours until finally the butter would form. My dad would give us kids five cents an hour to churn that darned thing and it was tedious, exhausting work! But a nickel could buy a lot of candy in those days. – Mack Williams, Forester, born 1929.

In the early part of the century there wasn't a science of meteorology and we didn't get weather predictions from the newspaper or the evening news. We just looked up at the sky and made our own guess, based on experience. We'd never heard of a cold front coming down from Canada, or a storm off the Carolina coast heading our way. If we saw a blue-black cloud coming from the northwest we might interpret it as a blizzard coming, but we never knew for sure until it was upon us. When we lived on the farm we had to hastily round up the animals and get them inside the barn. We had a lot of sudden summer rainstorms in the Midwest, and a cloudburst could send the creek over its banks ruining everything in its path. -- Herb Combs, minister, born 1920.

Country Women Checking the Mail

Every afternoon I would run down to the big mail box on a post by the road when I heard the roll of wheels and the stop of the buggy that told me the mailman had arrived. Before they started rural free delivery, or the "mail route," as they called it, we had to go into town once a week to get our mail at the post office. But now the postman would bring the daily newspaper, and sometimes a magazine for my mother, but the most precious piece of mail would be a letter. Sometimes it would be from my aunt Lilly in Indiana, or from my mother's friend in Virginia, or even something official from the government. Getting a piece of mail was such an exciting event in those days that it's hard to believe that I now throw out about half of my mail without even opening it. – Jenny Partridge, born 1933 in Idaho.

Got Milk?

When I was a kid in the thirties and forties the milkman came every week in a horse and wagon to deliver milk to our house. When the glass bottles were empty, we'd wash them and put them out on the porch for the milkman to exchange for full ones. When you put the milk bottles out you put the money on top, or you put out a milk ticket hooked on with a clothespin, and a note indicating how many you needed. I can't imagine that today because the milk or the money would surely be gone by the time we got up! The bottles had the name of the dairy imprinted on them so they were taken back to the milk plant, sterilized, and used again...and again.

It was whole milk of course, none of this nonfat or one-percent fat stuff we have now. The cream would float to the top because it was heavier, and then mom would carefully drain that off and put it in a container for our cereal or dad's coffee. If we kids got to the

bottle first we would eat some of the frozen flakes of cream on top.
We didn't know that fat was fattening in those days, and we didn't
know that it clogged arteries, so if we had it in any form, we ate it
and didn't feel a bit guilty. — Bill Oaker, retired writer, born 1931.

My grandfather, Albert Koopman, was proud of his new Dodge milk truck when
this picture was taken in 1956. He ran his own farm and dairy for over fifty
years. - Jeff Koopman, Northbridge, Massachusetts

Modern Living

In the early part of the century homes often looked gloomy, with heavy drapes
and mahogany or other dark wood-paneling. Furniture was often large and
ornate. The dining room was the centerpiece of the home, and usually had a
large table where the nuclear family, other relatives and drop-in visitors could
all assemble, eat and talk. Birthdays, holiday rituals and other festivities were all
celebrated around the dining room table. When wives stayed home, dinner was
usually served promptly at 5 or 6 p.m. when the man of the house came home
from work, and everyone sat down together to eat and share their day.

This homey scene, which gave a sense of structure and security to
the family, was seldom seen by the end of the century. Mom was no longer
home all day preparing a nutritious family meal. People sometimes ate with
trays on their laps, sitting in front of the TV. The kids were in and out, often
heating up something in the microwave on their way to "practice," and dad
may not be home at all but still at the office. The elaborate formal dining

room of the past was disappearing as family members ate in the den, the kitchen, or on the run.

> YOU MAKE THE BEST SPAGHETTI! BUT WHY DID YOU STEW OVER THE STOVE ON SUCH A HOT DAY?

> BUT I DIDN'T, MY DEAR! THIS SPAGHETTI COMES READY-COOKED—

and the sauce is better than I can make!

"WHO wants to slave in a hot kitchen this hot weather? I'm sure I don't! That's why I'm doubly delighted to have discovered Franco-American Spaghetti. It not only saves me work, but we actually like it better than the kind I used to make. My sauce never was as good as this. I think Franco-American has the *best* sauce I ever tasted!"

Just try it and see!

We might recite the long list of eleven different ingredients this glorious sauce contains . . . the big, luscious, flavorful tomatoes . . . the mellow Cheddar cheese . . . all the tangy spices and seasonings. Yet mere words can never express the most important thing of all that goes into it — the inspired chef's touch! But one *taste* reveals it — makes women

exclaim in surprise, "Why, this spaghetti is a lot better than mine!"

Costs less, too

Serve Franco-American soon. See what a hit it makes with everybody. And remember, Franco-American is not only easier and more delicious, but more economical, too. Actually, it costs less than buying dry spaghetti and ingredients for the sauce and burning fuel to cook them.

But that's only half the economy story. Franco-American is packed full of nourishment. It contains a rich supply of important food elements that are needed to build strength and energy, yet costs surprisingly little. Generous can holding three to four portions is never more than ten cents. Why not ask your grocer for this delicious spaghetti today?

In the past, most homes had a piano for entertainment and, on top of the piano sat framed photographs of all the family members, including extended family. Trinkets and art objects stuffed every cabinet and filled every corner. As the years went by the piano was replaced by a console radio and record player, then a hi fi, and finally a stereo with dual cassettes and Compact Disk player, housed in its own entertainment center.

The photographs were replaced with indoor plants, a novelty in the fifties, and furniture became modern art-deco. Simplicity was in. Synthetic rugs began to replace woolen ones, and the relieved housewife cleaned them with an electric vacuum cleaner, instead of hauling them outside, throwing them over the line and beating them with a broom.

Cool Inventions

One of the things I really like are dimmers that can be put on the light switches. I have them all over the house. We had an elegant chandelier in the dining room in my parent's house, but they're gone now in most houses, and I always hated turning on a bright light over the dinner table, so these dimmers are great. We have a night light in the bathroom so if you have to go in there in the middle of the night you don't have to put the light on full blast and wake yourself up. Of course those weren't invented in my parents' day. Sometimes we don't realize it's the little things like this that make our lives more pleasant. Even knowing that we have smoke alarms in all the rooms, and a fire extinguisher in the kitchen, is a blessing, so I don't have to worry so much about the kids. – Tracy Hull, dog groomer, born 1942, Arlington, VA.

Some things are so common we never think about them, but a calendar on the kitchen wall is a luxury we didn't have in the early part of the century. We had to rely on our memory or the newspaper, or see the calendar in the local bank to know what day it was.

One of the inventions I liked the most was pre-glued wallpaper. When I was a kid my mom had a fetish for changing the wallpaper every couple of years. It was a real chore because we always had to strip off the old paper, which would sometimes take days to accomplish. Then gluing the new stuff on was very messy and we'd get it all over us, so when I got my own home the only wallpaper I'd ever buy was the pre-glued kind, which wasn't available when I was younger.

And how about paper towels? What a convenience they are! Before their invention we used to keep huge bags full of rags under the sink for all the clean-up stuff, and then throw them in the wash. Pulling a towel off a roll to clean up little spills on the counter is sheer luxury to me. – Francine Lapides, born 1944, Felton, CA.

Good Housekeeping, 1932

Something that people today are probably not aware of is the evolution of the bed. In the past they were often very comfortable if you had down or feather beds, but they were extremely small! There was no such thing as a "Queen" or "King" size, or even "Full" size, and most of them were just slightly bigger than today's twin bed. Of course both mom and dad had to sleep together in one bed, and maybe two or three or even four kids might sleep in another one, depending on the family finances. It sometimes amazes me when I go to a historical museum where a bed is displayed how two adults could manage to sleep comfortably in one of them. Overweight people probably had a big problem trying to avoid rolling off the bed in the middle of the night. In the seventies waterbeds were the fad, but they often proved to be unreliable, causing landlords to charge an extra deposit if the tenants had one. Some apartment buildings even had regulations against them. And, when you decided to move, it took forever to drain all the water out of them.

I remember during the '60s many motels had coin-operated vibrating beds, called "Magic Fingers," that would massage you to sleep for a quarter. Fifteen minutes for two bits. They were really neat, and I thought they were sexy too! Then some people started vandalizing the coin machines and stealing the quarters, so eventually these disappeared from motels, along with coin-operated radios and TV sets, which soon became free.   – Patrick McAtee, respiratory therapist, born 1940, San Jose, CA.

I say Sissy! The Umbrella that boy has got was certainly not sewed with COATS COLORED THREAD See the seams have all washed White. Ours are firm as a Rock.

Until at least the sixties a sewing basket was as indispensable in every household as an iron. Everyone's mother had one and, if a kid were to rip off a button playing with the neighbor's children, their mother would promptly whip out her basket and sew it back on. A boy's corduroy pants often had patches at the knees that mom had sewn on, and dad's shirts lasted longer when she detached the frayed collars and cuffs, turned under the worn parts, and sewed them back on. Socks of course were darned when the heel wore out, and sis got a new dress for the school prom only because mom knew how to sew one for her. Almost every housewife had a sewing machine with a woven basket sitting beside it full of mercerized cotton thread, thimbles, needles and extra buttons. As clothes became cheaper and women entered the workforce, taking the time to mend a dress or darn a sock became a luxury for which few had time. As the cost of fabric increased, sewing a dress became as expensive as buying one at a discount store, and many of today's women would have no idea how to read a McCalls' or Vogue pattern.

An ad in the January, 1953 issue of "Better Homes and Gardens" urged husbands to *"Give her an O-Cedar Sponge Mop for Christmas! Keeps hands dry, and cleans floor faster. Only $3.95."* Today's woman would not welcome a broom as a Christmas gift; he may wear it over his head.

When we lived on the farm in Iowa in the thirties my mother cooked our meals on a wood stove, used a kerosene lamp to light the house in the evening, and washed our clothes on a washboard in the sink, using lye soap to get them clean. She boiled the water in an enormous black kettle which was also used for making the year's supply of laundry soap. She made all the familys' clothing, including even the mens' overalls, on her old Singer sewing machine that had a foot pedal which she pumped with her feet to make it go. Of course nothing was ever wasted in those days because most everyone was poor. When a child outgrew something it was passed on down to the youngest, and finally it was ripped apart and the material was reused for something else. Once a month dad would take mom into town in our horse-drawn carriage so she could go to the millinery store and get some more thread and fabric to make our clothes, and maybe even get a new hat that she could wear to church.

A washboard and old machine with wringer

Dad took care of all the outside chores, milked the cows, pitched hay, carried swill to the pigs, fed the chickens, built a barn, cut wood for the pot-bellied stove, trimmed the fruit trees and helped take care of the garden. We didn't have tractors or any other kind of heavy machinery, so everything had to be done ourselves with the help of a horse. My parents worked from sunup to sundown, and never complained. As children we helped churn the milk to make butter and cheese, picked the bugs off the corn and tomatoes, and did other chores, besides enjoying home-grown vegetables free of pesticides and playing outdoors in the fresh air a lot of the time.

Nobody was a lazybones on the farm, everyone had their job to do, and the work was never finished. Women certainly couldn't work outside the home, unless they were "old maids" and didn't have a husband and kids to take care of, then they might become schoolmarms. My mother had to sew clothes for herself and the children, darn socks, do a load of laundry every day, sometimes more than one, make her own bread, shuck peas, peel potatoes and do other chores from morning till night. In those days there wasn't any social stigma about child labor because the work had to be done, and everyone had to help, and we knew it, so we didn't complain much. The boys worked outside helping dad, and the girls stayed inside helping mom. And of course there were no movies, no radio, no soft drinks, and no plastic toys. All the toys we had were made by dad, or put together ourselves out of this and that. If your religion didn't forbid it, you could play card games and, if your parents could read, they would read you a story, mostly something from the Bible. We didn't have any schoolbooks because most families couldn't afford to buy them, so we only read them when we were at the schoolhouse.

We didn't have any music because we were too poor to afford a piano, but my dad had a harmonica that he would sometimes amuse us with. Of course we had a front porch like everyone had, and on Sundays when we couldn't work, after we got home from church we would sit out on the swing and watch for grandpa's wagon to come rolling down the dirt road. Then we would get to hear the week's news because of course we didn't have a telephone or a radio, so we never knew what had happened during the week until those Sunday visits. – Fay Ramsey, housewife, born 1925 in New Hampshire.

A Loaf of Bread, A Glass of Wine...

I think sliced bread was introduced about 60 years ago. First we had loaves that we tried to slice evenly ourselves, which never worked of course, and it was so hard we had to toast it to make it edible. We didn't have toasters that automatically popped the toast up in those days, so you stood over it until the toast started to burn, then quickly pulled down the latches on the sides of the toaster and turned each piece over. I remember when Gilianni's grocery store down on the corner started carrying sliced bread. We could buy a few pieces at a time, wrapped in waxed paper, so mom would save pennies and then we kids would run down and get five pieces of bread for supper each night. That was about 1939 I think.

The famous Wonderbread is still around but, thankfully, we now have lots of whole wheat breads to choose from. But I make my own bread with my home breadmaking machine, so I don't have to spend the morning kneading dough. My grandmother would have been overjoyed with that.

Most things were wrapped either in newspaper or waxed paper. The butcher had those huge rolls of brown paper that he'd wrap the meat in, but it didn't sit in a meat bin wrapped in see-through cling wrap like it does today, it was just protected by sliding glass, sometimes not even that. Aluminum foil to wrap food was quite an invention, and enabled us to keep food frozen in the freezer for a long time. And nobody asked that infernal question: "Paper or plastic?" when you got to the checkout counter because there wasn't any plastic.

Of course we didn't have supermarkets in the early part of the century, just family grocery stores, and then gradually a few larger markets began opening up. Fresh produce was one of the things I loved the most! In the thirties we seldom had anything fresh in Wisconsin in the winter. Most of the time we ate canned vegetables, either ones my mom had canned herself, or from the grocery store. They were usually fairly tasteless, and people were always afraid they'd get botulism from the tin cans if they didn't eat the food fast enough. Of course we didn't have Tupperware, Ziploc bags, or any other plastic containers to store it in, so nobody went to 'Tupperware parties' back then. – Jean Dixon, born 1930.

Good Housekeeping Ad, 1945

I remember when margarine first came out the government wouldn't let the manufacturers color it because the butter industry said it would compete with them and cause them to lose business. So it came in a pure white package, almost like lard, and there was a little red ball on top that you had to squeeze into the margarine if you wanted it to look more edible, like butter. Most of us did, so we had to spend about ten minutes squeezing and stirring that bag of red coloring into the margarine until the whole thing turned yellow. After a few years, the government relented and allowed margarine to be sold with pre-mixed color. – Patricia Griswold, homemaker, born 1940, Indianapolis, IN.

But Can She Cook?

Cooking appliances have changed a lot since our mothers had to sweat over a hot oven all day to prepare family meals. Pressure cookers were popular in the forties for preparing quick meals, but died out when some accidents were reported and people became afraid of them. Later we had small toaster ovens that could cook a cheese sandwich, or even a TV dinner, and then came the biggest revolution in cooking, the microwave. That was a great boon to working people in a hurry; or even the opposite device, the Crockpot, so food could be put in it in the morning and be ready in the evening without burning. And Teflon coated pans were a welcome miracle that saved a lot of dishwashing and pot scrubbing.

My sister, Mary Caldwell Murphy, cooking with her New Guardian Service Cookware in 1949. Evelyn Caldwell Sotir, Crystal River, FL

For lovers of coffee, no longer must it be boiled tasteless on the stove, but it can gently drip down into a glass pot or, for those who prefer a stronger brew, home espresso machines are available. If you want a cup of gourmet coffee you can drink it on the patio of an elite coffee shop in a foam cup which was invented in the fifties, and despised by many.

For dessert most every night my mom would open a can of peaches or pears preserved in thick, heavy syrup, because you just couldn't get fresh fruit then in the wintertime. It was such a pleasure when frozen vegetables were invented, and then more and more fresh ones became available, but nothing nearly like the display you see in the stores now. Since they invented refrigerated transportation we now have this incredible array of fresh vegetables and fruit but, if it's out of season, you can always buy the frozen kind. It was just a little jump from frozen vegetables to entire dinners that were frozen and could be quickly heated up in the oven, and later on in a microwave. Everything seems to be instant today, instant coffee, instant oatmeal, instant rice, and now we even have instant salads. It's convenient, but the nutritional value of some of these foods is debatable. – Carmela D'Angelo, medical transcriptionist, born 1932, Toronto, Canada.

A Diner's Wonderland

When I was about twenty years old and had my first job I used to eat lunch at the Automat in New York. It was on the west side of Broadway near Times Square. It was really quite chic with white marble tabletops, and a white tile floor. The best thing was the convenience! I used to try to go home from the office for lunch, but that was always a hassle. Now I could just walk a couple of blocks, put a few nickels in the slot, and choose from a wonderful array of food presented in individual glass compartments stacked up like little mailboxes. Seventy-five cents could buy a three-course dinner of macaroni and cheese or beef pot pie with cole slaw, a roll, a glass of milk, and a slice of lemon meringue pie. It was quite a bargain during the Depression. Local business people would go there for lunch, and soon even actors and other celebrities began frequenting it. By 1939 there were forty Automats in New York, serving about 800,000 meals a day. I don't know why they disappeared, but I suppose it was because of the emergence of fast-food chains that soon took over. -– Gary Albright, retired librarian, born 1932.*

As a child in the '40s, I was lucky enough to eat at Horn and Hardart Automats in New York City. My grandmother would take me there after we'd gone to a double feature. Clutching her hand, I felt fear and fascination as we entered the large, noisy restaurant. The first thing we did was exchange a dollar for twenty nickels, enough to buy dinner.

Not unlike postal boxes, the automat windows formed a huge wall of small, heavy glass squares framed in stainless steel. Behind those windows reposed a wonderland of food choices. There were sandwiches on soft, white bread, their centers bulging with ham, corned beef, egg salad or chicken. Other windows displayed plump, glistening hot dogs, bowls of soup and red-umber baked beans dripping from dark-green porcelain bowls. When I'd made my choice, I put the required number of nickels into the slot. With a snap, the window popped open. I'd reach in, grab the white plate and slide the treasure onto my tray. Just like magic, that window slammed shut and, in the empty space where my food had been

*whirled away, an exact   duplicate appeared. Balancing my tray,
I weaved my way back to grandmother and carefully slid it onto the
heavy, Bakelite table, It was yellow with wide, pale-green borders,
and I loved its smooth, worn feel.*

*My memories of the Automats are happy ones and, while
I wish they still existed, I know the food couldn't possibly be as good
as it was back then. Never again will twenty nickels buy so much
pleasure! – L.C. Van Savage, Brunswick, ME.*

*In the early 1960s while vacationing in New York, we stayed at
the old Martinique Hotel on 33rd and Broadway. When my sister,
Henrietta, looked out the window and saw the red lights of a Horn
& Hardart Automat, she could hardly wait to go there for dinner.
Many of our meals during that visit were right there at that
wonderful Automat. It was really a novelty putting our coins in the
slot, sliding open the door, and retrieving our food, while watching
another one quickly take its place. The coffee was superb and cost
only 5 cents. -- Gerald Palmer, Rochester, NY.*

Want fries with that?

J.G. Kirby's Pig Stand, the first drive-in restaurant, opened in Dallas in 1921. In
1935 Howard Johnson contracted with a friend to open a restaurant on Cape
Cod. Within a year, thirty-nine more Howard Johnson franchises had opened,
becoming the first franchised chain restaurants. By 1941 there were more
than 150 Howard Johnson restaurants stretched along the roads from Florida
to New England.

The architecture of Schaber's Cafeteria, on Broadway in downtown Los Angeles, was typical of the grand style of the cafeteria in its heyday. In the early part of the century, they were very swank with live music, appealing food and upscale décor. The cafeteria craze started in Los Angeles in 1905 when Helen Mosher opened a downtown restaurant where people chose their food from several selections at a long counter and carried their own trays to their tables. Using the slogans "Food That Can Be Seen," and "No Tips," the idea of not having to wait for a waiter to take your order and then deliver your food, quickly caught on. By 1920 the concept of self-service cafeterias spread internationally, even reaching France. They started fading away by the mid-forties as people moved out to the suburbs, and drive-in restaurants, and eventually simple, unadorned fast-food joints began replacing them.

When I was growing up, my favorite place to eat was Kresge's. My allowance was 25 cents and, after saving pennies to buy gifts for my parents, food for my canary, and an occasional magazine, there was little left. However, when I'd saved 10 cents extra...the price of a bowl of mashed potatoes and gravy, with a glass of water, a girlfriend and I would walk downtown to Kresge's for this special treat. Sometimes we even managed to have enough to buy a Coke. Our ultimate goal was to save 75 cents to get a turkey dinner with all the trimmings. That happened only once a year. – Sandy Flick, Toledo.

My father, Edward Oulund (far left behind the counter,) was the manager and a cook at Cooper's in Chicago in this 1939 photo. Customers could order 2 tenderloin steaks, 2 fried eggs, toast and coffee for a grand total of .55 cents. -Jack Oulund, New Castle, CO

The appearance in the late fifties of fast-food outlets such as McDonald's, Taco Bell, Burger King, Kentucky Fried Chicken, Jack-in-the-Box, Mexican and Chinese take-out food, all loaded with fat, were too tempting and convenient for the average person to resist. Also contributing to the increased popularity of "junk food" are working parents who are often too tired to cook, and the easiest thing to do is put the kids in the car and take them to a fast food place, which is much cheaper than eating in a restaurant. Home delivered food, the ultimate in convenience, was unknown until the sixties.

Since the 1990s obesity has become an epidemic in America even though weight loss salons, diet supplements and fitness clubs have become big business. Thousands of people are desperately trying to work it off, sweat it off and starve it off, but the end result seems to be people are becoming increasingly overweight. Low-fat and non-fat foods became the rage in the last few decades, but studies showed people were actually eating more fat than ever. But probably the biggest contributor to our ever-widening girth has been the advent of "snack foods," consumed in great quantity while lounging in front of the ubiquitous television.

My Aunt Vera was proud of being fat and thought it was sexy. – Janice Fields

When I was a kid in the '40s we weren't chubby little kids like some are today because first of all we exercised all the time playing outdoor games, instead of zoning out in front of the TV and,

secondly, we didn't have any fast-food restaurants where we could gorge ourselves on French-fries and double cheeseburgers. The most fattening food we ever ate was when mom would give us a dollar and send us down to the fish and chip store where we would eat loads of Halibut deep-fried in thick greasy batter. But that was a real treat; it only happened when mom was going to one of her meetings and too busy to cook dinner. – Fran Alrecht, artist, born 1933, Rochester, NY.

In 1923 Frank C. Mars invented the Milky Way and Curtiss Candy invented Butterfinger. Welch's put its first jar of grape jelly on the market, Sanka perked its first pot, and Pet Milk hit the stores.

Clarence Birdseye offered his quick-frozen foods to the public in 1929. Birdseye got the idea during fur-trapping expeditions to Labrador in 1912 and 1916, where he saw the natives use freezing to preserve foods.

Gerber started selling baby food in jars in 1929. Before that time mothers had to mix and mash their own.

The American Dream: Owning Your Own Home

Never before have Americans spent so much time and money on their homes. We are buying more and bigger houses, and decking them out in ways not even imaginable fifty years ago. Before the second World War, barely half of homes had a telephone, a radio, hot water, a flush toilet and a bathtub. By 1945, most had all these features. Backyard pools began showing up by mid-century, originally plastic ovals that sat on top of the ground and had to be hand-filled and drained, and finally pools sunken into the ground that one sees dotting southern cities when you fly over them. Many of these pools are heated by the sun, using solar panels.

By the end of the century single family homes were so expensive less than forty percent of the populace could afford to buy one. In the Bay Area of Northern California, particularly San Francisco, the median price was over $300,000, and climbing.. But the size has been increasing too. In 1949 the average single-family household was 4.2 people, and the average house was only about 1,200 square feet. Now the average family is only 2.8 people and the house is at least 2,500 square feet. The appearance of suburbs in mid-century helped spur the development of larger homes because people who had left crowded cities wanted space to spread out, both inside and out.

Former home of the Vondra Family, Stockton, Illinois, 1933.

This thirteen room house on a farm had seven bedrooms, a steam heating system and a full bath. We had two wood-burning stoves, one for cooking in the kitchen and a pot-bellied heater in the dining room. The house wasn't insulated so thick frost formed on our upstairs windows in the winter. — Elmer Vondra

CHAPTER FOUR

That's Entertainment!

When the twentieth century opened nobody went to a Beethoven concert or listened to a Mozart record because there were no classical recordings, and no symphony orchestras. There were some chamber music ensembles that played private concerts in the homes of the wealthy, and small theater orchestras, but the majority of people listened to band music, which was usually played outdoors, and was popularized by John Philip Sousa, composer of *The Stars and Stripes Forever.* The Sousa band went on a world tour in 1910, bringing its stirring music to Europe, Great Britain, Australia, Hawaii and Canada.

A century of unimaginable media capabilities opened in 1901 when Walt Disney was born and changed the world of entertainment forever. He opened the first cartoon studio in Hollywood in 1923, and created Mickey Mouse, the first of a long line of beloved creatures that delighted the child in us. He premiered Snow White, the first full-length animated film in 1937. Disney invented the theme park and opened *Disneyland* in California in 1955. His creative innovations have shaped our world and the way we experience it. Walt Disney died in Los Angeles in 1966, mourned by hundreds of creatures.

The first movie theater was established in Pittsburgh in 1905 and featured the longest moving picture at the time: *The Great Train Robbery*, which lasted all of twelve minutes. People were so fascinated they refused to leave the theatre when it ended, and watched it over and over. It starred Mary Pickford, "America's Sweetheart," the first film star, but the words she spoke could not be heard by theatergoers because talking pictures were not yet invented. *The Great Train Robbery* introduced a revolutionary concept: the story line.

Two of the film world's greatest stars were born that same year: Marlene Dietrich in Germany, and Greta Garbo in Sweden. "**Garbo Speaks!**" screamed the headlines when her first talkie, *Anna Christie* was released in 1930. And what did she say? These memorable words: "*Give me a whiskey, ginger ale on the side, and don't be stingy, baby.*"

In 1913 Paramount Pictures introduced its first movies, starring Charlie Chaplin in *Making a Living* and *Tillie's Punctured Romance*. Until "talkies" were created in 1920, the actors just mouthed any old words they could think of, sometimes it was just gibberish, and the director would give instructions aloud while they were playing the scene. The first movie with sound was released in 1927, *The Jazz Singer*, starring Al Jolson. Thomas Edison, who was the first person to create a movie studio, declared that "The talking motion picture will not supplant the regular silent motion picture... there is such a tremendous investment to pantomime pictures that it would be absurd to disturb it." He was a great inventor but he wasn't very psychic!

When I was ten, we used to visit my grandma in Mendon, Michigan, which is a very small town. On Saturday nights, they would show a free movie in a corner lot on Main Street. We took chairs or blankets to sit on. A man with a popcorn machine sold bags for five cents and, at the drugstore next to the lot, you could get an ice cream cone for only a nickel. So, if you had a dime, you had it made. –Joan Panno, Chicago, IL

In 1909 the first newsreels were produced and now people could go to a movie theater to see pictures of current world events, albeit a week late. Nevertheless, people found the idea of seeing live, moving pictures of events that happened across the world's oceans to be absolutely amazing! Along with newsreels, movie theaters began showing cartoons, designed by Disney Studios, before the feature movie. Donald Duck cartoons appeared in movie houses in 1934, often difficult to understand, but fascinating for their animation. The first Shirley Temple film was made in 1934 and she immediately became the nation's darling.

Sid Grauman's palatial Chinese Theatre, which still stands today, opened in Hollywood in 1927, with Cecil B. DeMille's *King of Kings* screening for 2,000 viewers. Price of a ticket: ten cents. The Academy of

Motion Picture Arts and Sciences was founded that same year, and is now known as the Motion Picture Association of America, which presents the Oscar Awards each year in Los Angeles.

Marlene Dietrich and Gary Cooper in "Morocco," 1930.

The first Academy Awards were presented on May 16, 1929. *Wings*, an epic film of romance, war, and daring in the air, staring Gary Cooper and Clara Bowe, was chosen as best film. Charlie Chaplin was given a special award for "his genius and versatility in writing, acting, directing, and producing *The Circus*. This was the only award the great Chaplin ever won.

Gone With the Wind, considered one of the great, enduring classics, brought "Technicolor" to the movies in 1939. The script was derived from Margaret Mitchell's best-selling Civil War novel that was over a thousand pages long. It was also one of the longest movies of the century, running three hours and forty-two minutes, excluding intermissions. Producer David O. Selznick acquired the film rights to the novel in 1936 for $50,000, a record amount for the first novel of an unknown author. Although this extravagant purchase was dubbed "Selznick's Folly," he proved to be psychic and his investment has paid off many times over!

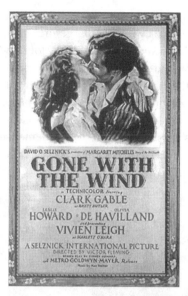

CinemaScope hit movie theaters across the U.S. in 1953, followed by stereophonic sound and wide screens to make the most of it. While providing the audience with a pair of special glasses, movies in 3-D were attempted in the sixties, but were a dismal failure. People found it awkward to sit in a theater for a couple of hours wearing a silly-looking pair of glasses.

Going to a movie at the drive-in was always my favorite place to take a date, because being in the dark in the privacy of your own car made it easy to smooch. I always picked a romantic movie that I hoped would turn the girl on, and it usually worked. Of course in the fifties it wasn't easy to have sex with a girl, but we did plenty of kissing, touching, feeling and groping. When I finally got married and had kids, the drive-in was still the best place to go because we didn't have to pay a baby-sitter, we could bring our own popcorn, and we didn't have to search for a place to park. We'd put the kids in their pajamas so if they fell asleep all we had to do was toss them into bed when we got home. It was a lot cheaper too if you had a large family, and you could make all the comments you wanted about the movie and it didn't bother anybody. Now we rent videos and have all the comforts of home —snacks, a handy bathroom, privacy, and comfortable clothing, but I really miss the drive-ins because there was something exciting about exploring 'forbidden fruit' in the back seat of the old jalopy. It was a Saturday night ritual I really enjoyed. –Jason Higgens, mechanic, born, 1941, Long Beach, CA.

The first drive-in movie theater was opened in 1933 in Camden, New Jersey. In 1948 Hull's Drive-in theater on Route 11 in Lexington, Virginia opened with *Wake of the Red Witch,* starring John Wayne. Saturday night visits to this outdoor theater were as much a part of family life in the Shenandoah Valley as the county fair or Little League. Families brought their own snacks and spread out in lawn chairs or blankets, while teenagers preferred to snuggle in the darkness of their car's interior. When land values escalated, Hulls closed and was to be demolished in 1998, but the townspeople so loved their landmark they organized a fund to purchase the drive-in for the community.

GLORIA SWANSON.

Courtesy TIME Magazine

Memories are Made of This

As a boy in Alhambra, California, in the days of silent films, I was smitten with cowboy movies, and spent a dime of my meager allowance every Saturday at the Granada Theatre. Music for the silent movies was provided by Alan Spur, a blind organist. He relied on us kids to let him know what the cowboys were doing on the screen. I'd sit alongside him on his bench, and sometimes develop

a crick in my neck from staring almost straight up at the screen.
When the inevitable shoot-'em-up chase scene began, I'd nudge him
with my elbow, and he'd usually start playing the "William Tell
Overture." – Wally Smith, Littleriver, CA.

Movies and the lyrics of certain songs are often connected with
significant events in our lives, and evoke memories of times gone by. As we
look back at some of the most popular songs and movies of the century, they
serve as reminders of special years: places we lived at the time, friends we
associated with then, perhaps nostalgic memories of sharing a movie with a
lover of yesteryear, and reaching out in the dark to shyly hold a hand.
Enshrined in our memories and captured forever on a piece of tape, these
sometimes great, sometimes humorous, sometimes emotional works of art,
and the people who made them, live on. Movies are a treasure trove of the
history of the twentieth century; the only century that has had its life and
thought preserved forever.

Some movies, such as *Norma Rae, National Velvet*, and *Lawrence of
Arabia*, were inspiring, some delightfully entertaining with sweet, doe-eyed
stars like Audrey Hepburn in *Sabrina* and *Roman Holiday*. Movies like
Psycho, Rosemary's Baby, and *In Cold Blood*, terrified us, highlighting the
violent side of mankind. Some were controversial, like *The Wild One* and *Easy
Rider* and still others, like *Marty, Sophie's Choice* and *The Color Purple*,
touched us emotionally. Now, in the latter half of the century, we have a
choice that didn't exist until the seventies: we can get dressed and go
downtown to a movie, or we can put on our P.J.s in the comfort of our home
and watch a video while skipping through the commercials and enjoying
our home-made popcorn.

Memorable Stars

Born in 1921, Lana Turner, the platinum-blonde "Sweater Girl" who loved
going to the movies, was "discovered" at the Top Hat Café, across the street
from Hollywood High. W.R. Wilkerson, publisher of the Hollywood Reporter,
caught sight of her, introduced himself and asked her to call talent agent
Zeppo Marx. She was hired for the magnificent sum of $50 per week. Thus
began a celebrated career that included five Academy Awards, but she is
probably best known for her portrayal of Cora in *The Postman Always Rings
Twice*. Later in life she became involved with a dangerous mob associate,
Johnny Stompanato, who was abusive. During one violent argument, her
daughter Cheryl, fearing Stompanato would kill her mother, fatally stabbed
him with a kitchen knife. The death was ruled a justifiable homicide. Lana
died of throat cancer in 1995 at seventy-four years old.

The last glamorous child-star of the thirties is the stunningly beautiful Elizabeth Taylor. Born in London, England in 1932, her impassioned acting and violet-eyed beauty has made her a legend.   Plagued by life-long health problems, including a benign brain tumor in 1997, Ms. Taylor has survived many tragedies.   She first achieved fame in 1934 at the age of twelve when she played the leading role in *National Velvet*, opposite Mickey Rooney.   In 1956 she appeared in the hit *Giant,* with James Dean, and in *Raintree County* with Montgomery Clift. She finally won an Oscar in 1960 for her flawless performance as a call-girl in *Butterfield 8*. She's famous not only for her acting, but also for her many husbands. In 1963, Elizabeth starred in *Cleopatra,* and her salary was said to be a whopping one million dollars. During this film she fell in love with Richard Burton, and quickly divorced Eddie Fisher, who had divorced Debbie Reynolds in 1959 in order to marry Liz.   She managed to survive the scorn which was heaped upon her from a disapproving society, and later received plaudits for her performance, along side Richard, in *Who's Afraid of Virginia Woolf?* Now in her older years, she devotes herself to causes such as The AIDS Foundation.

*On May 6, 1950, Liz Taylor wed hotel magnate
Conrad Hilton. Photo Courtesy of Los Angeles Times*

*I'll never forget seeing Elizabeth and Richard Burton in
Toronto, in 1963. I was taking a seminar at the King Edward Hotel
when they were staying there.   During lunch break I got into the
elevator to go down to the dining room and there they were! I tried
to be cool and didn't even look at them, let alone whip out a piece of
paper and ask for their autographs. I figured they deserved a little
privacy after the press had come down hard on them for leaving
their respective spouses to be together. Believe me, it was quite a
thrill to see someone I'd worshipped as a little girl when she starred
in "National Velvet!" I was surprised at how tiny she was since she
seemed so tall and impressive in "Cleopatra." He looked like
somebody out of the FBI's 'most wanted' files, wearing a tan
trenchcoat with his collar pulled up, and his face was pock-marked,
something you don't notice in the movies.*

*They weren't married yet, and they ostensibly had separate
rooms. There were actually people picketing outside the hotel with
signs calling them sinners, slut and immoral. She was so beautiful I
tried to keep from staring at her while I was eating lunch. I could
hardly wait to get back to class and tell the students who I'd seen.
– Jesse Marlbrough, born 1936, Hamilton, Ontario, Canada.*

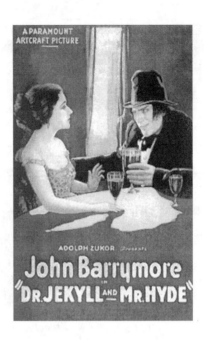

Immortalized by Dying

During the "Roaring '20s" Rudolph Valentino was the hot Latin lover of silent movies. An extremely handsome virile-looking man, he was portrayed as a dashing and seductive playboy, impossible for women to resist, both on and off screen. His premature death at the young age of thirty-one set off the most outrageous mass-mourning in the history of celebrity deaths. Nearly 30,000 people came to the funeral home where his body was displayed, crying, moaning, collapsing and causing a near riot. There were even reports that some people had attempted suicide to be with their beloved in heaven. His reputation as a heroic conqueror of women was so great that the name Valentino has become a synonym for romantic, debonair, playboy types.

Two superstars of the fifties were Marilyn Monroe and James Dean, both of whom died an early death, she in bed and he in a speeding car. Dean was killed when his Porsche Spyder went off the road late at night in 1955, and hit a tree. He was only twenty-four years old and at the height of his career. Marilyn Monroe was found dead in her bed on August 4, 1962, an apparent suicide at age thirty-six. At the end of the century, the cause of her death is still being disputed. Although they may have eventually faded into obscurity if they had lived, too soon taken from our midst, they are now immortal. We can only remember them as young, attractive, magnetic personalities who held for us a certain fascination while they were here.

Two other major stars of the '40s and '50s were Natalie Wood and Montgomery Clift, both of whom also had an early death. Throughout his life Monty, one of the great movie stars of the post-war era, was plagued by drug dependency, alcoholism, guilt and shame because of his homosexuality. A disturbed personality, who often appeared moody and brooding, he earned four Oscar nominations, and his unique style of acting influenced generations to come. On July 23, 1966, at only forty-six years old, his companion, Lorenzo James, found him lying on his bed, dead from "occlusive coronary artery disease." During his short life he played in eighteen movies, including *Suddenly, Last Summer, Raintree County, A Place in the Sun* and *From Here to Eternity.*

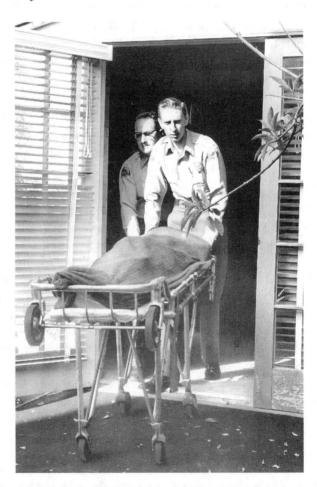

The body of Marilyn Monroe being removed from her home. Los Angeles Times, August, 1962

Death of a Princess

Grace Kelly first starred with Gary Cooper in *High Noon*, in which she played a mousey Quaker bride. Her performance in *Mogambo* in 1953 won her an Academy Award nomination and a Golden Globe for Best Supporting Actress. Her work in *High Noon* and a screen test for the film *Taxi* piqued the interest of director Alfred Hitchcock, who, with the aid of Edith Head, pruned Grace into his ideal of the elegant, beautiful blonde. Grace went against this image in the film *The Country Girl,* which won her the Academy Award for Best Actress in 1954. The success of the song "True Love" from the movie *High Society*, which she recorded with Bing Crosby, earned her a gold record. In 1956, she was voted the Golden Globe's World Film Favorite Actress.

Grace became a real princess in 1956, when she married Prince Rainier Grimaldi III of Monaco and became Her Serene Highness Princess Grace of Monaco. Because of her royalty, she was forced to give up her successful acting career, after she had made eleven films, including *To Catch a Thief* with Cary Grant and *Rear Window* with Jimmy Stewart.

Grace died tragically on September 14, 1982, leaving behind three children: Caroline, Albert, and Stephanie. She was killed in an accident when her car went off a road over the cliffs of Monaco, while her daughter Stephanie was with her. She was only fifty-three years old, and was mourned by hundreds of thousands of fans who still revere the memory of this beautiful, graceful, elegant princess.

When my brothers and I were little, mom would send us to the Sheas' Theater on Saturday afternoons. There was only one theater in town, and it showed a different movie every two weeks, so there wasn't a lot of choice. We walked there of course, a distance of about a half mile, and no one worried about our safety. It was during World War II, and the show cost a dime, but you could get in free if you brought some metal, such as pots and pans, or a piece of silverware which was melted down and used for making machinery. There were posters in the lobby warning people to keep quiet, not because of disturbing other patrons, but because 'The enemy may be listening,' and 'Loose Lips Sink Ships.' The show always began with the news of the world; the newsreel took about fifteen minutes and we would see moving pictures of the allies at war overseas. The action had taken place about a week before, and was shown in black and white. Other than the newspaper, that's how we found out what was happening in the world. Or, more precisely: what had happened. – Howard Yates, retired fire fighter, born 1935, NJ.

Natalie Wood was another of Hollywood's legendary movie stars during the '40s and '50s. A dark-eyed beauty, she made fifty films and earned three Oscar nominations until her untimely death in 1981 at age forty-three. When she was only nine years old she played in *Miracle on 34th Street*, and had appeared in fourteen movies by age twelve. The only childhood Natalie had was on the silver screen. She married Robert Wagner, one of Hollywood's hottest heartthrobs, when she was nineteen. On November 27th, 1981, Natalie and Robert had a sailing party on their boat off Catalina Island in southern California, where she fell overboard during the night, and drowned.

Even though I'm in my sixties now, I'll never forget "Rebel Without a Cause." That movie made superstars out of James Dean and Natalie Woods. I was a rebellious teenager when it came out in 1955, and I totally identified with Jimmy and Natalie, and my contemporaries did too because we were a disaffected and "misunderstood" bunch, just like them. Like Jim Stark, played by Dean, I had uptight, middle-class parents who loved me, but had no idea how to show it, and weren't capable of understanding my adolescent upheaval. And, like Dean, Natalie and Sal Mineo, I found friends my own age to form a substitute family with and act out my emotional disturbance in various ways, some of them risky. Although it wasn't explicit in the movie, it was apparent to me that "Plato," Sal Mineo's character, had a homosexual attraction to Dean, and I think he was probably the first gay character in a film. The actors in this movie were all born under an unlucky star, because all three died an early death under tragic circumstances, including Sal

Mineo, who was brutally and mysteriously stabbed to death in 1976 at the age of thirty-seven. I've seen 'Rebel" about twenty times, and I miss all three of the stars—they were brilliant actors. – Marjorie Romberto, Born, 1940, Windsor, Ontario.

Who was my favorite movie star? I'd really have a hard time choosing one, because I liked so many of them. I guess I'd say Laurence Olivier in "Hamlet," and also in "Wuthering Heights", both great, memorable roles. I always remember him as the dark and brooding Heathcliff that I fell in love with. I believe he was the greatest talent ever, although Richard Burton and Orson Welles were right up there too. Of course no one born in my era would overlook Jimmy Stewart, or Gregory Peck or Cary Grant, real gentlemen, all three of them. I was in love with John Garfield, who unfortunately died young. As for the women, I always thought Ava Gardner was the most beautiful actress, next to Liz Taylor, and Rita Hayworth was one of the sexiest, and I always admired Katherine Hepburn for her spunk. She lived life her way. As for male heartthrobs, I'd pick Victor Mature and that strikingly-handsome, swashbuckling Tyrone Power, especially in "Captain From Castille" and "The Razor's Edge." I was heartbroken when they died. My all-time favorite movie was "Casablanca" and I'll never forget Ingrid and Bogie. They were really the great actors of the time. – Maryanne Winters, retired psychotherapist, born 1935, Los Angeles, CA.

What's the Latest Gossip?

In the past, millions of teenage girls and housewives avidly read movie magazines every month, and a visit to the hairdresser always saw groups of women with dryers on their heads, and noses in the fan mags. They glamorized the stars, never ran pictures that didn't show them in their best light, and usually made allowances for any improprieties, such as having serial marriages. A little eccentricity was expected of people who were in the limelight. Some people made fun of these magazines, but they were tame compared to the tabloids we have now in the supermarkets, much of which is either an exaggeration or a falsehood. Movie and television stars are no longer people to emulate, but people to dig up as much dirt on as possible. The glamour their lives once held for more ordinary folk has been buried under the muck revealed or implied by the paparazzi, and the illusion of stars as gods and goddesses is gone forever.

My sister Shirley used to be crazy about movie magazines. She had a huge stack of them on the floor in one corner of her bedroom—"Modern Screen", "Photoplay," "Silver Screen," "Motion Picture," and anything else that was published about movie stars. She also liked trashy romance magazines like "True Confessions." The fan mags of the forties and fifties were full of sweet, syrupy stories about how wonderful the stars were, and they offered

mildly titillating stories of their romantic involvements (but nothing explicitly sexual). The stars were pictured as 'regular people' who had problems like everyone else, but their difficulties were always treated sympathetically. Shirley read every word she could about heartthrobs like Van Johnson, Cary Grant and Rock Hudson, and she also studied how actresses like Liz Taylor, Lana Turner, Joan Crawford and Rita Hayworth dressed and wore their hair. These women were our role models when we were growing up and many young girls fantasized about living a glamorous life like they did, and marrying a handsome movie star. – Brenda Livingston, homemaker, born New Jersey.

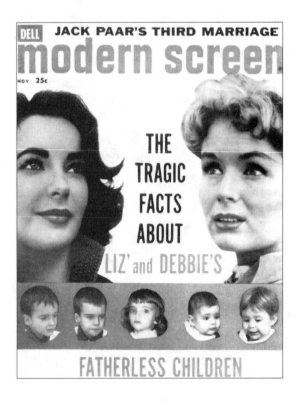

You Must Remember This…

Nothing seems to touch our emotions as strongly as music. Certain songs will always be associated with important events in our lives, causing us to feel nostalgic, or even longing for days gone by, that never will be again. They are a storehouse of memories encapsulated in a few lines of lyrics, and most people have favorite songs that they love to hear because the words touched them in some special way. Sometimes hearing a certain song can evoke memories that actually bring tears to our eyes. The lyrics resonate with meaning and are like snapshots of special moments. Some songs represent periods of our lives, such as our adolescence, or the years we were bringing up our children, or that lost romance.

Bing Crosby was one of the most prolific and respected artists in entertainment whose smooth, melodious crooning soothed a nation for decades. He was both a singer and a movie star who made enormous contributions to radio, television and films. His recordings of songs such as "White Christmas," (written by Irving Berlin), are perennial classics which will always have a place in our hearts. He had over twenty Gold records, including "Silent Night, Holy Night" "Pistol Packin' Mama" "I'll Be Home For Christmas" "Swinging On A Star" "Too-Ra-Loo-Ra-Loo-Ra" "Don't Fence Me In" "Sam's Song" "I Can't Begin To Tell You" "Now Is the Hour" "Dear Hearts and Gentle People" "Play a Simple Melody" and, with Grace Kelly, "True Love."

I can still get tears in my eyes when I hear Bing Crosby sing those wonderful old Irish songs like "Galway Bay" and "Danny Boy." As an Irish Catholic I was deeply moved by his portrayal of priests such as Father O'Malley in "Going My Way" and in "The Bells of St. Mary's" with Ingrid Bergman. He made me proud to be Irish and touched my heart with those marvelous performances. I also loved the old "Road" movies back in the '40s with Bob Hope and Dorothy Lamour..."Road to Morocco, Utopia, and Rio." "Holiday Inn" was also a great movie. We always play "White Christmas" every holiday and of course you can't escape hearing it in every store, but I never get tired of it and, apparently, neither do other people. Crosby was one of the greatest singers of popular songs that we've ever known, before or since. I liked Perry Como too, who was also a crooner with a smooth-as-silk voice, but Crosby had the edge on him. – Paulette Carter, Secretary, born 1933, Detroit, MI.

That Old Black Magic

In 1942 Frank Sinatra made his solo debut at the Paramount Theater in New York. Women lined up for blocks to hear him, and screamed and "swooned" when he sang. It was pandemonium unlike anything any singer before him had ever evoked. Sinatra was a part of our lives and our history for sixty years, evoking memories every time we hear such great ballads as "*All the Way,*"

"*That's Life,*" "*Stormy Weather,*" "*I'm a Fool to Want You,*" "*When I Was Seventeen*" and his signature song: "*I Did it My Way.*" As well as being an outstanding singer with a unique style, he was also an accomplished movie star. His contribution to our lives will never be forgotten.

Frank Sinatra, C1947 William Gottleib, Photographer
Courtesy Library of Congress

As recording equipment became more sophisticated, and evolved from thick, scratchy 78 rpm records to the high quality of today's Compact Disks, it seems that music has gone in reverse. The romantic ballads of yesteryear have "gone with the wind" and couples no longer dance together cheek-to-cheek, but each does his or her own thing on the dance floor, barely aware of each other. Mid-century music offered the promise of eternal love in such wonderful old songs as Nat King Cole singing "*I Can Only Give You Love That Lasts Forever,*" or Frank Sinatra crooning about "*The Nearness of You,*" or Mario Lanza's glorious tenor voice asking you to "*Be My Love, For No One Else Can End This Yearning.*" Yesterday's music was leisurely, slow and melodic compared to the blaring, grating sound of today's rock. Perhaps that is symbolic of the fast-paced life we live now.

As Time Goes By

At the end of the war the big bands began to die out and solo singers overtook the bands in popularity. In the '50s soloists such as Nat King Cole, Tony Bennett, Andy Williams, Diahann Carroll, Vic Damone, Sammy Davis, Jr.,

Billy Eckstine, Eddie Fisher, Dick Haymes, Frankie Laine, Peggy Lee, Tony Martin and Johnny Ray were the biggest hits. Laine and Nat King Cole, marked the ascendance of the popular singers over the Big Bands, and their phenomenal success set the pattern for Johnny Ray, Tom Jones, Elvis Presley, and the other musical idols who followed.

Frankie Laine's style was thrillingly new to the audiences of the late 1940s, based as it was on his deep love of jazz and the blues. When his recording of "*That's My Desire*" burst onto the scene like a musical firework in 1947, praise poured in from all over the world for this gifted and versatile artist, and he is still in demand today, twenty-one gold records later.

I'll never forget the day Frankie Laine came to our city! My girlfriends and I were just nuts about him. We went down to the Casino Theater on a cold rainy night and had to wait four hours in the rain. It was just miserable, but well worth it when he came on stage singing "Mule Train," one of his best. That was followed by "Jezebel," "Ramblin' Rose," and "I Believe," and by then we were swooning in the front seats. He was so handsome and virile; I was totally in love with the man. If he had touched me I'm sure I would have fainted. I loved Elvis too because he sang those wonderfully romantic songs like "Love Me Tender," and "Heartbreak Hotel," and it sure was sexy the way he moved! And I'll never forget the romantic songs of Nat King Cole, like "Unforgettable," and words like "I can only give you love that lasts forever..." We thought love did last forever in those days, and it often did. – Lorraine D'Angelo, born 1936, in Toronto, Canada.

Let's Rock

Bill Haley and The Comets launched rock-and-roll in 1953 with "*Rock Around the Clock*," and changed the music world forever. Slow dances where couples held each other close were replaced by couples dancing independently in front of each other. People began expressing fears that an insidious new strain of music was an ominous threat to family life and domestic tranquility. Millions of middle-class Americans felt the new sound was a clear and present danger, and would surely lead to the corruption of their children and the disintegration of society if it were not stopped. The mayor of New Jersey said: "We're not having rock-and-roll in our town, it's evil." Cries for the government to ban rock-in-roll forever began to reverberate throughout the states, from people over thirty. People forgot the waltz caused the same reaction in its day.

A Really Big Show

One of the chief purveyors of this offensive music was Elvis Presley, who shamelessly gyrated his hips in subtle sexual gestures while crooning songs with titles like "Hound Dog," and "Blue Suede Shoes." His movements were considered crude and obscene, and they obviously hypnotized teenagers in such a way that they began suggestively moving their bodies at concerts in undisguised imitation. Ed Sullivan, the consummate showman, launched a superstar when he had Elvis as a guest on his television show in 1953. While women screamed, the TV cameras moved away from Elvis' gyrating hips, concerned that viewers would find his gestures obscene. With his striking good looks, his slightly mocking sneer, melodic voice and sensual movements, Elvis became a megastar who sold more gold records than any performer before or since. When he died suddenly of a heart attack at age forty-two in 1977, the world was stunned; both women and men openly wept. It was almost as emotionally powerful as the day President Kennedy was shot. His home in Memphis, Tennessee, has become a shrine, and people from all over the world make annual pilgrimages to his graveside. Elvis is adored as much in death as in life, and there are those who claim he still lives, refusing to believe their hero wasn't invincible.

President Nixon and Elvis. Courtesy Library of Congress.

In 1964 a band oddly named "The Beatles," featuring four young men from England, first appeared in the U.S. on the Ed Sullivan Show. Sixty-eight million people tuned in to see what this phenomenon from overseas was about. The audience, largely females, screamed hysterically throughout the entire performance, and little actual music could be heard. Nevertheless, the Beatles were successfully launched in America as England's greatest rock group, universally loved, and their influence on music has been lasting.

In the seventies heavy metal bands such as Kiss, Ozzie Osborn, Judas Priest, and Iron Maiden, became popular, although many parents were shocked by the graphic lyrics. In the eighties it was 'gangsta rap' and 'hip hop' music, much to the dismay of parents who disapproved of the often violent and sexist lyrics. Warning labels began to appear on albums and C.D.'s.

When I was growing up everyone had a popular song that had special meaning for them; reminding them of their anniversary, or their first love, or prom night, or the boy who broke their heart; and these songs were little mementos in our lives that always rekindled those memories whenever we heard them. In the forties and fifties every significant event in our lives seemed to be linked to a popular song. During the war years it was songs like "Now is the Hour," "Over There" "As Time Goes By" and "You'd be So Nice to Come Home To."

And we could dance to all the songs then; snuggling up and melting into our partner's arms as Bing Crosby crooned; maybe even putting our head on our date's shoulder.

Now we have gangsta rap and heavy metal groups screaming something totally unintelligible that has no sentimental meaning. It's a good thing they print the words on some of the labels because I'd never be able to figure out what they're saying, and there's certainly nothing romantic about it. You can dance to some of the disco music but it's at arms length, so you might as well be dancing by yourself. That's a statement about the alienation of our times I guess. – Michelle Ringer, boutique owner, born 1937, Alabama.

Folk Singers and Groups

As the hippie movement began spreading across the country, the most popular singers in 1963 were Joan Baez and Bob Dylan. Some other sixties greats were The Kingston Trio, The Mama's and the Papa's, Jimie Hendrix, Stevie Nicks and Fleetwood Mac, Janis Joplin, Woody Guthrie, The Jefferson Airplane, and the Beach Boys.

In 1964 "The Twist" hit American discotheques, where "Go-Go Girls" set the pace. In dance halls and nightclubs, women in scanty clothing danced solo in cages set high above the stage.

Jayne Rosen, the second "Champagne Lady" to sing in Lawrence Welk's orchesra, from 1939-47

A Classical Romance

Not to be overlooked in our love of music is the enduring pleasure of the great classical composers, especially Beethoven, Mozart, Bach and Brahms. And, of course, the epitome of great music emphasizing the beauty of the human voice: opera.

I grew up in an Italian family. I really didn't care that much for the popular singers of the time, probably because both of my parents loved opera, and constantly played recordings of the great operatic singers, such as Caruso and Benjiamino Gigli, Risa Stevens and Maria Callas. Toscanini was the prominent conductor of the time and, through listening to his recordings, I developed a love for Beethoven. Because of that background, when I outgrew Johnny Ray and Frankie Laine during my teens, I turned to opera and the symphony for the joy of music. I'll always be grateful to my parents for developing in me a love of the most beautiful music of all time. When I hear groups like Iron Maiden or Kiss, screaming their outrageous lyrics, I can't understand why anyone would call that music. Nothing can compare to the glorious sound of a tenor like Domingo or a soprano like Marilyn Horne. Listening to them gives me goose bumps. – Adrian D'Angelo, photographer, born 1939, Toronto, Canada.

Glued to the Tube

The most significant media event of the fifties was the introduction of home television, which changed our entire psyche and culture. Before the 1950s when TV sets began appearing in homes, most information about the outside world came through the radio, and it was also the source of our greatest entertainment. Families who gathered around the set after supper on Sunday night felt the tension when the squeaking door opened on '*Inner Sanctum,*' or a serious voice warned us that "*The Shadow knows...what evil lurks in the hearts of men.*" Jack Benny amused us with his penny-pinching and violin playing, and Fibber McGee and Molly, George Burns and Gracie Allen, Our Miss Brooks, Bob and Ray and Jack Armstrong kept us laughing with their spoofs. At a time when a woman's place was in the home, there was "*Stella Dallas,*" "*Ma Perkins,*" "*The Romance of Helen Trent,*" and no less than sixty-one soap operas. Little Belle Silverman, who later became opera diva Beverly Sills, would cheerily warble: *"Rinso white! Rinso white! Happy little washday song!"* Not every woman was as happy about washday as she appeared to be.

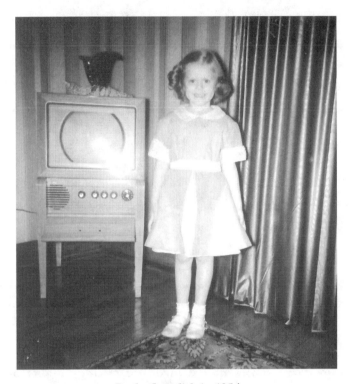

Paula Gramlich in 1954

Every Sunday night during the '50s, my parents let me stay up late to watch "The Loretta Young Show." She came into our living room via our Philco TV set as graciously as any princess. Like a dancer in a dream, she entered through the double doors and swirled in a cloud of chiffon. Loretta was everything a lady should be and, although I didn't have a chiffon dress, I tried to be as glamorous as any six-year-old can be when I posed for this picture.
– Paula Gramlich, Kansas City, MO.

Dr. I.Q.

Back in the '50s, after homework and chores were done, our family gathered around the radio to listen to "Fibber McGee and Molly," "Amos and Andy" and "One Man's Family". But our favorite program was "Dr. I.Q., The Mental Banker," and the star of the show was my brother, Lew Valentine. (above). This was one of the first radio quiz shows and it aired on Monday nights on NBC. — Madelyn Harris

I was born in 1940 and I'd barely gotten over the invention of radio when TV came along. I remember staring at the radio, turning it around and looking under it, trying to figure out where the sound was coming from. Then we got this incredible machine with moving pictures that showed cowboys and Indians running through our living room. We got our TV later than most of our neighbors, about 1955 I think, and we all huddled around it. Our parents sat on the couch with us kids on the floor, all of us absolutely hypnotized by the thing! I couldn't believe you could tell an entire story in less than half an hour.

It took about five minutes for the thing to warm up and I remember being so frustrated when the commercials interrupted the program, right at a crucial moment of course. My mom would yell at it: "OK, we'll buy it, we'll buy it, just let us see the rest of the program!" I loved watching the comedians, especially Sid Caesar and Imogene Coca, and "The Honeymooners." Another funny thing about sitting around watching it was that it made us hungry, so mom starting making popcorn for us, and that was the beginning of snacking and watching TV. —June Mulcahy, school principal.

As TV sets became more prolific, people were fascinated by them. If your neighbors had one and you didn't, you suddenly began visiting them more often. People would stop on the street to watch TV in store windows, hoping to catch a glimpse of this new wonder, especially if they were showing a baseball game. Having a television soon became a status symbol, and also gave teenagers something to do on their dates: stay home and watch TV together. This pleased parents who would much rather have Susie at home than necking in the back seat of the car. Bored adults now had a new way to spend their leisure time, and a new subject of conversation: "What's on tonight?"

Of course there were only a few stations, and no cable in the beginning, so you had to have a huge antenna stuck on your roof, which would invariably get turned the wrong way whenever there was a high wind or a storm. Then dad would have to get up on the roof and turn it while someone watching the set in the living room would yell to him: "that's better," or "worse," until he got it right.

Some Program Highlights

ABC (American Broadcasting Company) began broadcasting Saturday morning television shows for children on August 19, 1950, with two programs. Of course, not many people owned a television in the '50s, but it was a great substitute babysitter for those who did.

Game shows were very popular. In 1955 the *$64,000 Question* began with host Hal March. *The Phil Silver's Show* had its debut, the *Mickey Mouse Club* was first telecast on ABC, *Captain Kangaroo* began on CBS, and *The Honeymooners* began a long run with Jackie Gleason, Art Carney and Audrey Meadows.

My 3 siblings, Judy, Charlie (with Petey the parakeet on his head,) and Kathy, watching TV after school. Our favorite program was The Mickey Mouse Club. -Gayla Baggett, Hendersonville, TN

Westerns reigned supreme in the '50s and '60s. The earliest westerns were for kids, typified by Roy Rogers. But in 1955 *Gunsmoke* began a twenty-year run and was the first successful adult western. *Wagon Train* debuted in *1957* along with *Maverick* and *Have Gun, Will Travel*, which glued people to their sets for years, hating to miss an episode. *Rawhide* started its seven-year run and *Bonanza* became the first Western in color in the '60s. *The Virginian, High Chaparral, Cheyenne* and *Big Valley* were also popular '60s westerns. Cowboys set the standards for right and wrong, and always got the girl and caught the bad guys, who were easy to distinguish. None of their guns were fully automatic, and they never killed the wrong person.

People finally tired of westerns and doctor shows began to replace them, such as *Ben Casey* and *Dr. Kildare*. We also had Ed Sullivan, who brought us an upgraded type of vaudeville show. Then in the mid-sixties we had spy shows, such as *The Man From U.N.C.L.E.*, *Mission Impossible*, *I Spy*, and *The Avengers*. Bill Cosby became the first black lead on prime time TV in 1965 on *I Spy*.

In 1956 the first soap opera *As The World Turns*, was broadcast, and it still runs today. All three networks covered the Chicago Democratic Convention that year. In 1957 *Perry Mason* and *Leave it to Beaver* began on CBS.

Art Linkletter is another great entertainer of TV and radio who lifted our spirits for over sixty years with such shows as *People Are Funny* and *Kids Say the Darndest Things*. His current lecture tour is entitled *Old Age Is Not for Sissies*, which is also the title of his 23rd book. Linkletter was the only person in TV history to have five shows concurrently on network TV.

Another bonus of TV has been re-runs of old movies which we may not have had a chance to see. With the invention of video recorders we can now tape these and watch Hepburn and Tracy, Newman and Taylor, Orsen Wells in "Citizen Kane," or even the sultry, sexy Ava Gardner, right in our living rooms.

Children who grew up before the invention of TV had to be creative out of necessity, so they invented games which usually involved a lot of interaction with siblings or the neighborhood children. It was sociable and mind-expanding. But television is really a solitary pursuit; even though there may be other bodies in the room, we can politely ignore them. And we don't have to use our imagination or creativity; it's all done for us so that we can live vicariously. Television is the greatest mood-altering drug ever invented and, just like heroin, we let it entertain us in a state of complete passivity.

TV has been a boon to the sick, the elderly, and the shut-in. It has allowed us a fascinating glimpse into a world most of us would never get to see: capsules blasting into space and men walking on the moon, news of the world, documentaries, exposés such as governmental waste, the marriages, divorces and death of celebrities, other countries and other cultures, elephants wandering the African plains, lions and cougars in southeast Asia, bringing us awareness of endangered species and environmental issues we may never have known. At the beginning of the century when conflicts broke out in Europe, Asia, or other continents, we didn't hear about it for several weeks, sometimes even months, if at all. Now the nightly news brings these events into our living rooms as they are happening, for better or for worse.

Some highlights from the world of art and entertainment:

In 1906 Picasso's "blue period" began, and the art world, as well as laymen, were astounded. His paintings were considered scandalous and outrageous, if not a complete joke perpetrated on a foolish public. Not only did he shock the sensibilities of lovers of classical art, the average person laughed at his unrealistic impressions and declared any child could draw as well.

1904   The first radio transmission of music came from Graz, Austria. That same year saw the first telegraphic transmission of photographs, from Munich to Nuremberg, by Arthur Korn. Two years later the first radio program of voice and music was broadcast in the U.S. and, in 1920, KDKA Radio in Pittsburgh began the first regularly scheduled commercial broadcast. Mass production of radios started in 1922.

1907   The Ziegfeld Follies were staged in New York during the '20s and '30s, and were the largest and most extravagant musical revue of all time. A typical production included huge sets with revolving stairways, glittering chandeliers and girls descending from the rafters in flower-decked swings. When the show went on the road the massive scenery and costumes required ten to twelve railroad cars, plus a few more for the cast and crew. Famous stars who were in the Follies at one time were Al Jolson, Will Rogers, Eddie Cantor, Fanny Brice, Jimmy Durante, Bert Lahr, Fred Allen and Billie Burke, who was Ziegfeld's wife and played the good witch in *The Wizard of Oz.*

1907   Comics first hit the newspapers when the San Francisco Chronicle published "Mr. Mutt," which later became "Mutt and Jeff."

1908   Harry Houdini, the most famous magician and escape artist of all time, introduced his sensational "Milk Can Escape" in St. Louis on January 27th. He offered rewards to anyone who could successfully restrain him. He escaped from handcuffs, leg irons, straightjackets, jails and prison cells, packing crates, coffins, the famous 'Water Torture Cell,' and even being buried alive. In most of these escapes, there was never a sign of how he did it.

On October 22, 1926, when Houdini was performing in Montreal, a man came into his dressing room while he was resting on a couch.The young athlete asked if Houdini could actually withstand punches to the stomach. Before Houdini could prepare himself by tightening his stomach muscles, the athlete began punching him in the mid-section. Although he didn't know it, Houdini's appendix was ruptured. He completed his show in Montreal and then collapsed on the way to Detroit, and died of peritonitis.

In 1981 Walter Cronkite, one of Americans most popular and respected newscasters, retired from regular television broadcasting.Ten years later,Johnny Carson retired after twenty-five years on *The Tonight Show*. He, and many people in the audience, had tears in their eyes as this well-loved American icon gave his last performance.   His sidekick for thirty years, Ed McMahon, wrote about his time with Carson in his 1998 book: *For Laughing Out Loud.*

In 1985 the Live Aid Rock Concert held simultaneously in London and Philadelphia, and beamed to a worldwide audience, raised over sixty million dollars for African famine relief. The artists played for free and included Paul McCartney, Madonna, Bob Dylan, U2, the Beach Boys, Dire Straits and Phil Collins.

In 1997 Ellen Degeneris came out as a lesbian in her sitcom 'Ellen,' and also in real life in an interview in *Time* Magazine, and on 'Prime Time Live.'" She made history as the first ever openly-gay woman in a TV series. Forty-two million people watched the show, which was loudly protested by the religious right.

In 1975 Sarah Caldwell became the first woman conductor of the Metropolitan Opera House in New York City.

CHAPTER FIVE

Fashion:

from Glamour to Grunge

Always wear gloves as well as a hat to church, and also on the street in a city. Always wear gloves to a restaurant, to the theater, when you go to lunch, or to a formal dinner, or to a dance. Always take them off when you eat. - Emily Post, *Etiquette,* 1955

Germaine Pfister Colvin, Topeka, KS, 1940

The symbol of refinement for women in mid-century was the ubiquitous hat and white gloves. No well-dressed lady would be seen publicly sans these items, and many a comment was made about her particular choice of hat. Although less rigid than the Victorian days, this "perfectly dressed" outfit reflected the button-downed woman of the day, who was ostensibly the perfect wife and mother, who knew which floor wax was best, and could make a great martini.

I'm so glad the casual look came into fashion and I can be more myself now without worrying what the neighbors will think if I go out to dinner without the obligatory hat and white gloves. It was the uniform of the day back in the '50s, and you didn't want to be seen in public without them. I compared it to the tyranny of neckties that men are enslaved to. The whole get-up was so prissy, and besides that they were hot and sweaty when you had to wear them on a humid summer day in New Jersey. And of course a proper lady had to wear the long elbow-length gloves with anything formal. It was expensive too because naturally they had to be spotless, and that meant constantly washing them until they were ready to fall apart, and having a half-dozen on hand for daily wear.

But I have to acknowledge Jackie Kennedy looked pretty classy when she'd go to a dance in a formal gown and gently pull off those long white gloves. Or, when she'd wear those little pill box hats and short white gloves for daily wear. But for me, that's a fashion statement I'm glad to be rid of! —Margaret Coppel, born 1935, New Jersey.

Fashions always reflect the mores of the time. In a hundred years we have gone from overdressed females in high-collared, ankle-length dresses, to underdressed females with mini-skirts and exposed midriffs. Men have gone from wearing starched white shirts, vests, ties and jackets, to colored shirts with casual pants, and even jeans, to the office.

Many companies that still require shirts and ties have instituted "casual Fridays," when employees may wear what they want, within reason. In some schools the attire used to be uniforms, but is now "the grunge look." T-shirts worn untucked, with personal messages written on them, jeans or baggy pants and, for males, one of the ugliest fashion statements: baseball caps worn backwards. A single earring worn on the eyebrow, nose or ear, is also fashionable on campus. Although New York has retained the traditional annual Easter parade, which includes a display of beautiful and expensive finery, particularly showcasing women's elegant hats; in most big cities it has now been eliminated. In 1996, a national magazine declared that Haute Couture was dead; casual attire for business, and grunge the rest of the time, was in.

Anne DeLacy's millinery shop on Park Avenue in New York in 1932, catering to the matrons who wore custom-designed hats.

When I was a little girl, on Easter Sunday my mother would dress my two sisters and me in fancy new clothes, and parade us down Main Street after Mass. I think she wanted to impress people with her good taste and affluence. I didn't really know what the parade was for, something to do with Christ's resurrection and the Easter bunny, but I loved my pretty little dresses which usually had a lot of lace on them, and we got to wear fancy hats, and just show ourselves off.

After the parade mom always took us to a nice restaurant for Sunday breakfast (there was no "brunch" then,) where she strictly enforced the rules of etiquette according to Emily Post. We had to be very careful to use the right silverware, not push food with our thumb, and never, ever, put our napkin in our plate when we're done, but put both our knife and fork horizontally across the top of our plate to indicate we were finished eating, and graciously thank the waitress for everything she did. Then we went home where our grandparents had hidden some colored eggs in the yard, and I had a great time trying to find them before my sisters did.

I always really enjoyed dressing up and looking very feminine, but now the casual or sloppy look is in, and if you wear an expensive tailored outfit, you're often overdressed. There was a

*parade downtown in our city last month and everyone was so shab-
bily dressed my sister said: "All you have to be to walk in this parade
is ugly!" I had to laugh because it sure looked that way, but nobody
else seemed to mind. It's a sign of the times I guess, but hard to
accept for someone brought up in my era when appearance was
everything and you wouldn't even go to the grocery store without
putting on your make-up. – Ava Powers, former magazine model,
born 1941.*

In the early twenties the boyish silhouette of the Gibson and Flapper
girls was popular. By 1925, women freed themselves of their corsets, drawers
and bustles, although they still wore girdles. The etiquette of the forties and
fifties dictated that men wear their fedoras in public, which they tipped
whenever they passed a lady. A youthful rebellion occurred in 1943 when the
"Zoot Suit" (with reet pleat), often worn with a long chain dangling from the
belt, became the popular attire among hepcats. When Jitterbugging and then
Bebop became popular in the forties, bell-bottom pants were often seen on
the dance floor.

Fashion statements now gone: bell-bottom trousers, ladies' veils, men's
spats, broad ties and wide lapels, the fedora, brown derbies, pocket watches
on chains.

*When my brother Ed and I made our confirmation in 1944 we had to wear dark
blue suits, complete with knickers. - Donald Barth, Naugatuck, CT.*

Smother that Sneeze

At the beginning of the century, a handkerchief was indispensable for ladies and gentlemen, preferably white linen and monogrammed at the corner. Women's handkerchiefs were usually dainty and trimmed with lace. It's hard to believe today that people carried around pieces of cloth that they blew into, pulled out even at the dinner table, and then put back into their pocket or purse to reuse. When Kimberly-Clark introduced "Kleenex™ Facial Tissues" in 1934 they were sold to help women remove cold cream from their faces, the popular moisturizer of the day. Instead, thousands of people began using them to blow their noses and then throw them away. The company quickly changed its advertising to promote this new and unexpected use, and Kleenex™ became a household word.

Nylon was invented just before the second world war, and was unveiled by the Du Pont Company at the New York World's Fair in 1939. It was the first textile fiber made entirely from chemicals. When nylon stockings went on sale in 1940 women rushed the stores in New York City and bought 72,000 pairs the very first day. After the attack on Pearl Harbor, nylon was needed to make parachutes, belts, tents and other military uses, so women donated their nylons and reluctantly went back to rayon and cotton hosiery.

Ad in Good Housekeeping, 1949

Polyester "drip dry" clothes appeared in the seventies, making life much simpler for people who didn't have time to iron. It was the rage for many years, until a movement started urging people to go back to natural fibers, such as wool and cotton.

Pantyhose, invented in the sixties, made it harder to get out of one's underwear. Men hated them but women loved them because they didn't have to be always tugging at their nylons to keep them up, and they no longer needed garter belts.

I bought my first girdle when I was only sixteen back in 1944. It had some boning and elasticized front panels for extra control of my barely noticeable tummy, and of course it had garters to hold up my stockings. Although it was constricting, it was a big improvement over the corset my mother wore with stays that laced up the back and left her barely able to breathe. After pantyhose came on the market, they soon developed some with an elasticized "control top," and an all-in-one girdle and panty. Then came bodysuits, and pants with built-in tummy control. Not many women wear girdles anymore, and when you get to be my age you're thankfully free of all that nonsense. – Dawn Thomas, department store supervisor, born 1928, Maine.

Ad in Good Housekeeping, 1934

Joan Crawford pioneered women wearing bare legs, abandoning her stockings when hemlines reached the knee in 1926. At the Wimbledon championships that same year, teenage tennis star "Billie" Tapscott was booed for appearing on court with her legs bare.

Zippers, which were invented in 1891, began to proliferate in clothing in 1913, making it easier to get in and out of things.

The Unfashionable Statement

In northern states in winter a fur coat was *the* status symbol, as well as being the warmest garment you could wear in sub-zero temperatures. During the seventies animal rights' activists changed women's pride in owning a fur coat, especially expensive mink, ermine and sable, into shame for harming animals. In 1973 Congress passed the Endangered Species Act, which banned trade in endangered wildlife. Activists also succeeded in changing some of the inhumane ways that animals were kept in captivity for research, and persuaded many cosmetic companies to cease testing their products on animals, and stop using ingredients derived from animals. By the 1980s fur was no longer fashionable, and many women who felt either intimidated or sympathetic to the cause, began wearing synthetic furs, which were just as warm.

In 1999 some animal-rights' activists in Beverly Hills, California, proposed that all fur products have a label that stated the way the animal was killed, such as by electrocution, clubbing, and so forth. This idea was greeted with great derision by the fur industry, who suggested that all food products should then declare how the chickens, lambs or cows were killed.

When my mother died she left me her full-length mink coat, and I was absolutely thrilled to get it! People who live in Canada can appreciate how cold it gets, and fur is about the only thing that will really keep you warm. Besides that, I wanted to wear it to opening night at the opera, and show off with all the other ladies in their expensive finery. What a shock I got when we arrived and were surrounded by an unruly group of screaming ragtags calling us murderers, and shouting that we were guilty of animal cruelty. One woman even got her mink stole splashed with paint. After that trauma, I put the coat in storage and I've never had the nerve to get it out since. – Patricia Wysocki, actress, born 1957, in Montreal, Canada.

Ad in Good Housekeeping, 1934

Less and Less Fabric, More and More Skin

The bikini bathing suit was introduced in 1946 to loud cries of "obscene," and many parents forbade their daughters to wear such skimpy attire on the beach. Micheline Bernardini made fashion history when she modeled the first bikini at a Paris fashion show in July of '46. She subsequently received 50,000 fan letters approving of her choice, almost all from men.

Many people were horrified in 1964 when the mini-skirt came into fashion. This was followed by "hot pants," and then the micro-mini, which further shocked the sensibilities of many people. Three years later some women were parading even more bare skin covered only by a thin string called a "thong" bathing suit. Once again, loud cries of "obscene" and "it should be banned as immoral" were heard. Some thought it was the end of civilization as we knew it, and it was, compared to the decades before.

Twiggy, an anorexic-looking British model, took U.S. fashion by storm in 1967, and girls everywhere began starving themselves in emulation.

Walking on Stilts

The basic high heel hasn't changed much for women, although more and more information has been released documenting how unhealthy it is for one's back. Platform heels were in fashion in the '50s, and they were agonizingly painful. Women throughout the years have sacrificed comfort for beauty when it comes to shoes, and many have paid the price in their older years.

Tennis and running shoes became popular in the seventies, and certain brand name sports-shoes became so expensive there were a few students who were almost willing to kill for them.

I remember back in the thirties when mom would take us to the store to get a new pair of shoes, we would put our feet into a little box they had on the floor which would show our bones. The shoe-fitting fluoroscope consisted of an X-ray machine and a fluorescent screen that emitted light when it was struck by the rays. When you tried on your new shoes you put your foot into it and you could look through the viewer at the top and see your bones light up within the outline of the shoe. Your parents and the shoe salesman would then take turns looking at the fluoroscope and determine whether the shoe fit. My brother and I got a great kick out of looking at our bones, and we were constantly putting our feet in and out of it. I wonder now how much radiation we were exposed to before they realized the danger of this device, and the medical profession had them banned as unsafe. Now, instead of the X-ray machine, at certain upscale shoe stores, customers can have their foot measurements read by a computer scanner, and can then order handmade shoes indefinitely without being refitted. — Ray Tolentino, *winery owner, born 1930, Detroit, MI.*

Women Trying on Shoes in 1945

My sister and I went to our first dance in 1948. I wore a beautiful blue satin dress with three crinolines under it so it really flared out. My sister helped give me my first home permanent, and I thought my hair looked great, although it was a little flat. Hairdressers didn't know about teasing and backcombing then, so the way it came out after the perm was what you were stuck with. We both wore long, dangling rhinestone earrings which were the fad then. I thought I looked terrific but, when I look back at the picture taken at that dance, I really looked like a dork!

We took a streetcar to the dance because of course we didn't have a car. When we got there the boys were all standing on one side of the room, and the girls on the other, and a few couples were dancing in the center. Even though we had to stand there looking like we were really enjoying ourselves, I felt more sorry for the boys because they had to walk all across the hall to get to the other side and ask a girl to dance. Once in awhile a girl would say no, and the poor fellow had to walk all the way back, with his buddies grinning and poking fun at him. Of course, once the other boys saw she rejected one of them, she never got asked again for the entire night.

That meant you usually had to dance with any dweeb that asked, or you hugged the wall for the rest of the evening.

I saw a few boys from high school that I really liked, but naturally you didn't dare approach a boy in those days, you had to wait until he decided to ask you to dance. –Or not. If he were too shy to ask, or not interested, you were just out of luck. That seems strange today when girls can calls boys and ask them out; no more waiting by the phone hoping someone who has never even noticed you will somehow get your phone number and call. It was acceptable back then for girls to dance together until a boy cut in, so at least my sister and I didn't waste the whole evening because we did some dancing together. —To the fast music of course, we wouldn't dream of dancing close together, someone might think we were lesbians. – Ingrid Wurtz, pianist, born 1933 in New York.

We were all dressed for the senior prom in 1956 when my dad took this photo of me, my best friend, Mark Eaton, and our dates, Carol Dunbar and Carolyn. I don't remember Carolyn's last name because she didn't go to our high school. The cummerbunds Mark and I are wearing match our plaid bow ties, which was quite non-traditional at the time. Richard Crisafulli, Algood, Tennessee

Haute Couture

Gabrielle 'Coco' Chanel opened her first millinery shop in 1912, and became one of the premier fashion designers in Paris, influencing fashions around the world. She replaced the corset with casual elegance. Her fashion themes included simple 'Chanel' suits, and trousers for women. Her chemise set a fashion trend with its 'little boy' look. Chanel herself dressed in mannish clothes, and designed more comfortable fashions which other women found liberating. She introduced her signature 'little black dress,' usually worn with a strand of pearls, which is still a fashion staple for women today. In 1922 she introduced a perfume, Chanel No. 5, which became an overnight, very pricey, sensation.

Christian Dior's 'New Look' appeared in 1947. To achieve the feminine shape required by his designs, bras emphasized high, well-separated and pointed breasts. The 'merry widow,' a long-line bra that gave shape to the bosom and nipped in the waistline, was worn with a garter belt, eliminating the need for elastic girdles. Starched cotton or nylon net crinoline half-slips, or lingerie petticoats with full ruffles and camisole tops, were worn under full skirts.

Women's fashions are influenced by social, economic, and political forces. When women gained the right to vote and gradually improved their legal position and economic status, their clothes expressed these changes. Technological advancements led to new materials for clothing, and these goods were reflected in fashions. As women increasingly went out to work, time-saving advances such as polyester, pre-shrunk and 'no-iron' fabrics became popular. During the '70s when feminism was on the rise and women were competing with men in the business world, popular fashions included ties and tailored, mannish clothes. Fashion has always been symbolic of societal changes in women's roles.

In the fifties manufacturers began making jeans for women and, by 1970, after demonstrations from the emerging women's movement, pant-suits become acceptable everyday wear for females. At first, corporations resisted the idea of women wearing pants to work, stating it would be unladylike, but perhaps also because certain males would no longer be able to ogle the secretaries' legs. Feminists eventually prevailed, although many companies had rules that they could only wear matching "pant-suits," and not a blouse or sweater with pants. A female reporter who showed up for a press conference called by President Nixon in 1971, was scolded by him for wearing a pant- suit, which he considered unseemly attire for the White House.

*Marjorie McGrath with little Lorraine returning
from buying a hat in 1934*

*I remember going to the office in Toronto in the fifties, which
is a very fashionable city. I worked as a secretary for a stockbroker
on King Street downtown. Unlike the West Coast, where jobs usually
start at 8 a.m., in the east we usually didn't have to be there until
nine; probably because of the bad weather in the winter. Five
mornings a week I would stand in the bitter cold, and sometimes
even be bombarded by pellets of freezing hail, waiting for a
streetcar. We didn't have running shoes and tennies for women in
those days, so you either wore your high heels or boots. Either one
was a pest because if you wore boots you had to carry your shoes.
And of course we women weren't allowed to wear slacks, so there we
stood, in our little skirts and nylon stockings, freezing our asses off!
Personally, I prefer the casual look of today where you can wear
running shoes to the office and keep them on all day if you want.
– Cecelia Martinez, administrative assistant, born 1937.*

The late sixties also saw some bra-less women protesting what they
considered male oppression that caused them to strap themselves into
restrictive undergarments such as brasseries and girdles, in the name of
fashion. Feminists held bra-burning ceremonies around the country in the

early seventies. But, by the nineties, bras were highlighted in a big way: the "Wonderbra" was introduced, and became an overnight sell-out. This look could be accompanied by bright red lipstick, black fingernail polish, and two-inch fake nails, which were another innovation of the nineties.

A Bad Hair Day

Hair products have undergone a tremendous evolution. Bobbed hair was in fashion for women when the century began. Bobbie pins weren't invented until the thirties, so lucky was the woman who had naturally curly hair, and didn't have it falling in her face. There was no liquid shampoo until about the forties, so hard-to-lather bar soap was used instead, but we usually only washed our hair once a week. It wasn't considered good for the hair to wash it too often and, since there were few cars to pollute the atmosphere, and the air quality wasn't as bad as it is now, that seemed sufficient. The fifties saw the introduction of the backcombed, heavily teased bouffant hairdo, popularized by Priscilla Presley when she married Elvis in 1967.

Charles Nestler, a Swiss-born hairdresser, started giving permanent waves in his London shop in 1906. They cost $1,000 and took eight to ten hours. Home permanents were introduced in the late fifties, and they're still a big seller today. Electric hair curlers, curling irons and blow dryers came along in the sixties, freeing millions of women from sleeping on hard curlers. This was followed by home hair-coloring, mousse and hair spray. For men there were toupees, hair implants, and hair-coloring that can be done gradually at home, week by week. And now we have red, orange, and green hair; the hairless skinheads, dreadlocks, worn mainly by African-Americans, and weird spiked haircuts like the Mohawk. One wonders how they sleep in them.

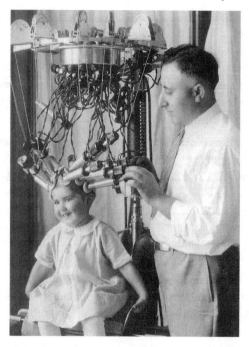

My mother-in-law, Rose Chrest Lundholm, had her first "hot wave" in 1926, when she was only two. Her father, George Chrest, manned the menacing machine at his shop in Iron Mountain, Michigan. Although she's smiling, she looks as though she's about to be electrocuted! – Trish Lundholm, Florence, WI.

When I married Tom in 1957 there were no curlers that you could plug in and heat up and have curly hair in ten minutes. Because my hair is very fine and won't keep a curl, I had to curl it at least three times a week, even though I had a permanent. I hated going to bed with my new husband with my hair wrapped in curlers, and then having to sleep on those hard, uncomfortable things all night long. The first year we were married I would wait until he fell asleep and then get up and go into the bathroom and roll up my hair. Then I got up before him to take them out so he wouldn't see how awful I looked. Many housewives at that time would wear their hair

in curlers to go shopping because it took all day to curl it, and it would be ready when their husbands got home from work. There were a lot of different kinds of turbans you could get then to cover the curlers, but I always thought they looked really tacky. Except of course, the white one Lana Turner wore in "The Postman Always Rings Twice." She made them more fashionable, but anything would look good on her.

I remember when I got my first permanent wave in 1949. I went to the Elizabeth Arden Salon where they had long dangling electric wires coming down from the hair dryer that were clipped on your hair. It looked like an electric chair and I was really afraid I might get electrocuted. The curlers singed my hair and made it all frizzy, but that was better than having it totally straight and stringy, with no body.

When Toni came out with the first permanent home wave I was in heaven. In fact I was so thrilled I volunteered to give a testimonial about it on the radio, and they gave me two free boxes of home perms. But my favorite invention of the twentieth century was electric curlers. – Nancy Michelson, R.N., born 1932, Orlando, FL

Oh Those Peepers!

Eyes came in for their share of beautification too. During the Marlene Dietrich and Jean Harlow era, eyebrows plucked pencil-thin were the fashion. Then movie stars like Joan Crawford made dark heavy brows chic. In the '70s and '80s black eyeliner, and mascara that promised to triple the size of your eyelashes were very popular. In the nineties salons were promoting permanent eyeliner that would stay with you till the grave, supposedly helpful when you got too old to draw a straight line. But by then, you may not care whether you have eyeliner on your eyelids or not, and you might look ridiculous if you do.

In 1915 lipstick became available, retailed in a metal cartridge container by American cosmetician Maurice Levy. A year later women were also polishing their nails with varnish introduced by Cutex.

Not only do people want to look good, they also want to smell good. At the beginning of the century, there was no such thing as deodorant. Anti-perspirants appeared in the '40s along with the radical idea of taking a shower every day instead of once a week. People thought bathing too often wasn't good for the skin. Expensive perfumes also became popular in the forties, and Chanel No. 5 was ushered in with a colossal advertising campaign that convinced many women it was worth $150 an ounce.

The Fat Lady Doesn't Sing

Aerobic and fitness spas sprang up everywhere in the sixties, as people became more health conscious, and strove ever harder to lose weight. In the fifties Metracal™ was the first to offer canned liquid meal-substitutes whereby a woman could bring her lunch to work, drink it in two minutes, and be hungry for the rest of the day. Weight Watchers™ made a huge splash in the seventies with "eat all you want" balanced meals. This was quickly followed by a plethora of expensive diet centers providing their own pre-packaged meals and 1,500-calorie-a-day diets, even though overwhelming evidence showed that if you lost weight that way, you wouldn't keep it off, and would likely gain back even more. But, if all else fails, one can always try liposuction to suck out the fat, or stomach-stapling to prevent the fat from getting in. Hope remains eternal when it comes to weight loss.

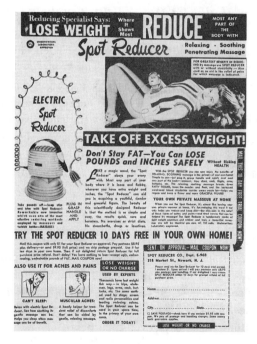

Ad in Intimate Romances, 1952.

I worked as an office clerk in Indianapolis in the early fifties when Metracal™ hit the market. Almost all of us girls immediately went on it. It was really torture because it only lasted about an hour and then you were starving again. We'd sneak in a few crackers here and there, and then go home and eat like a horse at dinner. Of course that defeated the purpose, but we were so convinced that there was something magical about this little can of powdered milk, sugar and soy protein that we stuck to it. Naturally the weight we lost from starving all came back on, but it wasn't until the eighties that we found out that starving yourself half to death didn't work for permanent weight loss. Then I went on the all-protein diet, and then the all-fruit diet, then just vegetables and salad, then that Beverly Hills Diet, just pineapples and papaya, and then the all-rice diet, then just eggs and grapefruit, then Weight Watchers, ™ *then liquid protein —that one was dangerous— then Jenny Craig,* ™ *and finally just broccoli soup. In between I did the shots at the doctor's office, I heard they came from a pregnant woman's urine, but they caused me to lose a pound a day, so I was thrilled. But it all came back within a year. Guess what? I now weigh the most I ever have in my life; but now I don't care! – Betty Goodwin, retired teletype operator, born 1935.*

Plastic surgery and body-piercing were in vogue by the end of the century. More and more men were having cosmetic surgery to look youthful, and it was acceptable for men to wear a single earring and not be considered gay. Tattoo parlors were an invention of this century, originally first used by sailors, and then mostly by members of gangs, but later also men and women in love who might want to tattoo each other's names somewhere on their person. This became quite an embarrassment if they broke up, and a sore spot with the new partner who had to look at the constant reminder of the ex.

The Changing World of Fashion

As world events affected women's status and roles, the changes were paralleled by changes in outer and underwear. As for the 'rules of fashion,' which were once so rigid that people would agonize before going to work, or even to visit friends, in case they were not appropriately dressed, there no longer are any rules. A pair of jeans and a T-shirt, or just some sweats, will do fine for most anything these days, even the opera.

Miss America Organization, 1932.
Courtesy Library of Congress

Miss America 2001
Angela Perez Baraquio of Hawaii.

CHAPTER SIX

Understanding Your Mind and Saving Your Soul:

from Sigmund Freud to Jerry Falwell

PSYCHOLOGY

The idea that there is a part of our mind that is "unconscious," or hidden, was a totally foreign concept until the twentieth century. Great literature, such as Sophocles' *Oedipus Rex*, and Dostoyevsky's *Crime and Punishment*, alluded to the idea, but it wasn't until the thirties that it was popularized by Sigmund Freud. Of course we forget some things, but the theory that traumatic incidents were repressed by unknown mechanisms, and could only be brought to light through a strange process known as "psychoanalysis," was astonishing, and some considered it laughable. Many people, including those in the medical profession, initially scoffed at the idea, and the Church opposed it because it threatened the concept of free will, upon which the idea of committing sin is based.

Freud and His Daughter, Anna in 1913. Courtesy Library of Congress

Freud, a doctor of neurology, was born in Vienna in 1856, but his ideas were not widely known until the 1920s. In 1917 he published *An Introduction to Psychoanalysis,* followed by *The Interpretation of Dreams,* and opened a window on the unconscious where, he said, lust, rage and repressed impulses battled for supremacy. When his theories were introduced to America in the thirties they were met with disbelief, vitriolic criticism and attempts at censure. He shocked Victorian prudishness by using terms such as "penis envy," "anal-retentive personality," and "castration complex." Such words were not used in polite society. He declared that even infants had sexual feelings, and children went through an "Oedipal Phase," during which they loved the parent of the opposite sex, and unconsciously wished to do away with the same-sex parent. In place of the devil, Freud postulated that human personality was comprised of an "Ego," the conscious part of the self, an "Id," which was an unconscious reservoir of instinctual, animal-like drives and, instead of an innate moral consciousness instilled in us at birth by God, he speculated we had a "Super-ego." The latter was formed by internalizing the dictates of parents, the church, and other authority figures of our childhood. In 1927 Freud published *The Future of an Illusion,* in which he questioned the veracity of God as an anthropomorphic being residing in heaven. Heretical ideas indeed!

Undoubtedly Herr Freud, with his theory that human personality was governed by unconscious determinants which could be uncovered through a process called "free association," had a profound effect on the outlook and mental health of people born in the twentieth century. Even though a number of his ideas have now been discredited, the foundation remains intact, and Freud was most assuredly one of the world's distinguished intellectual giants who had a profound influence on civilization. One of his greatest contributions to society was making people aware that parenting styles had a lot to do with how a child's personality developed. Before his time this was thought to be largely a result of one's nationality, being a "bad seed," or the influence of God or Satan.

Carl C. Jung

Carl Jung, a Swiss psychiatrist born in 1875, was a disciple of Freud, but disagreed with his ideas about human sexuality, broke from him, and began work on his own interpretation of human nature, which included man's spiritual side. In 1912 he published *The Theory of Psychoanalysis* and, although he wasn't as popular as Freud, his ideas have been carried on by many therapists today who are practitioners of Jungian Therapy. Jung died in 1961.

The Talking Cure

During the fifties people who experienced emotional distress and could afford it, found themselves on the psychiatrist's couch. He (almost always male) was a medical doctor who could prescribe drugs if necessary, and sat behind or beside the patient scribbling notes throughout the session. For all the patient knew, he could have been figuring out his taxes, because there was little feedback. Nevertheless, patients continued to spend a fifty-minute-hour on his couch four or even five times a week, sometimes for several years. For people who were functional and didn't need hospitalization, but suffered from neuroses, there was no other alternative except the family doctor or local priest, neither of whom were much help in dealing with severe emotional dysfunctions.

Psychoanalytic theory of the structure of human personality was intellectually fascinating, but in actual practice it did little to alleviate the patient's suffering. Most of the insight the patient achieved came from his or her own revelations while "free associating." As Freud himself said in 1926: "The future will probably attribute far greater importance to psychoanalysis as the science of the unconscious than as a therapeutic procedure."

The ubiquitous leather couch, once the hallmark of psychoanalysis, is now seldom seen in the psychotherapist's office, and the famous non-committal "hmmm," has been replaced by a therapist seated directly across from the "client" and perpetually inquiring: "How do you feel about that?"

In 1957 when I was twenty-seven years old I decided to see a psychiatrist because I was feeling depressed a lot. I realize now the reason was that I had four kids and was stuck in the house all day. The biggest event of the week was when I had to go to the store to get some more diapers. When my husband came home from work he played with the kids for about five minutes, ate his supper almost in silence, showed no interest in hearing about anything I'd done that day, and then retired to the living room with the newspaper. I really couldn't blame him for not being interested in my day, because I thought it was really boring myself.

I hoped the psychiatrist would help me understand why I wasn't absolutely delighted to be a wife and mother like my girlfriends appeared to be. I lay down on his leather couch three times a week and just started talking about anything because he didn't ask me any questions or give me any direction. All he did was grunt "mmhmm," and mutter an occasional "go on" when I was silent. I never got any feedback from him, and it started to make me paranoid. Each week I was getting more nervous that I wouldn't have anything to say to him, and he'd think I was wasting his time. I kept wondering: "Does he think I'm crazy?" "Does he like me?" "Does he think I can't be cured?" I really started feeling hopeless, and also guilty because I was spending a lot of my husband's hard-earned money. Finally I quit before it made me more neurotic than I already was. I went out and got a part-time job, and started interacting with adults and that helped my self-esteem, and my depression cleared up.

Years later when I was married to my second husband, we went to a marriage and family therapist for couple counseling. The experience was totally different. She sat in a chair in front of us without a desk in between, and discussed our problems with us. She taught us some communication skills, gave us some homework exercises to do, and lots of feedback on how we interacted with each other. It really helped. – Anita, advertising executive, born 1927, Edmonton, Ontario, Canada.

Salivating Dogs

Ivan Petrovich Pavlov, a Russian physiologist, laid the groundwork for behavior therapy in 1927 by his work with animals called "Classical Conditioning" or "Conditioned Reflex Theory." Every time he gave a dog a treat he'd accompany it by ringing a bell. In a very short time the dog would start salivating the moment it heard the bell ring. This ushered in a new era in psychology, behavioral manipulation or management, but it wasn't applied in a therapeutic setting until the sixties. Traditional psychoanalysis was later challenged by "behaviorists," such as B.F. Skinner, who thought neurosis was learned behavior that resulted from some trauma, and was not the result of deeply-buried repressed memories of childhood.

Skinner, and other behaviorists who followed him, developed therapeutic interventions such as reinforcing the desired behavior, and punishing or ignoring that which was unwanted, until the patient learned new ways of reacting to the stimulus. This was called "Stimulus-Response Theory," and proved capable of changing inappropriate behavior, such as phobias and obsessive-compulsions, much more rapidly than spending five years lying on the couch free-associating three or four times a week. The patient may not know the cause of his or her dysfunction, but the important thing was, the symptom was gone. Behaviorists said the symptom was the cause. Behaviorism was also very helpful to parents and schoolteachers who learned how to handle unruly children by not paying any attention to Johnny when he was acting-out, but vigorously reinforcing him when he was being good. This is just the opposite of what most parents tend to do.

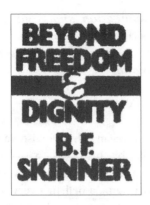

In the fifties several states passed laws that permitted certain licensed people who were not medical doctors, such as psychologists, social workers and marriage and family counselors, to practice psychotherapy. In 1964 a new type of therapy: "Transactional Analysis" was introduced with the publication of Dr. Eric Berne's *Games People Play*. It also became a popular parlor game as lay people attempted to diagnose whether their interactions with others were Parent/Child, Adult/Parent, or some other combination of these. By the seventies there was a plethora of new approaches to therapy, such as psychodrama, crisis intervention, group therapy, hypnosis, biofeedback, body therapies such as Polarity and Bioenergetics, Gestalt therapy, Psychosynthesis, imagery, affirmations, art and movement therapy.

Psychoactive drugs are now widely used to achieve quick results, especially anti-depressants such as Prozac and Zoloft, and anti-anxiety drugs such as Xanax. In the sixties psychotropic drugs such as Thorazine and Stellazine were very effective in helping schizophrenics to function well-enough to leave mental institutions and lead independent lives. With the advent of "managed health care," long-term therapy such as psychoanalysis was replaced by brief, goal-oriented treatment because HMOs wouldn't authorize payment, and "quick fixes" with medication became more popular. By the end of the century, cognitive behavior therapies became the predominant method of short-term treatment.

A fascinating new therapeutic approach termed Eye Movement Desensitization and Restructuring (EMDR) was developed by Dr. Francine Shapiro in Palo Alto, California in the nineties. Although it has been heavily studied and researched, no one is quite sure why it works. But to date EMDR has proven to be the quickest and most effective therapeutic technique ever developed for certain psychiatric problems, particularly anxiety disorders, such as post-traumatic stress syndrome and phobias.

Some psychobabble of the last half of the century:

"Thank you for sharing"

"I'm here for you"

"I'm working on it"

"You need to have closure"

"I'm in recovery"

"You need to process that"

"I hear you"

"I'm dealing with my problems"

"Get in touch with your inner child"

"You're in denial"

"You're just resisting"

"You need a shrink"

"I'm getting centered"

"Be present to your feelings"

Adult Children of Alcoholics (ACA's)

Substance abusers

Co-dependent

Freudian slips

Men are From Mars, Women are From Venus

RELIGION

At the beginning of the century religion pervaded everyday life, and greatly influenced people's conduct. Often the church constituted the entire social life of the neighbors in rural areas, so true believers and unbelievers alike attended, or they would never see anyone other than their immediate family. People came from miles around to celebrate weddings, weep at funerals, and participate in every other social function the community held. Because it was necessary for young people to meet each other in order to continue the human race, church picnics, Fourth of July celebrations, and money-raising suppers were well attended. Dancing was often not allowed as it was considered a wicked invention of the Devil that stirred up one's passions.

Charles Darwin, British Naturalist

The fundamentalism that dominated the first two decades of the twentieth century was challenged by the theories of three great geniuses: Einstein, with his theories of time, space, and relativity, Freud, with his theories of sexual repression and unconscious determinants governing our behavior, as opposed to the devil or simple sinfulness, and Darwin, with his nineteenth century theory of evolution that appeared to undermine the very foundation of the Bible, and its six-day account of creation.

Darwin's radical theory was challenged in 1925 at the famous Scopes trial in Tennessee, a state which had passed a law prohibiting the teaching of evolution in public schools. Teacher John Scopes was accused by two schoolboys of violating that law, and William Jennings Bryan, the famous trial lawyer from Florida, came to prosecute him and uphold traditional moral values. Clarence Darrow, another well-known lawyer, headed the Scopes defense, proposing the heretical notion that the Bible need not be taken literally. A jury of local farmers who had to be informed what the word evolution meant found Mr. Scopes guilty. During the trial William Jennings Bryan died, and presumably found out for himself whether or not the Bible was literally true.

I went to a Methodist church as a child in the twenties. The sermons were very tedious, but they were delivered in colorful language about God's punishment of eternal hell-fire, where we would be gnashing our teeth and continuously smelling burning flesh. This certainly served to frighten us about the evils of sin. The preacher usually banged on the pulpit a lot as he screamed at us to "Repent Ye Sinners," and "Believe on the Lord Jesus Christ or you will be condemned to eternal damnation." We knew that God carefully watched every single thing we did, including what we might do under the covers in the dark. So, when our parents weren't there to see us, God was, which kept our hands out of places where they didn't belong.

We lived on a farm and, getting everyone dressed in their Sunday best, and piled into a horse and buggy for the long trek to church, was an all-day affair. The whole event actually took an entire weekend because the night before everyone had to have a bath and get their hair washed, and that meant filling up the large metal tub with water heated on the stove. Then we had to have our clothes ironed by the flat-iron that mother kept heated on the stove.

When we arrived we had Sunday school first, then the sermon, followed by hymn singing, Bible reading, and a prayer meeting, then socializing afterward, all of which took the better part of a day. On the way home father would quiz us kids about whatever portions of the Bible we had studied in Sunday school, so one had better pay attention.

Walter and Minnie Worrell in 1903 on their way to church.
Photo from Dayne Shaw, Germantown, OH

What I did like about church was that I got to see other kids and, even though most of us were very shy, we could spend some time bashfully interacting with them while learning more about the Bible. Girls quickly caught my fancy and sent me fantasizing about love and lust, but one had to be very careful not to reveal that they had any impure thoughts. I had plenty of them, and just being able to interact with girls sent me fantasizing about sex until the following Sunday when the cycle began all over again. The only thing I knew about females came from the pictures of underwear I'd seen in the Sears' catalog, and my father telling me how a girl got pregnant. That was to make sure I never got one in that condition.

When I became a teenager I was allowed to go to the carefully supervised local Methodist dance on Saturday nights where everyone was chaperoned, but the most sinful and devious of males would secrete a bottle of liquor somewhere on their person, and share it in the bathroom stall with their closest friends. If they got caught, they knew right there and then what hell was! – Ned Henderson, retired railroad train operator, born 1919, Ohio.

Saving our Souls

One of the earliest renowned moral guardians was Aimee Semple McPherson, who was born in Ontario, Canada, moved to southern California, and started her revivals in the early twenties. After gaining a national reputation as a faith healer, she opened the Angelus Temple near downtown Los Angeles, which had a huge rotating lighted cross that could be seen for fifty miles. A special "miracle room" displayed crutches, braces and wheelchairs that had been thrown off by people who were healed during her sermons.

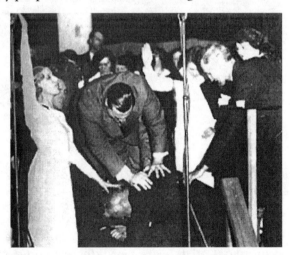

Aimee Semple McPherson Restores a Blind Man's Sight at a Service in Los Angeles. C1929. Courtesy Library of Congress

Sarah Comstock wrote in "Harper's" magazine, 1926: "Aimee Semple McPherson was one of the most famous female evangelists in the world. Described as 'dynamic, irrepressible, and complex,' she's been called the "most tragic figure in America. At the same time, she satisfied Americans' needs for spiritual satisfaction, sensationalism, and sex appeal."

However, in the early forties Sister Aimee fell from grace. She was vacationing on a beach near the Pacific Ocean in California with her secretary when she suddenly disappeared. When she turned up in Mexico a month later she claimed to have been abducted, but neither the police nor reporters believed her story. It was later learned that she had been seen in Carmel, California with a married man, whose wife subsequently divorced him. Sister Aimee continued her "Foursquare Gospel" mission after this scandal with a much-reduced congregation. She died in 1944 from an overdose of barbiturates and is buried at Forest Lawn Cemetery in Glendale, California. The Angelus Temple in Los Angeles is still a church for the Foursquare Gospel, which today claims over two million members worldwide.

Moving Further Right

The nineties saw the rise of the "Religious Right," which was mainly comprised of white, fundamentalist Christians. Rev. Pat Robertson founded the Christian Coalition in 1988, which has become a force in conservative politics, with nearly two million members, and more than 1,900 chapters. They have pushed a constitutional amendment to ban flag burning, defended the right to bear arms, and urged the government to crack down on illegal immigrants.   Some fundamentalist Christians were also known as evangelicals, born-agains and, less kindly, Bible thumpers. They attached themselves to the Republican Party and used their money and voting power to dictate as much policy as possible. Among other things, they insisted that Republicans support a constitutional ban on abortion, oppose legislation which would allow gays to marry, or even give them any rights through legalizing civil unions or Domestic Partnerships, and reintroduce school prayer, which was outlawed by the Supreme Court in 1962.

In 1982 Rev. Jerry Falwell announced the formation of the Moral Majority to pursue the interests of the religious right, and return the country to so-called "family values." He had thousands of followers, collected and spent money lavishly to keep up a relentless campaign for his agenda, and to discredit anyone who opposed it.

Television became a boon to preachers who wanted to preach their interpretation of the Gospel, attracting thousands of followers, and millions of dollars. One of the most prominent evangelists, Jim Bakker, who was head of the enormously popular "Praise the Lord," television network, resigned after accusations of adultery, and misuse of funds. In 1989 he was convicted of a $3.7 million fraud and was sentenced to forty-five years in jail. He served only four-and-a-half-years and was released in December, 1994. His wife Tammy, who was part of his ministry, and was ridiculed for using excessive make-up, divorced him and remarried. Jessica Hahn, a church secretary who charged that she had been coerced into having sex with Bakker, went on to become a Playboy centerfold.

Jim Bakker

In 1987 Evangelist preacher Oral Roberts declared that God would "call him home" if he didn't raise $4.5 million dollars. He averted this disaster by successfully raising the money.

In 1988 Jimmy Swaggart, an extremely moralistic television evangelist, admitted visiting a prostitute. He tearfully apologized to his flock for straying from the path but, a few months later, was again caught visiting a hooker. He soon disappeared from the TV screen.

Catholicism

I went to school at Catholic convents when I was a kid; not just a regular Catholic school, but boarding schools for girls only, where

I was taught exclusively by nuns. I was infatuated with the sisters and their mysterious ways as they came silently gliding down the hallways with their heads down, looking neither left nor right. As a child I always wanted to be a nun, and wear the distinguishing habit that commanded so much respect from everyone. Then, after the Second Vatican Council in 1962, the Church declared that nuns could wear civilian clothes if they wanted, and suddenly the mystique was gone, and they were the same as everyone else. By that time I had discovered boys and given up my pre-adolescent desire to spend the rest of my life secluded in a convent.

Not all the nuns were loving, kind and spiritual. Some, particularly those who were schoolteachers, could be very harsh and punitive. One of Sister Augustine's favorite punishments was to give you a sharp crack on your knuckles with a ruler if you weren't paying attention in class. If she wasn't close enough to do that, she would throw chalk at you, and it was just by sheer luck that she never put out anyone's eye. There were even times she screamed at us (young ladies don't raise their voices) while we stood in embarrassed silence frozen at the blackboard unable to do long-division.

Nuns in the early part of the century were often ultra-conservative, puritanical, anti-sex and extremely modest. One suggested that we should wear a bathing-suit when taking a bath so that we wouldn't be tempted to touch ourselves "down there." Sister Mary Thomas would stand at the doorway when we entered elementary school in the winter and would hike up the skirt of our uniform with her ruler to make sure we were wearing our bloomers underneath. Girls were warned not to wear patent-leather shoes because boys might be able to see the reflection of their underwear in the shiny surface. Other nuns said such far-out things as "The Blessed Virgin cries when she hears a girl whistle," and "chewing gum is an offense before God." Of course one was never to enter a non-Catholic church because the parishioners were apostates who would not be allowed to enter the kingdom of heaven. Jews and atheists, of course, would not be allowed in because they had rejected Jesus as their savior. Apparently heaven was filled only with Catholics, even though their God was a Jew while on earth. Fortunately, the Catholic Church has evolved a lot since I was a kid. – Angeline Guiliani, parent and grandmother, born 1939, Spokane, WA.

My maiden aunt Dorothea decided to become a nun in 1964.
She is shown here dressed in her habit as a novice. She was
40 years old at the time and couldn't tolerate the freezing winters
in an ancient stone convent in Montreal, so they transferred her to their
Trinidad house. There she couldn't take the heat, and the bats that
came out at dusk, so she decided she didn't want to be a nun after
all, and left the order. – Loretta McGrath, Toronto.

After the cultural revolution of the sixties, membership in religious orders began to drop, and both nuns and priests left their orders in droves. Young women, who sometimes had entered the convent because they had few other choices, just as some young men entered the army for a career, now had many more opportunities. Some nuns left because they opposed the Vietnam war and the Catholic Church's support of it, and some were offended by the Church's position on celibacy, birth control, divorce and abortion. When feminists began stressing that women were oppressed by men, including the patriarchal hierarchy of the church, some nuns became resentful of their dependency on priests and demanded the right to become priests themselves. The Church refused and lost more sisters.

When I was a kid in the forties, my aunt got married to a non-Catholic and they chose to marry in the Protestant church down the street because he wasn't willing to convert. Our family couldn't attend the wedding because Catholics were forbidden to go into a Protestant church in those days. Even close association with a Protestant could taint one's soul. My mother said my aunt would go to hell for marrying outside the Church — the only true Church that is. – Billy Joe Harrison, former radio announcer, born 1929, Wichita, KS.

The Second Vatican Council convened by Pope John XXIII which opened in Rome in 1962, resulted in many changes in Catholic liturgy and lifestyle, and diminished some of the reverence and mystical experience surrounding the church. Masses were permitted to be said in languages other than Latin, nuns were no longer required to wear the traditional long black habits, and the Eucharist could be served to the congregation by lay people. This alienated many Catholics who were attracted to the esoteric nature of the historical ritual, and it resulted in a mass exodus of priests and nuns that has created a continuing shortage. Some dissidents formed the Catholic Charismatic Movement.

By the nineties there were fewer than 100,000 women in all the Catholic religious orders combined throughout the United States. And there were more nuns over the age of ninety than under thirty, causing a crisis within the Church to support these aging women who could no longer contribute their labor.

CULTS

Drinking the Hemlock

There are hundreds of religious cults around the world, and several have encouraged suicide-pacts to enter the next world in a hurry. In one of the worst disasters of the century related to religious beliefs, Jim Jones, leader of a California-based religious cult, led 917 people, including himself, in a murder-suicide in Guyana in 1978. His followers were forced, or persuaded, to drink poison-laced Cool-Aid. Shortly before the tragedy occurred, U.S. Representative Leo J. Ryan and four other Americans were shot to death when visiting the cult's commune in the jungle.

The Immolation Scene

At the compound of the Branch Davidians, a religious cult in Waco, Texas, a raid on February 18, 1993, by agents of the Federal Alcohol, Tobacco and

Firearms Administration led to a shoot-out and ten deaths, including four ATF agents. This disastrous attempt to arrest David Koresh, the cult's leader, for alleged firearms violations, marked the beginning of a fifty-one day siege. It ended on April 19th with an assault by the FBI, and a conflagration, set by the Davidians, that incinerated more than eighty men, women and children who had barricaded themselves inside the compound. People watched the burning of the buildings on TV in stunned horror, and many wept.

Nearer My God to Thee

In 1997, four days before Easter, thirty-nine men and women who were members of a religious cult called "Heaven's Gate" committed mass suicide by consuming a mix of Phenobarbital and Vodka. The twenty-one women and eighteen men ran a business from their rented home near San Diego as designers of Internet Web sites. They packed their bags as if for a trip, including driver's licenses and passports, and put them at the foot of their beds. Then they drank the fatal mixture, placed purple cloths over their faces and lay down on their beds to die peacefully. They believed they were going to be taken to another planet by an alien spacecraft which was supposedly following the comet Hale-Bopp as it passed over the earth. It was the worst mass suicide on American soil in history.

Unconventional Beliefs

Near-death experiences came out of the closet with the publication in 1975 of *Life After Life* by Dr. Raymond Moody. The phenomenon became the object of scientific study when hundreds of people began reporting near-death experiences which had similarities, such as floating through a tunnel, seeing a white light and meeting the spirits of dead relatives. Since then a plethora of books have been published on the subject and several research projects have begun. Although Christianity teaches there is a life after death, people seem to have difficulty believing this, and often denounce it as superstition.

UFO's

Unidentified flying objects, or "saucers," were first sighted in 1917 in Fatima, Portugal. The next reported sighting was in 1947 by pilot Kenneth Arnold who saw a set of nine strange-looking objects darting across the sky over the Cascade Mountains in Washington State. In 1965 the residents of a small Pennsylvania town claimed they were invaded by a UFO, and they have been constantly reported throughout the second half of the century, often by very credible people. The government has always come up with some explanation for them, but many people strongly believe we have been visited by aliens from other planets.

In 1947 there was a crash of a large disk in Roswell, New Mexico, which was found lying on its back. The Army investigated and hauled everything away. Radio announcers declared the Army had captured a flying saucer. It was reported by a photographer at the scene that there were four strange-looking creatures, which he dubbed freaks, lying by the craft crying. One was dead. In July, 1947, an autopsy of two of the creatures allegedly took place and, in May, 1949, a third autopsy was filmed. This film continues to be controversial. A former U.S. senator, and a base commander at Wright Patterson Air Force Base, said they thought the government was withholding the truth, and the alleged cover-up has intrigued experts to this day.

Crop Circles

Although crop circles have appeared from time to time throughout history, they began appearing abundantly in various places, principally farmlands in England and America, in the eighties. These are precise and unusual circular geometric shapes made in fields of wheat, corn or barley, which has somehow been mysteriously down-trodden during the night. They have perfectly drawn circumferences, are hundreds of feet in diameter, and have intricate, complex patterns. As an art form, they are beautiful and astonishing. Various explanations have been given for them, including fraud and the downwind from a helicopter, but none has been satisfactory. Many people believe they are signatures left by alien crafts. In spite of numerous efforts to catch or photograph the perpetrators, they or it have left no trail.

Scientology

According to this church, centuries ago, an evil, intergalactic warlord named Xenu kidnapped billions of alien life-forms, chained them near Earth's volcanoes, then blew them up with nuclear bombs. Supposedly, the souls of these murdered people, called "thetans," are now possessing the bodies of everyone on earth. It is purported that all our negative thoughts and faulty memories are due to these body thetans infesting us and influencing us mentally. On the advanced levels of Scientology a person "audits out" these thetans telepathically by getting them to re-experience being exterminated by hydrogen bombs.

The church was founded by L. Ron Hubbard who imagined he was a great man of history. "All men are your slaves," he once wrote in a diary entry. After flunking out of George Washington University, he became a pulp science-fiction writer. In 1950 he published *Dianetics: The Modern Science of Mental Health.* The theory of Dianetics promised to cure almost any physical and mental ailment by cleansing people's memories of traumatic past experiences so they could arrive at a "clear" mental state. Timed to capitalize on a growing national fascination with psychotherapy, the book was an instant best-seller. In 1954, as the book's success began to fade, Hubbard founded the Church of Scientology, telling his son that the way to make a million dollars was to start a church.

Hubbard and his followers developed a reputation for intimidating critics and church defectors. Anyone who is against Scientology is called a "Suppressive," and may be subject to harassment by members and the numerous extremely-litigious staff lawyers. In 1967 Hubbard sent a "Policy Letter" to his followers in which he stated that people who are against Scientology are "Fair Game" and "May be deprived of property or injured by any means by any Scientologist without any discipline of the Scientologist. May be tricked, sued or lied to or destroyed."

In 1963, federal agents, suspicious that Hubbard's therapy might pose a mental- health risk, raided the church's Washington, D.C., branch. The IRS concluded that Hubbard was skimming millions of dollars from church funds and revoked Scientology's tax-exempt status. (The church won back that status in 1993 after a long, fierce campaign.)

Meanwhile, the church's paranoia and vindictiveness culminated in an elaborate operation, which Hubbard dubbed "Snow White," to spy on and burglarize multiple federal offices, including the IRS and the Justice Department, with the aim of stealing and destroying government documents about Scientology. The Scientologists even planted moles in some federal offices. In 1983, eleven church leaders, including Hubbard's wife, were convicted and sentenced to prison for the conspiracy.

Though Hubbard was named as a co-conspirator, he was never indicted, and he died of a stroke in 1986 in Big Sur, California. The church claims to have 8 million members.

EDUCATION

At the beginning of the century only about twenty percent of people completed high school, whereas in 1995 seventy-nine percent of people were high school graduates. In 1918 Missouri became the last state to ratify the "Compulsory School Attendance" law, making it a crime for parents not to send their children to school. Some parents, particularly in rural areas, thought it was more important for their children to help out on the farm, than to get an education.

A Classroom from the '40s, with a pot-bellied stove in the corner and inkwells on every desk.

In 1910 only three percent of adults completed four years of college, almost all were males because women were often denied entrance. In 1940 the U.S. Census listed nearly ten million adults as virtually illiterate! By 1995 twenty-two percent of Americans held a baccalaureate degree, and more women than men were enrolled in college.

Education is now a huge industry where educators and Congress and taxpayers battle over money, and schools provide services other than education, such as coaching, driving instruction, babysitting, and policing juvenile delinquents. The public school system employs hundreds of thousands of people throughout the country, including cooks, maintenance workers, administrators, coaches, nurses, bus drivers and counselors. School districts now vie with each other for equipment and, depending on the wealth of the community, they either have very little or somewhat more than that, but they never have enough. Teachers, parents, and kids often have to provide their own paper, pens, notebooks and other supplies.

This picture is of grades 1-8 in the one-room Brown Center School
near Janesville, Wisconsin where I went to school in 1951
– Marilyn Johnson, third from right in the front row.

Education had another crisis at the end of the century: the nation's schools were crumbling. At least sixty percent of schools around the country are in need of repair. It is estimated that fourteen million kids in America now attend schools which put their education, their health, and sometimes even their lives, in jeopardy. Nobody knows where the money will come from to rectify this sorry state of affairs.

My teacher rode to school on a horse, and we kids walked, but my dad would drive us if it were raining. A two-mile trip in the car over unpaved roads took a half hour. By 1924 there were some buses but, if you lived more than two miles from the schoolhouse, you had to walk. There was no kindergarten; grades one-to-eight were combined, so there were children from ages five-to-fourteen in one schoolroom. Our teacher had to get there early to shake down the pot-bellied stove, arrange the kindling, throw in some kerosene and coal, and get the place warm before we arrived. School in those days began at nine o'clock, and let out at four. After teaching about thirty-five pupils by herself all day, and preparing lessons and homework for them, before leaving she had to clean the blackboards and sweep the floors. For all this she was paid thirty-five dollars per month. —Amy Levitt, retired schoolteacher, born 1919, Salinas, CA.

Throughout the century educators argued about the best way to teach math, using the "new math" or the old, and whether teaching reading and spelling by standard methods was better than teaching phonics. At one time children were put into "tracks," but kids soon figured out that Track One meant you were smart, and Track Three meant you were dumb, so that was judged to be discriminatory. I.Q. testing was also challenged as being biased in favor of white students, and prejudiced against minorities. Other standardized tests were deemed to favor boys over girls. The arguments continue.

Courtesy Library of Congress

When I went to school in the thirties spelling was held in high-esteem. We took a test every day, and every Friday there would be "spelling bees" where the winners would be rewarded with cookies donated by someone's mother. In fourth grade we were asked to spell words such as occurrence, elucidate, elocution, occasionally, Mississippi and vociferous. We were also required to divide into syllables and mark diacritically words such as retrieve, defiance, propagate and remittance. And we had to know the meaning of words such as obsequious, deviated, mollify, laudatory, ubiquitous and mitigate. And of course we all spent hours writing on the blackboard and on paper, learning the rules of fine penmanship. Round and around and around went the endless circles as we practiced the proper formation of cursive letters. Flowery and precise penmanship, we were told, was the mark of an educated, literate person, one of grace and refinement.

School in those days focused almost exclusively on reading, writing and arithmetic. Of course we had to memorize the multiplication tables and learn how to add and subtract, including fractions. We didn't have cash machines that automatically calculated your change when you bought something like they have today. If you were a salesperson in a store you had to figure out the change yourself when someone gave you ten dollars for an item that cost $3.54. When I think back on the type of questions we had to answer in arithmetic I'm really astounded that we learned such things as figuring out the interest on a nine percent loan for $7,000 for a period of three years and two months, and how to change four pecks, six quarts and one pint to bushels.

In my day there was no such thing as social promotion, you either passed or you flunked, and nobody said anything about failing damaging your self-esteem. School was tough back then and you really had to apply yourself and do your homework if you wanted to pass into the next grade. We didn't have "special ed," or even tutors for kids who couldn't keep up, other than one of the smarter kids in the class who might be assigned to help you. Naturally some kids weren't as smart as others, or didn't apply themselves, and they failed a grade, so they had to repeat it. Their parents just accepted that; nobody marched down to the school and threatened litigation if little Jenny got held back a grade. Same thing if Billy got himself into trouble – his dad didn't bail him out; you accepted the consequences of your actions, and your parents usually sided with the school district. That taught us responsibility.

In 1950 illiteracy in the U.S. was only 3.5 percent but it's nearly fifty percent now. Today employers complain that many high school graduates can't spell, write a decent letter, or do anything but the simplest arithmetic. In fact, I recently read a shocking report in the paper that stated almost one in four American adults have such low basic skills that they can't fill out a job application, figure out a bus schedule, total a bank deposit, or even understand a newspaper editorial. It sure makes you wonder what's going on the schools today. – Patricia McCullough, retired personnel manager, born 1927, Buffalo, NY.

In 1954 "Brown vs. The Board of Education" was a landmark Supreme Court case that overturned the "separate but equal" doctrine that had prevailed in public schools until then. The 9-0 decision banned desegregation in public education, stating that "separate but equal facilities are inherently unequal," and ordered integration "with all deliberate speed."

In practice however, integration wasn't very workable as thousands of children were bussed to schools many miles from home, and couldn't attend one in their district only a block away. School chums were no longer your neighborhood friends who lived down the street; they lived on the other side of town, and you only saw them at school. By the end of the century many school districts acknowledged that bussing children outside their districts was disruptive, and began admitting them to neighborhood schools.

Thurgood Marshall became the first African-American Supreme Court Justice on October 2, 1967. Marshall won the most important legal case of the century, Brown v. Board of Education, ending the legal separation of black and white children in public schools. He spent nearly twenty-five years on the Court, and retired in 1991. When he died on January 24, 1993, many people felt the nation had lost a valuable leader and a pillar of justice.

"Affirmative Action" programs were instituted in schools throughout the country in order to achieve racial balance. In 1995 California passed an initiative banning the use of racial preferences for admission to colleges. Regents of the University of California system voted in 1995 to eliminate race as a factor in admissions, and instituted a race-neutral policy in 1997. Some other states followed, or began an investigation of the practice.

I went to a rural school in Kansas in the forties. It was a one-room schoolhouse with grades one-to-four on the left, and five-to-eight on the right. We always started off every morning by bowing our heads and saying the Lord's Prayer. Usually the kids in the higher grades would help those in the lower ones because the teacher was too busy to monitor all of them. Of course children were well-behaved in those days and they did what the teacher said and didn't sass her. Teachers were respected by both students and their parents or this system would never have worked. If a kid did

talk back to the teacher they would promptly get the strap and be sent home with a note for their parents, which often got them the strap again. Corporal punishment was accepted both at home and in school, but the favorite method was making you stand in the corner with your back to the other students, a humiliating and tedious experience.
– Richard Woosley, accountant, born 1936, Palm Springs, CA.

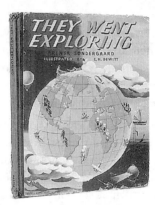

In 1971 the Court prohibited corporal punishment in schools. A year later the U.S. Supreme Court outlawed prayers in public schools on the grounds it violated the Constitution's ban on establishment of religion. Separation of church and state was emphasized, and no religious symbols were allowed in public places.

In my elementary schoolhouse there was a pot-bellied stove to keep us warm, and one of the boys was in charge of making sure he brought in enough wood to keep it going. Even though it was a co-ed school, there was a door marked "Boys" and one marked "Girls." We went in separate doors and then sat down together in the same room, which seemed pretty silly. But at recess the two genders always split-up. Each student had an ink-well at his or her desk, and that could mean trouble if a girl with long hair or pigtails sat in front of a mischievous boy! Along with the ink-well went a penholder with a steel point and a piece of fabric called a 'pen wiper' which was used to dry the pen after use so that it wouldn't rust.

Instead of scrawling graffiti on public walls, in those days boys would use their jack knives to carve initials or linked hearts into the wood of their desks. Teachers had to be constantly on the lookout for this kind of mischief, which was about the most serious trouble a kid would get into. – Karen Broadbent, piano teacher, born 1922, Arlington, VA.

By the end of the century so many kids were carrying weapons to school that some schools installed metal detectors to prevent them from bringing guns or knives into the classroom. Lockers and backpacks were randomly searched, sometimes by drug-sniffing dogs. In some inner-city schools, teachers who feared their lives were in danger if they didn't do it, automatically passed students to the next class, even if their grades didn't warrant it. Some kids got a high school diploma who could barely read it.

A 1912 classroom with a stern-looking teacher

When I went to school in the late forties all the male teachers wore neckties and the female teachers wore long skirts and heels. We kids were always clean and our clothing was pressed, otherwise we'd be looked down on by both teachers and the other children. Everyone wanted to conform in those days, and most of us were governed by the opinions of others. At least our parents were. Teachers threatened to keep a kid back a grade if they failed, and they did it, so we usually studied hard to avoid this dire fate. Being sent to the principal's office was mild compared to the fate that awaited the student when he or she got home! Double jeopardy!

During school we didn't dare ever talk back to our teachers; being rude in class was tantamount to a mortal sin. When I hear about some of the things kids today say to their teachers I'm really shocked. I don't know how the teachers can stand to be treated so rudely. – Eric Shearer, salesman, born 1930, Grand Rapids, MI.

In 1982 T. Cullen Davis, who was crusading against sex education in schools, came up with the following list comparing the worst problems in today's school with those of forty years ago: According to this list, in the forties the top problems were:

1. Talking
    2. Chewing gum
    3. Making noise in class
    4. Running in the halls
    5. Getting out of turn in line
    6. Wearing improper clothes
    7. Not putting paper in wastebaskets.

And now they are:
    1. Drug abuse
    2. Alcoholism
    3. Pregnancy
    4. Suicide
    5. Rape
    6. Robbery
    7. Assault
    8. Bullying and verbal abuse

In Calgary in 1942 the building and classroom walls at my school were all drab grays and browns, some just concrete without any paint on them. Contrast that with the bright yellows and blues and greens of classrooms now! Rows of desks were bolted to the floor, and took up most of the room. Now in elementary school kids often sit around the teacher in a semi-circle, sometimes not even with desks, but on a carpet on the floor.

In the back of my schoolyard there were two outhouses, one for the boys and the other for the girls, but sometimes teachers would refuse to let a student leave the room thinking he or she just wanted to escape for a moment. Her judgment wasn't always accurate and would be followed by a trickle on the floor, which was succeeded by muffled laughter.

We all had to wear clean, neat clothing or our classmates might look down on us. In our school they didn't make us wear uniforms because most rural families couldn't afford them. But we never went to school in sloppy, baggy-looking clothes like they do now or the other kids would ridicule us. And there was no such thing as running shoes, or tennies, or sports-shoes. People didn't run anywhere; we got plenty of exercise walking four miles to school! During the summer we wore sturdy shoes likes Oxfords, and during the winter we wore boots.

Unlike the mixture of ethnic groups and different languages we have in schools today, we were all white, and I never saw a black person until I was ten years old. And I certainly never knew anyone from countries like Iran or Pakistan or Israel because they didn't have those names then, and nobody from far-off lands like Persia or India ever seemed to make it to the U.S. Not that I knew of anyhow. Now we have bi-lingual education and "English as a Second Language," and even "Ebonics," a term for black slang that has been proposed to be taught in some inner-city schools.

Our school was fortunate enough to have a complete set of the Encyclopedia Britannica that someone's father had donated, and I loved to sit in the corner at recess and look through those books, which I found utterly fascinating. Now I have all of those huge volumes compressed on a single CD ROM on my computer!

If a child who lived on a farm went on to high school he had to board with a family in town during the week, and usually do some chores around the house in exchange. Very few people went to high school then, and certainly not girls. I went to business college and got a secretarial certificate, so I could get a job; one of the few available to women in those days. – Teri Picard, retired legal secretary, born 1936 in Calgary.

Ethel and Wilmer, relaxing and educating themselves
by reading magazines in 1937 in Wisconsin

I grew up in the thirties in a small mining town in southeastern Ohio. We didn't have any luxuries in those days, and we didn't expect them. We even had to buy our own schoolbooks, which usually cost a quarter each. We also bought our own writing tablets, which cost a nickel, and penny pencils, which we kept in our desk at school. Occasionally we could afford a five-cent box of crayons for coloring on Friday afternoons. Those crayons had to last the entire school year, so we learned to take care of them.

Families with several children passed the books down each year to the next child in line, and it was a hardship when new textbooks were printed, and everyone had to buy the new ones. As the youngest child, I often wished I could have a new book, instead of always getting a used one.

At Christmastime we sometimes got a storybook. I remember getting Horatio Alger Jr.'s "Do and Dare" and "Brave and Bold," which sold for the exorbitant price of ten cents' apiece. Then I discovered that other people received books occasionally, so I began borrowing from them. I found a bonanza when one family had a whole bookcase of hardbound volumes. I began my early reading pleasure with "The Bobbsey Twins" series by Laura Lee Hope. How I envied the Bobbsey family who had such fun and even went on vacations; something unknown in my family.

In the second grade I earned "The Tale of Brownie Beaver", as a reward for spelling achievement. In the third grade I earned Louisa May Alcott's "Little Women." Even though we were poor, my life became rich because of my literary interests, which even included an encyclopedia! – Rose McAffee, Senacaville, OH.

Many colleges, and some high schools, no longer publish yearbooks. On some campuses Blacks, Hispanics and other ethnic groups, publish their own yearbooks, thus splitting up the school into various factions and creating a non-inclusive climate. Other schools, in keeping with the cyberspace times, are publishing their yearbook on a CD-ROM or a video, thereby saving a great deal of expensive paper. But computers have to be booted up to display the sentimental memories, whereas a hard-bound collection of nostalgia can sit on a coffee table, or be readily available on a bookshelf, whenever one wants to be reminded of what used to be (before children had guns) the carefree days of school.

In many ways life was harsher in the first half of the twentieth century but, if you think it was simpler, you'd be right.

CHAPTER SEVEN

Hi Ho, Hi Ho,
It's off to Work We Go

In the early 1920s, Freeda Bogad and her new husband boarded a bus in New York to go to Los Angeles, where they heard you could buy a house for practically nothing. Discovering this tale to be untrue, her husband found work at a fruit stand for $1 a day, and Freeda walked downtown to work at a factory that had a hundred women sitting in front of sewing machines. She sewed cotton blouses in a hot, dusty room with windows that wouldn't open, for $1.50 a week. On Friday nights, after a week of grueling work, she would trudge up five flights of stairs to the family's one-room apartment and hand over her entire pay-envelope to her widowed mother. Then she would ask for a nickel to go to a movie, but most of the time the family couldn't afford it.

The first part of the twentieth century belonged to manufacturing and the businessmen who ran the companies, and the second part belonged to computers and the men and women who designed them, and the software that operated them.

At the beginning of the century, the average U.S. worker made between $200 and $400 per year. A competent accountant could expect to earn $2,000 per year, a dentist $2,500 and a veterinarian between $1,500 and $4,000. To put such low wages in perspective, sugar costs four-cents a pound, coffee fifteen cents a pound, and you could buy a dozen eggs for only fourteen cents.

General Motors was once the symbol of corporate dominance, both admired and detested. By the end of the century it was just a husk of its former self, and is now a symbol of post-industrial America. Because the company was so huge and profitable, it could afford to pay higher than average wages and offer generous pensions. It was also grossly inefficient. Today, as corporate America faces ever-intensifying world competition, GM's share of the automobile market has fallen by half.

Office with files in cartons, 1937

In the early 1900s, J. Pierpont Morgan, a financial genius, created the U.S. Steel Corporation, by far the biggest business in the world at the time. Oil was struck in Beaumont, Texas in 1901, and inaugurated the Texas Oil Company, which became the largest oil refinery in the world. That same year

Samuel Gompers formed the first union: The American Federation of Labor. Manufacturing was the engine that powered the economy, and made certain astute businessmen enormously wealthy.

At the beginning of the century the majority of people lived on farms but, as a result of the growth in industry, a migration to the cities began. Hired farmhands made about fifty cents an hour, working seven days a week, ten hours a day. Small family farms began disappearing as large corporations moved in, mass-producing food with machines, spraying it with pesticides, and increasing production with chemical fertilizers. The quality of food, and even the taste of some foods, such as tomatoes, deteriorated.

My mother, Mary Baboski, raised chickens and they were often our main meal. I'm standing between my parents in this picture taken in the late 1920s. In the background is her old washboard, mops and a clothespin bag. There's a milk bottle on the steps. - John Baboski, Pen Argyl, PA

A Car in Every Household

In 1913 Henry Ford pioneered the assembly line in his car factory and revolutionized the world by mass-producing automobiles. Ford, who had little regard for the judgments of history, completely altered society, lifestyles, commerce and history itself by creating the Model T and selling it to the masses. He upset other businessmen when he proposed paying workers the huge sum of one dollar an hour, and some people thought he would destroy capitalism by so doing. Instead, the automobile became the fulcrum for a new economy. Prior to the introduction of the Model T, most people had never been more than twenty miles from their homes. Cars spurred travel, pushed the growth of cities outward and eventually helped create suburbia, in addition to smog and traffic congestion. Ford never imagined the chaos that would exist when millions of people clogged freeways morning and evening during commute hours.

Brother, Can You Spare a Dime?

Capitalism was dealt a severe blow on "Black Friday," October 28th, 1929, when the New York stock market crashed, and the business slump began that was to become the greatest depression in history. The U.S. Stock Exchange collapsed, banks closed their doors, and millions of people lost their life savings. U.S. securities lost $26 billion in value, and a world economic crisis ensued. Men who once owned large businesses were selling fruit on street corners, and some even committed suicide. By 1932 about one-quarter of the U.S. labor force had no income at all, and unemployment lines in New York and other major cities stretched for blocks. The YMCA in New York's Bowery was feeding 12,000 people a day.

A relief program during the Depression tied welfare to work. These men had to show tickets that proved they had been working in order to qualify for food parcels. Courtesy Los Angeles Times, January, 1933.

It was impossible to find a job during the depression. My brother and I were both laid off and we would get up at the crack of dawn every morning and go down to the docks, or to any place where we thought there might be a possibility of work, and we'd stand in line for hours, along with hundreds of other hungry people.

We hoped for anything we could get, no matter how hard or dirty, or how little it paid. I had a wife and three kids to support in those days, and all we had to give them to eat was watery soup and potatoes. My youngest daughter got bitten by bed bugs because the place we lived in was a flea bag, but it was all we could afford. I used to go around the city collecting bottles that I could turn in for a few pennies, much like the homeless do now. Of course our parents helped out, but they didn't have much either. It was a terrible time for everyone, and those who couldn't take it committed suicide.
— Kevin Jameson, retired Teamster, born 1914, Pennsylvania, PA.

Dorothea Lange's famous photograph, "Migrant Mother" taken during the Great Depression, 1936. Courtesy Library of Congress

From 1935 to 1940, Lange's photographs made the country aware of those who were suffering most during the Depression, especially families of migrant farm workers who sought work in California after losing their own farms in states such as Oklahoma and Arkansas.

"I saw and approached the hungry and desperate mother of seven children, as if drawn by a magnet," said Lange when asked about one of her most famous photographs. "I do not remember how I explained my presence or camera to her, but I do remember she asked no questions. I did not ask her name or history. She told me her age, that she was thirty-two."

Lange sent her photographs to newspapers across the country, free of charge. The images she took soon became symbols of the Great Depression.

Just before the Depression started, I graduated with a B.A. in engineering, but it took me eleven months to get a job. If I hadn't been able to live at home with my folks, I would have been out on the street. Families took care of each other then, out of necessity. I was happy to get a job that paid me forty-cents an hour, with no unemployment, pension or medical benefits. If the boss asked me to work overtime, I did it without complaint and without extra pay because I was grateful to have a job and he knew it. If I complained, he could replace me by the next day, and the new man would be willing to work as many hours as the boss wanted. – Ralph Edellson, retired electrical engineer, born 1912, Rochester, NY.

The Depression began to recede by 1934, helped by President Roosevelt's programs. At the same time war was building in Germany, and the depression finally ended when the United States got involved in World War II and began extensive government programs to build planes, bombs and other artillery.

In 1933 the U.S. Securities Act was passed to protect investors from another crash of such magnitude by providing information on new securities issues. The following year the Securities and Exchange Commission was formed to police Wall Street. That same year the U.S. Supreme Court ruled in favor of a Minimum Wage Law for women and, in 1941, labor laws were established restricting the work hours of children aged sixteen to eighteen. After years of labor groups protesting long working days, in 1938 President Roosevelt signed into law the eight-hour work-day, and the forty-hour work-week. No sooner was this done than groups began demanding a thirty-hour work-week. Although many attempts were made to introduce laws, by the end of the century, the forty-hour work-week remained the standard.

My first job in the fifties was at a furniture company in Oklahoma, where I was secretary to the office manager. I worked in the credit department on the fifth floor, and would take the elevator up in the morning. It was run by a friendly young black fellow named Sammy who would punch in our floor numbers and open and close the doors for us. But. in the sixties the elevators were automated; Sammy lost his job, and we had to punch in our own floor numbers.

Nobody had cubicles back then. The bosses, all males of course, each had an office with a window, and the secretaries and typists were all neatly lined up in rows and rows of desks. Everyone had a lamp on their desk because we didn't have florescent lighting then, which I don't think is very good for you anyway. Employees, especially the female clerical staff, were closely monitored. If you were even five minutes late the boss would give you a dirty look and a warning. Everyone was neatly dressed too, no slacks or tennies. Every company had a dress code then: dresses and heels for the ladies, and white shirts, ties, jackets and, in the winter, vests for the men. In the fifties a successful businessman went to work wearing a starched white Van Heusen shirt that cost two dollars.

One of the things I hated most was typing several copies of columns of figures on that old Remington-Rand. Because it was manual, you really had to pound on the thing to type a lot of copies at once. It's strange but nobody got anything like 'carpel tunnel syndrome' even though we pounded on that typewriter all day long. There weren't any copy machines back then, and there was no "white-out" either, so we used carbon paper. But, if you made a mistake, you had to take an eraser to every one of those copies, hoping you wouldn't tear a hole in the paper or you'd have to type the whole thing again. But one nice thing about those old typewriters, they never crashed, they kept working even if the power went out; you never lost any data, and you didn't have to call in the repair man every month or so to fix the thing. Then the automatic typewriters came along and the difference in ease of use was unbelievable. Years later we even got the self-correcting ones which were a real pleasure, and then the electronic typewriters, and now there's a computer on every desk. – No more erasing, and it even checks your spelling!

Pecking Away at the Typewriter

I remember when the Rolodex was invented in the fifties, it was really a neat thing to have instead of keeping books of lists with everybody's address. Then when a company moved you had to erase the old address and pretty soon your book was a mess. But now it's all in the computer database. Post-it notes are great too, instead of everything attached with paper clips that tend to hook onto things. I had a huge adding machine on my desk that was plugged in of course because we didn't run things with batteries then, and a dictaphone that I worked with a foot pedal. Now I've got a calculator that fits in the palm of my hand, and runs on a little battery. Of course the engineers in the office figured out their calculations by using a slide rule. Some of today's engineers have never even seen one; everything's done on the computer. – Marjorie McGrath, retired secretary, born 1940, Ann Arbor, MI.

In 1935 a subscription to TIME magazine was five dollars a year.

I remember when the ball point pen was invented in the '40s. What a blessing! Before that we used fountain pens which meant there always had to be an inkwell handy. In school that was dreadful because the ink was always being spilled when you tried to refill the wells, and you got ink all over your paper and hands. But there was some mischievous satisfaction if you happened to sit behind a girl with long hair, and you could dip her hair into the inkwell and get a suppressed giggle from the other boys. If she reported you to the teacher you'd get the strap, but sometimes you could get away with fibbing and claim it had been an accident.

The Parker fountain pens were developed in 1939, and I got a Parker 51 for $10 in 1941 and used it for forty years without ever having to repair it. I still have it, and it's a magnificent pen.

The first ball point pens were pretty messy because they leaked ink all over the place. And we didn't just throw them out when the ink ran out, we would buy refills and reuse them. Pocket protectors were invented for men who liked to keep their pens in their pocket and not have their shirt stained with ink. – Bobby Bernstein, former bank manager, born 1918, Long Beach, CA.

The Inflation that Changed our Lifestyle

In 1973 a petroleum products shortage created rationing of gasoline and resulted in lines at gas stations for several blocks. The situation was so severe that some American cities declared only even-numbered license plates could get gas on one day, and odd-numbered plates the next.

The law firm that I worked for as a paralegal had thirty-five employees in 1973, and of course every one of us needed to have gas in our cars. The boss assigned hours each day for individual employees to leave the office and go wait in the gas lines. Sometimes it could take up to three hours to get to the front, and you were often only allowed up to ten gallons no matter how big your gas tank. It was a very frustrating time, but fortunately people weren't as hot-tempered then as they are now. Most of us chatted with other people in line, or simply read a magazine. I got caught up on a lot of the reading I needed to do for my job, so I really didn't mind it. And besides that, I was paid for the time I had to wait in line. – Anthony Negrette, attorney-at-law, born 1952, Miami, FL.

By the end of 1974 at least 100,000 people in the U.S. were unemployed, and worldwide inflation resulted. Inflation dramatically increased the cost of fuel, food and materials. Economic growth slowed to near zero in many countries, and unemployment reached record highs. By 1975 the unemployment rate in the U.S. reached 9.2%, the highest since 1941. The interest rate on home mortgages rose as high as twenty-one percent in some parts of the country, thereby denying home ownership to millions.

George, a newsboy for the Milwaukee Journal with his dog, in Jefferson, WI. 1929

I think life really started falling apart for a lot of people around 1974; that's when many of us got laid off from jobs we'd held for years. Especially those of us who worked in defense for government-contract employers like Lockheed, which had always been stable long-term jobs. Prices started skyrocketing and most of us weren't prepared for it. The 'Women's Movement' had started a few years earlier and women were just beginning to enter the work force in large numbers, instead of being stay-at-home moms. I was really glad my wife had a job because I suddenly didn't have one anymore, and we had a huge mortgage to pay. It was hard on my ego as well as our financial situation because engineers like me had always been very employable, and we changed jobs whenever we felt like it because there were so many available. Not anymore! Life just smacked us in the stomach without any warning. – Jack Henderson, engineer, born 1951, San Diego, CA.

Some 1950 Wages

Factory Worker $12/day

Steelworker $26/day

Stenographer $45/week

Key Punch Operator $35/week

Legal Secretary $60/week

Schoolteacher $3,000/year

Babysitter $.35/hour

Will I Run Out of Money When I'm Old?

In 1940 I bought a hot dog at Coney Island with all the trimmings: mustard, pickles, onions, etc., for a nickel. Last week I bought the same size dog at the Chicago airport for $3.05. But it was just a wiener and a bun. There was a bottle of ketchup and a jar of mustard on the counter to put on myself. –– Teri Martin, retired auctioneer, Louisville, KT.

In 1935 The Social Security Act was signed into law by President Roosevelt to pay retirement benefits at age sixty-five. The majority of Americans had only one wage-earner in the household, and in 1935 the average male died at age sixty-two, and the average female at sixty-five, so not many people received benefits. Now that people are living much longer, the program is predicted by go broke by the year 2042 if something isn't done to change the way it's distributed. In 1994 Congress raised the age for full benefits from sixty-five to sixty-seven for those born after 1947. A great flood of so-called 'baby-boomers,' people born from 1946 to 1961, are expected to retire in the next ten years, and Congress is struggling to figure out how to pay their benefits. In 1950 sixteen persons supported each person receiving benefits. By 1996 it was only three. Projected for the year 2030: two.

After the inflation crisis of the seventies people began investing in huge numbers in mutual funds and other stocks and bonds, rather than putting their money in bank savings accounts. Before this time the stock market was a place mainly for large investors. The government promoted investing for retirement with the introduction of Individual Retirement Accounts, Keogh's and company 401K plans, which provided for tax-free savings until retirement.

Millions of people, however, will not have any significant retirement income beyond Social Security, because they failed to save. Boomers who are struggling now to stay in the middle class will continue that struggle into retirement. Thus, Social Security will be enormously important in keeping many of this generation's elderly out of poverty, but its fiscal future is in doubt.

A 1930s small business office with stove, safe and print wallpaper.
Courtesy Library of Congress

When my dad retired in 1968, he had a small company pension and a little monthly check from social security. My mom didn't have anything of her own because she'd always been a housewife. But their house was paid for because they bought it for $8,000, and they rented the upstairs flat to bring in a little extra money. They weren't rich, but they were comfortable, and I didn't have to worry about them because they had enough health insurance to cover any emergency.

But my husband and I are very worried about how we're going to be able to afford to retire. We're in our late fifties now, and we still have a $90,000 mortgage on the house. We haven't been able to save much because we had to put two kids through college. Now we regret we didn't at least start putting away $100 a month twenty years ago, which would be a nice little nest egg now. Harold had a company pension until a few years ago when the company suddenly closed its doors and declared bankruptcy. It's in the courts now, but it doesn't look like anybody will ever get their full pension. This devastated us!

I started working as a teacher's aide right after the kids went to kindergarten, but I've never made a lot of money because I didn't have a college degree or any particular skills. Now I'm tired and would like to quit, but I'm afraid we're both going to have to work until we're at least seventy years old. – Rosalie Anderson, born 1953, Houston, TX.

Downsizing – the Demise of Lifetime Jobs

In 1987, on "Black Monday," the New York Stock Market crashed again, but not nearly as seriously as it did during the Great Depression. Wall Street's 'Dow Jones Index' fell by 508 points. In order to prevent a similar crash, or one as severe as the crash of '29, changes were quickly made to automatically shut down the market if trading got overheated and reached a certain critical mass. Another nationwide recession occurred in 1989 when hundreds lost their jobs due to the economic slump. Real estate prices dropped dramatically, and many people lost money on their homes. Ph.D's tried to get assembly-line and grocery store checkers' jobs. This national recession lasted about five years and companies tried to survive by eliminating staff, especially middle-management. "Downsizing," a euphemism for layoffs, became the buzzword of the eighties. Nearly thirty-percent of U.S. workers lost their jobs from 1990 to 1995 because of downsizing or company shutdowns. Cost-conscious corporations, wanting to reduce the number of full-time employees, began hiring freelancers, temps and consultants. A huge market opened for temporary workers as companies kept a skeleton staff and hired for the job of the moment, thus they avoided having to pay benefits, such as health insurance. Corporate America had changed drastically, never to return to the old model.

I walked into the office one morning and, without any warning, found a pink slip on my desk. My boss didn't even have the good grace to call me into his office to let me know there was going to be a layoff, and I was one of twenty. I was told by the Human Resources lady that I had to leave that very morning—no time for saying goodbye to old friends—just clean out your desk and leave. A security guard even accompanied me to the front door, as if I might steal something, or foul up the computers. It was really humiliating and added to the pain of being basically fired.

I lost a job in the '70s due to staff cutbacks but, back then, I was given two weeks notice—time to look for another job—and my boss called me into his office to personally give me the bad news, apologized, and said he'd give me a great letter of recommendation. I had time to say goodbye to my co-workers, who took me out to lunch and gave me a little farewell gift. It was so much more humane than the way it's done today. – Carole Nash, bookkeeper, born 1941, Seattle. WA.

Good Housekeeping, 1935

We have now come not just to the end of the millennium but also to the end of an era, the post World War II era, which was one of incredible industrial and economic growth. The U.S. has changed radically since the fifties, and America is operating under a new model. Gone are the days of corporate paternalism when a man stayed with his company his entire working life, and felt secure in the knowledge that he could always take care of his family, and have a pension at age sixty-five so that he, and his one and only wife, could enjoy their retirement comfortably. Even though most families now have working wives contributing to the finances, many people still feel vulnerable.

My husband worked for his company, a manufacturing plant, for thirty-five years and fully expected to leave at age sixty-five with a sizable pension plan. Rumors of downsizing had flown around the plant for months, but it never occurred to Frank that he'd be let go after so many years of dedication. He was loyal to the company, but it wasn't loyal to him, instead he was tossed away like an old winter coat. He got a good severance package, but he spent two years looking for another job, so that was all used up. After two years without finding anything he was totally depressed, and couldn't even make the effort anymore to look. The reality was nobody was going to hire a fifty-five year old former plant manager, and we had to accept that.

I was working as a nurse at one of the large hospitals in our city, and that kept us going. But then "managed health care" descended on us and I too was laid off, along with 157 other registered nurses at that hospital in San Jose, California. What saved us financially from having to struggle along on our reduced retirement savings was the equity we had in our house. We sold our home in Northern California, which was now worth more than twice what we'd paid for it, and moved to Oregon, where we got the same size house for $100,000 less, and we put the extra money into a retirement account. Frank never did find another job, and so he officially, but reluctantly, retired at fifty-five. He died six years later.
– Martha, R.N., born 1940, Oakland, CA.

Dick Johnson, Office Manager at Adams Furniture Co. in the '40s

Striking Out on Our Own

Instead of relying on the corporation to take care of us, the introduction of 'Small Business Loans,' in the forties helped many people open their own shop, store, or restaurant. Business owners are getting younger because those born between 1961 and 1981, the so-called Generation X-ers, are launching businesses in greater numbers than did their predecessors. A Roper Organization poll taken in 1995 showed that thirty-eight percent of college students said owning their own business was the best route to success.

This generation is the most left-alone generation in history. It's the first generation with both parents working at the same time.

They've been home alone, watching TV. And this has translated in the workplace. They want to be left alone to do their own thing. – Bob Losyk, author of "Managing a Changing Work Force."

The New Corporate Environment

Years ago when I was an office manager, the boss was always called the president; now he or she is the Chief Executive Officer, the accountant is the Corporate Financial Officer and the Personnel Office is now Human Resources. But I suppose the biggest change is the incredible executive salaries. The gap between the lower levels and the executives is staggering! It's really hard for me to believe that some of these top execs are earning <u>millions of dollars</u> a year! And right outside his office is his secretary, without whom he'd be totally lost, and she's making $25,000 a year. It's really a disgrace, and nothing but sheer avarice. – Philip Rosalindo, CPA, born 1956, New Jersey.

Other innovations of the latter part of the decade: Silicon Valley computer companies in Northern California, and similar companies in other states, gave employees stock options which, in the nineties, produced hundreds of nearly-overnight millionaires. Profit-sharing with employees, and so-called "Dot-com" Internet startup companies, made a lot of people wealthy. Layoffs, mergers and hostile take-overs, which often resulted in downsizing, became epidemic, and venture capitalists vied with each other to fund products, mostly technology, that they believed would eventually make them a fortune. And it did, until the so-called "Dot-Com Bust" of the late 1990s, when everything collapsed. Dot-com companies were a collection of start-up companies (mostly based in a region of California between San Francisco and San Jose, named "Silicon Valley,") selling products or services somehow related to the Internet. They proliferated in the late 1990s dot-com boom, a speculative frenzy of investment in Internet and Internet-related technical stocks and enterprises. The name derives from the fact that many of them have the ".com" TLD suffix built into their company name. By the end of the century, the majority of them were out of business, and their employees were out of a job.

I never thought I'd have to learn to type because I always handed over anything that needed typing to my secretary. Now only the head-honchos have a secretary anymore in the big computer company I work for. Excuse me, I mean administrative assistant. With word-processing software we can compose our own letters and, because a lot of engineers seem to have difficulty with spelling, we just use our computer spell-checkers to do the job. If it's too burdensome to compose a letter, we can simply send a short e-mail memo to everyone at once. I don't even need a secretary to answer the phone and screen my calls because my voice-mail does it for me, although it's tedious writing down all those messages when I've been out of town for a week.

These days administrative assistants don't make the coffee for the men in the company, or sharpen our pencils, or dust off our desks, and they don't buy gifts for the boss' wife, so those are other conveniences we males don't have anymore. And, because we work in these little cubicles, I don't even have the pleasure of watching the gals walking around the office in their dressy clothes and high heels. It's sort of de-humanizing; just me and my computer all day long, and very little live interaction with other humanoids. No harmless flirting, that's anathema these days, no males gossiping about the secretary's attributes, and no fun. – Gary Arnold, computer programmer, born 1951, San Mateo, CA.

1930s Bank in Toledo

Can You Trust Your Bank?

During the first half of the century, not many people kept their money in a bank. After President Roosevelt closed the banks during the depression, some people were afraid to leave money in them. Most working-class people felt more comfortable with cash, and expected their weekly pay to be given in an envelope full of dollars. In those days they seldom worried about walking home from work, or taking public transportation and being robbed before you got there; but the local pub was a big temptation for some. Paychecks became common in the early fifties, but even by the end of that decade only about half of working Americans had checking accounts, and the other half would cash their check at a bank or grocery store, sometimes buying money orders to pay the telephone company or the landlord. Money that wasn't spent on daily living needs, was usually kept in a drawer or box, or even under the mattress. Purchases were always made with cash. If one couldn't afford an item, it was put on layaway until fully paid. It was a simple way to do business because you didn't have to worry about balancing a checkbook, waiting to see if a check cleared, or being overdrawn at the bank.

When I lived in Memphis in the thirties, banks offered free personalized checks, toasters and steak knives to attract depositors. When I opened an account I was issued a passbook. The teller sat in a cage, complete with vertical metal bars, and entered my transaction with a fountain pen. Every time I made a deposit or withdrawal I handed her my passbook and she would write in the amount, then rubber-stamp the date, and sign her initials. She then hand-recorded the amount in the bank's ledger. Good handwriting and an ability to do simple math quickly and accurately was a must for a bank employee. If she made a mistake, she usually had to make it up out of her own paycheck. And I always had to go to my own bank branch, because you couldn't get your money from a bank where you didn't have an account. – Patrick Mahoney, retired truck driver, born 1912, Memphis, TN.

The drive to convince people to put their money in banks was so successful that, during the seventies, banks became burdened by the billions of checks they now had to handle annually. They persuaded some customers to let them transfer funds electronically, authorizing the bank to pay the mortgage, the gas bill, the car payment, and so forth, without having to write a check. The Social Security Administration now deposits over 400 million payments directly into client's bank accounts, saving the cost of drawing up checks. This system also helps the elderly avoid being the victims of theft on the way to the bank with their monthly check.

In the past, getting some money usually meant waiting in long lines at the bank to cash your check or withdraw some funds. The advent of ATMs changed our lives dramatically. The first one was installed in a New York bank in 1973. Armed with only a little plastic card, a person can usually withdraw cash at any hour of the day as easily in Acapulco as in downtown Los Angeles. One need only be careful that someone across the street isn't capturing your identification number with some spy gear as you enter it into the computer, or standing behind you with a gun at your back, persuading you to take out more than you had planned.

I earned 35 cents an hour when I worked at this Kroger Store in Holland, Michigan. That was enough to put me through college. I'm the second from the left in this 1930 photo.
- John Schuiling, Grand Haven, Michigan.

All People Aren't Created Equal

In the first half of the century schools taught there were only three races in the world: Caucasian, Negroid and Mongoloid, and everybody had to fit in one of those three, no exceptions. There were no categories on the national census, or on application forms, for "mixed race," "Pacific Islander," "Southeast Asian," or "non-Hispanic white," such as we have today. In the past a person's nationality was the same as their fathers. Even though mom contributed one-half of our chromosomes, she didn't count; you were what your dad was, and you also got his last name.

Before 1964, a company could legally ask your nationality and religious affiliation on employment applications and, if they didn't like your religion or ethnic group, they simply wouldn't hire you; no reason given. Employers could also ask your age, marital status, the number of children you had, and if you planned to have more. If they thought you were too old for the job, you were told they wouldn't hire you because of that, and you had no recourse. Or, if you were a female applying for a traditionally "man's job" you were simply told they didn't hire women for that category. This type of blatant discrimination changed after the Civil Rights Act of the sixties.

When I got my first job in 1945 I was hired to work in a typing pool. My application was a single page, and all they wanted to know was where I went to secretarial school, and then I had to take a typing and shorthand test. There were no questions about college, or even high school, because very few women graduated from high school in those days, and almost none went to college. After all, why waste education funds on someone who was only going to get married and have babies? There was a question about my religion, and another asking my nationality. At the bottom of the application it said: "Only girls of good moral character will be employed by this firm." In those days, if they didn't like the color of your face, or if you were too fat or too old, they simply didn't hire you, no reason given, and there was no such thing as suing for discrimination. Married woman often weren't hired because they were afraid you'd quit as soon as you conceived, which often did happen. If a girl got pregnant, married or not, she was automatically fired. If you really needed your job, you tried to cover it up as long as possible. Of course if you weren't married, you were fired for being an immoral woman. – Kay Jackson, retired clerk-typist, born 1926, Grand Rapids, MI.

In 1974 AT&T banned discrimination against homosexuals. Prior to this announcement gay people could be fired, or refused to be hired, for their homosexuality alone, no matter how qualified. Some states still allow homosexuals to be fired solely because of their sexual preference. Until the late sixties an employee could be fired for being a Communist. Jessica Mitford, author of "*The American Way of Death*," was fired by the San Francisco Chronicle because of her Communist affiliation.

Dawn and Sherry in 1975.

The last three decades have seen numerous lawsuits filed against corporations for discriminating against women and minorities. The largest settlement on record was in 1996 when Texaco Inc. settled a job discrimination suit, filed by black employees, for $176 million in cash, and other considerations.

I remember back in 1941 or '42 when the Village Green apartments first opened and I took a bus from Hollywood to see the models. I liked the complex at once and would have loved to move in, but I was told very sweetly by a sales rep that they were renting only to Protestants. The reason, I was told, is that they didn't want any bickering between possible Catholic tenants and, I assume, though he didn't say so directly, Jewish ones either. I have never forgotten that initial rejection. – Francine Lapides, Los Angeles, CA.

Sexual Harassment: Offensive Behavior on the Job

Back in the thirties and forties men often hired their secretaries based on their looks, and few men would hire a fat or homely girl unless she had exceptional skills. My boss used to try to put his hand under my skirt whenever I sat beside him to take dictation, but, fortunately, my skirt was long so that was hard to do. I would squirm out of his way, maybe playfully slap his hand, and try to cajole him into leaving me alone, but I couldn't afford to really complain about it because he'd simply fire me. And, when I went to find another job, he could legally say anything he wanted about my performance. If he wanted to punish me for declining his advances, he could just say I was a bad employee, and make it difficult for me to get another job. Women didn't have any rights in those days so you had to learn how to use your so-called 'feminine wiles' to get out of awkward situations without offending your boss. Thank goodness those days are gone! – Ethel Klopmeyer, retired supervisor, AT&T, born 1934, New Orleans, LA.

Although sexual harassment in the workplace, perpetrated mainly by men against women, has gone on since the beginning of organized business, it exploded into a national issue in 1992 when Clarence Thomas was nominated to the Supreme Court by President George Walker Bush. At the Senate Judiciary Committee hearings, Anita Hill, a black professor from the University of Oklahoma, accused Thomas, also black, of sexually harassing her when she worked for him ten years earlier. Two days of charges and countercharges sparked the most ferocious debate ever witnessed at a Senate hearing, and polarized the country. It was his word against hers, although there were also three other women who claimed to have been sexually harassed by Thomas, but their testimony was not allowed to be presented during the hearings. The female accusers gave credible testimony to the FBI; they seemed to have little to gain, and a great deal to lose by coming forward. Thomas, however, had a great deal to lose when he denied the charges.

In the end Thomas prevailed by accusing the all-white panel of an old-fashioned "black lynching," even though his accuser was also black. The members backed off and approved his confirmation by one vote. Many felt that, not only did we now have a Supreme Court Justice who had engaged in sexual harassment, but also one who was willing to perjure himself to obtain his goal.

The positive outcome of this debate that fascinated millions of viewers watching it live on TV, was that sexual-harassment came out of the closet, and became a national issue. President George Walker Bush signed a civil rights bill that finally allowed victims to collect punitive damages in harassment cases.

CHAPTER EIGHT

Health and Medicine:

Doctors Don't Make House Calls Anymore

Annie McPherson, born Dec. 17, 1933, at home.

Is there a Doctor in the House?

At the beginning of the century, if a doctor came to the house, he probably was not college-educated. Instead, ninety-percent of all physicians attended medical schools, many of which were condemned by the government and the press as "substandard." As time went by the public demanded that doctors have more education, and faith in them began to increase as they became more skilled.

Before the 1960s doctors made house calls in the morning before they went to the office, and then again in the evening on the way home, and they were also available on weekends for emergencies. At the beginning of the century ninety-five percent of all births took place at home, so the doctor visited the home to deliver the baby, often with help from a midwife. By mid-century doctors were held in high respect, and people tried not to call them unless it was absolutely necessary, especially at night. When he arrived (and it was always a man), he was treated like royalty, usually offered coffee, cake or cookies, and the housewife cleaned the bathroom and put out her best towels for him to wash his hands. Although doctors lacked examining equipment that was not available in the home, they felt they could learn more by visiting the household environment. Parents felt reassured when he studied their child's tongue, used his stethoscope to hear her lungs, then took her temperature and pulse while consulting his pocket watch, and pronounced Julie simply had a mild fever and would be better tomorrow. "If not, bring her down to the office in the morning."

As cities grew larger, taking the time to drive to a patient's home became increasingly impossible. The advent of "specialists" after the war spelled the demise of the family doctor, who was both a physician and a surgeon, and cared for the entire family from birth through adulthood. By the middle of the fifties, as technological equipment expanded in doctors' offices and hospitals, few were willing to rely on their black bags for a diagnosis. By 1957 house calls were only eight percent of doctors' visits, and soon there were none. People no longer had a regular doctor, but might see a variety of specialists, depending on their symptoms. Many people felt fragmented by this development because they no longer had a family doctor, but a revolving group of strangers.

High Tech House Calls

By the end of the century, some computer-literate doctors were sending and receiving email from patients, a big time-saver for both. For overburdened parents, emailing their pediatrician and getting some instant advice about Susie's fever, instead of packing her into the car and driving an hour, can be a real help. Instead of taking time off work to visit the doctor's office, harried business people can talk to their doctor right from their office computer, get a prescription for their sinusitis or allergies, which is e-mailed from the doctor's office to the pharmacy. This method may be too impersonal for some patients, and even some doctors, who prefer face-to-face contact, but it seems like an idea whose time has come in our hectic world.

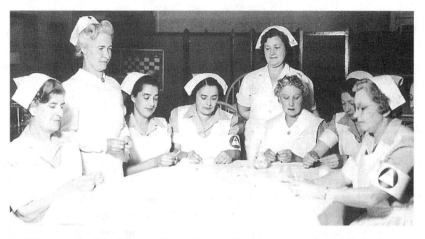

My aunt, Lucille Gimse, of San Diego, CA was a nurse's aide. She's third from the left in this photo of a group of volunteers patiently making cotton swabs during World War II. - Jean Beam, Knoxville, TN.

Few People Went to a Hospital

At the beginning of the century hospitals were used only for severe emergencies, such as surgery, complicated labor, or a bad accident. Because "miracle drugs" hadn't yet been invented, there really wasn't much a hospital could do for you, and most people just stayed home and were cared for by their families. Mother, and maybe even grandma, were usually at home and could look after a sick patient. Those who could afford it, could hire a "practical" nurse who would stay in the home for 12-hour days, providing skilled care.

"Exploratory surgery" was a dreaded phrase which meant we don't know what we're looking for, so we'll cut you open, look inside, and hope we can diagnose the problem. These days, of course, we have huge, expensive machines that use cameras and TV screens to do the exploring for the doctor, sans cutting.

Private rooms in a hospital were only for the rich. Most people stayed in wards that had about ten beds, and were tended by a single nurse. Some hospitals in big cities even had wards with twenty beds, cared for by two nurses. In addition to her regular nursing duties, she also did the work usually done by nurses' aides today, such as changing bed linens, taking temperature and blood pressure, and even scrubbing floors. Unlike modern hospitals, there were no central nursing stations with monitors that sound an alarm when something goes wrong, so nurses had to carefully watch their patients.

In the past, hypodermic needles were cleaned and re-used on several patients until they became so dull they could no longer be sharpened on a sharpening stone. In wasn't until the middle of the century that the hospital staff realized re-using needles was spreading infection, and disposable needles became available.

One thing that hasn't changed: nobody has designed a hospital gown that doesn't expose a patient's back end for all to see when walking down the corridor!

I am a doctor. Not a pediatrician, not a gynecologist, psychiatrist, internist, ophthalmologist or dermatologist. Just a plain, ordinary, garden variety general practitioner—a family doctor, if you will... When I make a house call, I learn more than just the temperature of the bedridden one. I check up on the health of the whole family. I practice preventative medicine. I may suggest father cut down on his cigar smoking, or content himself with nine holes of golf on Sunday. I might propose we do something about little Judy's excess fat or get to work on young Billy's pimples. – Francis Hodges, M.D., Colliers, August 6, 1954.

Germ Warfare

When the century opened the five leading causes of death in America were: 1) Pneumonia and influenza, 2) Tuberculosis, 3) Diarrhea, 4) Coronary disease and 4) Strokes. The average life expectancy was a mere forty-seven years. In the nineteenth century calling for a doctor could be a mistake, and might do more harm than good. You could become a doctor without any college, knowing no chemistry, very little anatomy, and never having participated in an autopsy. Although the situation started improving in the twentieth century, in the early decades a good many general practitioners were still uneducated and inadequate. Many doctors in the 1920s still doubted the germ theory and were diagnosing symptoms being caused by such things as female hysteria.

People were not very conscious of hygiene in the first half of the century. In public restrooms there were racks that held cloth towels that were pulled down in circular fashion, so that they often got reused if the roll wasn't immediately replaced. The same bar of soap was used by everyone who frequented the restroom because people weren't very conscious of how germs were transmitted. Liquid soap eventually replaced the bars, and toilet paper replaced old cut-up newspapers. Now we even have toilet seat covers for the meticulous who don't want to sit where some stranger recently sat.

Ad in Good Housekeeping, 1935

Saving Lives

When the century opened, there were few physicians, and almost no drugs. By the end of the century there were an astounding number of advances in medical science, and an astounding number of drugs, raising new hopes for cures of chronic and terminal illnesses, and at the same time raising medical costs astronomically.

Every summer my parents sent us kids to a farm that took in boarders, and those were the happiness days of my childhood. We climbed trees, milked cows, and helped the farmer build a new barn. But one day I stepped on an old rusted nail and it went about a half inch into the bottom of my bare foot. We feared lockjaw, but we didn't have tetanus shots or antibiotics then so the farmer's wife just cleaned it out with soap and water, then some hydrogen peroxide, and then put iodine all over it, and bandaged it up. Sometimes people died from little accidents like this. My friend's grandma died because she got a wooden sliver imbedded under her fingernail, and she never had it removed, and it got infected and killed her. I was lucky, my wound healed right-up with no trouble. – Nancy Renalto, retired real estate agent, born 1937, Oklahoma.

The first part of the century was dominated by infectious diseases, which were largely controlled by the discovery of vaccines in the '20s, sulfonamides in the '30s and penicillin in the '40s. These wonder drugs, particularly penicillin, which was discovered in 1928 by British bacteriologist Alexander Fleming, changed the course of human existence. When it was finally recognized years later for what it was—the most efficacious, life-saving, infection-fighting drug in the world, it forever altered the treatment of bacterial infections. Fleming was knighted by King George VI, and won the Nobel Prize for Medicine.

The advent of vaccines and antibiotics, along with breakthroughs in public health, surgery and anesthesia, heralded a golden age of health care compared to what had been before. In less than a century, science learned to cure, treat or prevent an incredible list of diseases, ranging from polio and typhoid, to syphilis and gonorrhea. Because of antibiotics and increased sanitation, internal parasites were practically eliminated as a cause of disease and death in advanced countries.

Yeast. A primitive "cure" for a host of illnesses. Good Housekeeping, 1934

Polio: the Terror of Summer

Paralytic poliomyelitis was a frightening viral disease that struck tens of thousands of people during the first half of the century. A major epidemic struck America during the twenties. President Roosevelt was stricken in the summer of 1921, during one of the worst outbreaks in history. In New York City nearly ten thousand people were infected, and two thousand of them died. Hysterical families tried to flee the city, but were turned back by police. Many hospitals were so fearful of the contagious nature of polio that they refused to admit patients. Mothers organized the "March of Dimes" to raise money to fight the disease.

Summertime was a time of fear in the forties and fifties because polio once again stalked the neighborhood, crippling and killing children, and everyone knew someone who got it. Mothers were very paranoid about where their children went, and who they associated with, because no one really knew how it was spread or how to prevent it. It was a terrifying scourge which attacked mainly children, and was transmitted like a plague in public places, such as the schoolhouse or public pools. Many people died or were partly paralyzed, and some lived for months in Iron Lungs. These were the forerunners of respirators, and were huge, black, ugly, barrel-like machines that compressed and released lungs too weak to breathe for themselves.

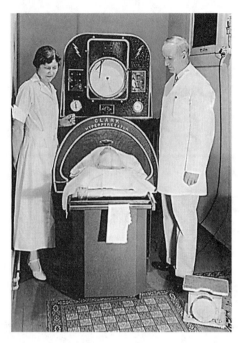

Iron Lung, 1938. Courtesy Library of Congress

In 1949 Dr. Jonas Salk, an American bacteriologist, with funding from the March of Dimes, started research to develop a vaccine. Six years later he announced the success of a serum vaccine, and hundreds of thousands of children were inoculated across the U.S., which finally stopped the epidemic of this crippling disease. Two years later Dr. Albert Sabin developed an oral vaccine. In 1991 only nine cases of polio were reported in the western hemisphere.

There is seldom a kid who doesn't get an infection from something and, before antibiotics came into widespread use in the forties, parents used mercurochrome and iodine and hydrogen peroxide, and hoped for the best.

Vaccines were developed that staved off a host of childhood diseases, such as diphtheria, whooping cough and tetanus, but there are still no vaccines for childhood killers such as diarrheal diseases, acute respiratory infections and malaria. Epidemics such as polio and the black plague were replaced by heart disease, cancer and strokes as the primary killers of people but, by the end of the century, infectious diseases once again reared their hideous heads, particularly in the form of AIDS, but also in the form of antibiotic resistant viruses and bacteria.

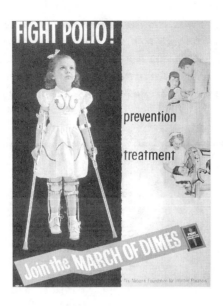

FIGHT POLIO!

prevention

treatment

Join the MARCH OF DIMES

In 1925 a doctor came to our elementary school to test everyone for diphtheria because cases had been reported in the town. I remember he put the same stick in everyone's mouth. Soon after that a dozen children in my class came down with diphtheria. My little sister, Beverly, was diagnosed with it, so everyone in the house was quarantined and a yellow sign was put on our door so nobody would come in, and we couldn't go out. The same thing was done if someone in the house had scarlet fever, another contagious disease of the time. Mom made a separate room in the attic for my sister so she wouldn't contaminate the rest of us.

Beverly died of diphtheria when she was only seven years old. There was no such thing as immunization then, but an anti-toxin was available as a treatment. It was new and our country doctor wasn't familiar with it so he didn't want to try it. Mother gave us sassafras tea to help build our resistance. When my sister was buried all the neighbors came to the graveside, but they wouldn't get close to the family or hug us, fearing they might get it from us.

Because we didn't have antibiotics or even an aspirin in those days, mom had a bagfull of remedies for most common illnesses. For a cold she made a fiery mustard plaster and put it in a cloth on our chest to burn it out. In the morning when the cloth was removed our chest would be beet-red, but the fever had broken and we were on our way to getting well. For rheumatism she had a stinky linament that assaulted one's nostrils for hours, and "female problems" were helped by Lydia Pinkham's tonic. If your tummy was upset, you had to down a glass of warm water mixed with bicarbonate of soda. Of course castor oil was a favorite for almost everything, and iodine was used for every cut. — Irene Morgenson, born 1938, Louisville, KT.

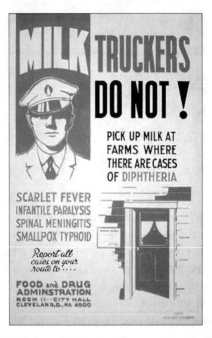

1936 Poster. Courtesy Library of Congress

TB: Not just in the last act of an Italian opera anymore.

In the early 1900s the best treatment doctors could prescribe for tuberculosis was bed rest, nutritious food, sunshine, fresh air and isolation from others. Until the middle of the century, TB was an indiscriminate killer, taking over 100,000 lives each year in America, until antibiotics finally brought it under control. But, in the last two decades of the century, it has once again become a killer, particularly among those with already weakened immune systems, such as AIDS patients, the homeless, and the poor. It began making a comeback in the U.S. in the late 1980s because of the overuse of antibiotics and the appearance of new strains that are resistant to a variety of drugs. In New York City nearly one-third of TB patients are infected with drug-resistant strains.

The tubercle bacilli are now one of the world's leading killers, causing eight million new cases and three million deaths every year. This has been partly attributed to the expansion of international transportation and the massive migration of peoples from undeveloped countries where the disease has not been controlled. The increase of homeless people living on the streets without medical care has also contributed to a resurgence of TB. Many doctors are urging the government to restore funding for the old TB-control programs, and even revive sanitariums so that infectious patients can be quarantined during treatment.

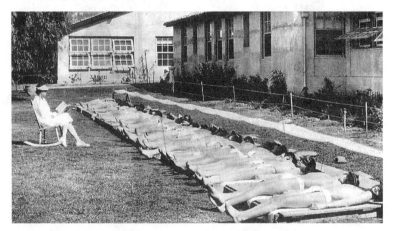

Men Having Sun Therapy for T.B. at a Sanitarium in 1928.
Courtesy Los Angeles Public Library.

Not only has TB been reincarnated, so have other infectious diseases, such as malaria, whooping cough, cholera and yellow fever; and the emergence of new killers such as AIDS and the Ebola virus, threaten to undermine recent advances in health care. Ebola, a contagious hemorrhagic fever that surfaced in 1977, re-emerged to kill 245 people in Zaire, Africa, in 1994. The hepatitis C virus, which causes liver cancer, and was discovered in 1989, is another new disease which is spreading rapidly.

A Triumphant Discovery!

The discovery of insulin in 1922 by Drs. Banting, Best and MacLeod, has saved the life of thousands of diabetic patients. At that time people with diabetes were treated with spoonfuls of cooking oil! Although insulin isn't a cure, it can control the disease and extend life. Without it, people with type I diabetes would slowly starve to death.

Banting, Best and MacLeod were Canadian doctors who first injected insulin into a fourteen-year-old boy in 1922, and saw that his blood glucose levels dropped. By the end of 1923 it was being produced commercially and used to treat diabetes in most western countries.

The 1930 graduates of The Holy Family Hospital School of Nursing in Manitowoc, Wisconsin wore caps and heels.

Slowly, over the years, my fellow nurses and I gave up wearing our caps, and those crisp white uniforms evolved into pastel tops and colorful jackets with white slacks and jogging shoes, which were more comfortable. We wanted to look less clinical and authoritarian. Doctors, nurses and technicians became part of a "health care team." In some hospitals, everyone from housekeepers to nurses started wearing "scrubs."

One day I entered a patient's room just as she was asking the housekeeper for a pain pill. When the housekeeper explained she wasn't a nurse, the patient complained that everyone in the hospital looked the same to her. She asked: "Why don't you wear white uniforms anymore? And what happened to your caps? I used to love seeing nurses in their caps."

When we wore them, there was no mistaking a nurse for anyone else. But nurses no longer wear caps for many reasons: they often became dirty and were difficult to launder. Sometimes they got caught on new kinds of medical equipment. I don't wear my cap anymore, but I still have it. It's a reminder of my connection to a group of dedicated nurses who wore their caps with pride. — Cynthia Frozena, Manitowoc.

Going Under the Knife

For most of the twentieth century, tonsillectomies were the most commonly performed surgery in America, with hernia repairs second, appendectomies third, and hysterectomies fourth. In 1963 a large-scale study was done in England that reported the average child whose tonsils were removed was no better off than the ones who kept their tonsils. But it wasn't until about 1980 that doctors in America began reducing the number of tonsillectomies, either because they finally got the message, or because they were reluctant to give up a procedure that had provided a nice little income.

When I was a kid my siblings and I all had our tonsils taken out. It was just automatic because doctors thought they had no usefulness, so as soon as you got a bad sore throat, off to the hospital you went, and they yanked them out. When you were recovering from the surgery the nurses always gave you lots and lots of vanilla ice cream to soothe your sore throat, and everyone made you feel special, so it wasn't so bad. For most of us kids this was our first introduction to the mysteries of hospitals, nurses and doctors. — Anita Ferguson, housewife and grandmother, born 1936, Louisville, KY.

The latter half of the century brought "trauma centers" to our major hospitals, to deal with the increasing emergencies of people who had been violently assaulted or shot, injured in car accidents, or overdosed on drugs. Due to technological advances, paramedic units can send images and data from remote accident locations to the hospital so that emergency room personnel can know what to prepare for.

Out of Hospitals and Onto the Streets

One of the most dramatic medical advances of the sixties was the development of psychotropic drugs, which controlled, but seldom cured, many of the most severe psychiatric illnesses. As a result of this, in 1981 the governor of California, Ronald Reagan, ordered the state's large mental institutions to be closed, and so-called "half-way houses" were opened to accommodate the released patients. Other states soon followed suit, and huge, antiquated institutions for the mentally ill were shut-down all over the country, and the patients were mainstreamed into the community in smaller homes. Unfortunately, there were not enough homes available, nor sufficient funding, and many of the mentally ill who either had no place to go, or refused to continue taking their medication, began wandering the streets and created an epidemic of homeless people.

It wasn't affordable enough for her.
Courtesy Los Angeles Times.

There's a homeless man living on the street and sleeping in the doorways of local businesses, a few blocks from where I live. Every morning when I walk my dog before I go to the office, I see him leaning against a building, usually loudly yelling something unintelligible, and flailing his arms wildly.

Once I walked by him with my little dog and he shouted "Good Morning" to me. I just ignored him and kept walking. He suddenly jumped in front of me and growled: "I said Good Morning!" "Good Morning, Sir," I replied, as politely as I could.

This man is mentally ill, and shouldn't be on the street, because he's obviously incapable of living a normal life, and he could be dangerous. For all I knew, he could be carrying a knife. In the past he would be put in a mental institute, where at least he'd get a bed and three meals a day and, hopefully, some psychiatric help. It's a disgrace that we treat our mentally ill this way. Or, I should say, that we don't treat them; we've gone from the snake pit in the early part of the century, to abandonment now. – Dawn DeCelles, psychologist, born 1945, Upstate New York.

Outliving our Resources

At the end of the twentieth century, the average American could expect to live at least thirty years longer than people did at the beginning. The biggest health story of the century was the evolution of modern sanitation, including clean drinking water, which has saved countless people from dying of infectious diseases. As a result, the average person in the developed world lives to a good old age instead of dying before their sixtieth birthday. The benefit is that people now have time for increased leisure, which was extremely limited in the early part of the century when people worked twelve-hour days, seven days a week, then died soon after retiring, if they got to retire at all.

But living longer has actually created problems for society in many ways and has affected fundamental domestic issues, such as Social Security and Medicare payments, employment of the elderly, inheritances, and family pressures related to caring for aging relatives. At the turn of the century, the average Caucasian lived only about forty-eight years, for a black man it was 32.5 years. By the end of the century, life expectancy for women had risen to seventy-nine years, almost seven years longer than men. In actual fact, many people live into their eighties and even nineties and, although still rare, it's no longer astonishing to find people over 100 years old. The big question now as we begin the twenty-first century is: "Who will be the caretakers of this aging population, and who will pay for their support?"

Leaving Home to Die Somewhere Else

The twentieth century also saw the advent of nursing homes for the elderly. Instead of being cared for by family members, sick and elderly parents and grandparents who once were taken care of at home and died in their own beds, often die now in nursing homes. Many of these facilities are understaffed by caretakers who are overworked and underpaid, and patients are sometimes strapped into beds and wheelchairs, and given drugs to sedate and quiet them until they die. Hospices, where the dying are treated with great care, sprang up in the eighties and offered an alternative to cold, clinical hospitals.

When my grandma was seventy-four years old in 1945, she got really sick and her family doctor came to the house and examined her, and said she'd have to go to the hospital for some tests. My grandma hated hospitals and had never been in one, but she was so sick she reluctantly went. While there she was told she had inoperable cancer and had probably had it for a long time, and so they sent her home to die, without any treatment. My grandpa and my mother took care of her because she got so weak she couldn't walk around anymore and, about four months later, she died at home. It was really a nice way to die because she wasn't hooked up to machines, didn't have any tubes stuck in her, and she wasn't forced to linger long beyond the time her body was ready to go, and she was in her own home surrounded by her family. So she just died peacefully in her sleep without any fuss.

Two days after the funeral my eighty-year-old grandpa, who had also been ill, just didn't wake up in the morning, so we buried him beside her. We missed them both terribly, but we were grateful that we didn't have a mountain of medical bills to pay, and we didn't have our lives interrupted for months, or even years, by having to transport them both in and out of hospitals, and watch them go through the agony of radiation and chemotherapy, and all the other trappings of the medical profession forcing you to stay alive no matter how sick you are. Back then when you were old and had lived a full life, you went quietly when your time came, and you didn't cling to a miserable life pumped full of poisonous drugs just so you could stay on earth a few more months or years, distressing everyone around you watching you die inch by inch. Maybe it was because we so strongly believed in a heaven back then, which was a much more religious time, that death was easier for us to accept, because we knew that we would be reunited with them again someday.
— Priscilla Flanagan, age seventyish, former bank teller, Oakland. CA.

One of the changes I'm really happy about is that we no longer display the bodies of the dead in our front parlors. When my grandfather died we lived on a farm in New Hampshire, and we put his body in the coffin in our living room for all the relatives and neighbors to see, and it stayed there for three days. As a little kid I dreaded going to bed at night with that dead body downstairs; it really spooked me! — Jerry Petruno, retired chauffeur, born 1930.

Rather than being the natural end of an elderly person's life, death began to be seen as a medical failure, to be avoided at all costs. "Living Wills" became necessary so that terminally-ill people could legally instruct their doctors when to stop medical care, and let them die in peace.

I urged my mother to draw up a living will because she had always said she never wanted to end up with tubes in her body, and machines controlling everything. But, like a lot of people, she never got around to doing it, and I think she was really relying on me to take care of it at the hospital. But I couldn't. The doctors were afraid *of a lawsuit, and they refused to pull the plugs even though my mother, who was eighty-seven years old, lay there in a coma for four months. It was heartbreaking, but they absolutely refused to let her go. My family and I were totally exhausted from trips to the hospital, and arranging to sell her house and other goods so we could pay for the escalating costs when the insurance ran out. When she finally died, my husband and I had contributed $35,000 to the cost of keeping her vegetative body alive with machines for four months after she had essentially died. It was really criminal. – Martha Kristof, teacher's aide, born 1940, San Diego, CA.*

Self-Medicating

At the beginning of the century marijuana, heroin and morphine were all available over the counter at corner drugstores. According to one pharmacy's ad: "Heroin clears the complexion, gives buoyancy to the mind, regulates the stomach and the bowels and is, in fact, a perfect guardian of health."

1930s Poster. Courtesy Library of Congress

I'd Walk a Mile for a Camel

Lung cancer was first attributed to cigarette smoking in 1953. The FDA estimated 3,000 Americans die a year from lung cancer, and approximately 40,000 from heart disease, due to smoking. In 1971 cigarette advertisements were banned from U.S. television, but not from magazines. Not much else was done about it until the eighties when "stop smoking" campaigns began in earnest. Smoking was soon banned in most states in restaurants, public buildings, hospitals, work places, and even some outdoor events. The airlines followed suit and banned smoking on all domestic and international flights. It's hard to believe now that we were once crammed into a small space and subjected to the smoke from passengers in the back rows, being recirculated throughout the plane. Flight attendants had to inhale it on every flight.

Selling cigarettes to minors has always been illegal, but in the forties and fifties people weren't as concerned about it as they are now. It was rumored that smoking would stunt your growth if you did it before eighteen or so, but parents freely smoked in front of their children, even in a closed car, and nobody thought anything about it. When my brother and I were in our late teens, he would write a note that he signed with our mother's name asking the local grocer to sell her son a package of cigarettes for her. They were only nineteen cents a pack then, and Larry would take the note to the store, and they always gave them to him without question. – Patrick Hershenhorn, vice-president, manufacturing, born 1945, Portland, OR.

By the end of the century only about twenty-five to thirty-five percent of people smoked, compared to about forty-to-forty-five in the 1950s, and these were mostly considered pariahs who were unable to control their addiction.

Popeye says:"Eat Yer Spinach So You'll be Strong and Healthy Like Me!" ©*King Features Syndicate*

Ad in Good Housekeeping, 1934

I've been smoking for forty years, and I have no intention of quitting. This is one of life's great pleasures as far as I'm concerned. When I grew up everybody smoked - Humphrey Bogart, Lauren Bacall, Ingrid Bergman, Katherine Hepburn, even debonair Cary Grant. It was sophisticated, and it gave you something to do with your hands at those infernal cocktail parties. Nobody told us there were health dangers. Doctors didn't tell me to stop smoking when I was pregnant, and I even smoked cigarettes while I was nursing my baby and, thank goodness, there's nothing wrong with him. I smoked in the hospital recovery room after my delivery.

My doctor knew I smoked because I used to smoke in his waiting room, where there were actually ashtrays for smokers. And he didn't say a thing about it, because he smoked too! – Caroline Kristoferson, self-employed business woman, born 1948, Maine.

One More for the Road

Our attitude towards drinking has changed dramatically. Drunkenness, once the butt of jokes on radio and television, personified by Dean Martin, became serious business when a group called *Mothers Against Drunk Driving* began their campaign in the seventies to educate people. Motorists who had formerly gotten off with little more than a slap on the wrist now found themselves facing huge fines, enormous insurance increases, and even jail time. Being drunk in public became something to be ashamed of, instead of something to brag about on Monday morning at the office.

Bob's Bar and Grill, 1986, Omaha.

Bedding Down with a bug: Sexually Transmitted Diseases

The United States has the highest rate of sexually transmitted diseases of any developed country. Each year these diseases cause thousands of deaths and such serious health problems as cancer, miscarriages and birth defects. The most common "STDs" include chlamydial infection, syphilis, gonorrhea, herpes and hepatitis B virus. Gonorrhea infects 150 of every 100,000 Americans, compared with three of every 100,000 people in Sweden and 18.6 per 100,00 in Canada. One-fourth of the estimated twelve-million new cases that occur each year involve adolescents, who are at greater risk because they are more likely than adults to engage in unprotected sex.

> *When my husband and I got divorced, I went back into the dating scene and was absolutely terrified. It was the seventies and people were having sex with each other on the first date. It was such a different world from the one I lived in when I met my husband. Of course I was a virgin in 1956 when we married, as most women were. After the divorce I joined a singles group and met a man my age who was also divorced.*

We dated for about six weeks when I decided I really cared for him a lot and was willing to have sex with him. AIDS wasn't around then, and we didn't use a condom because I was menopausal so I wasn't worried about getting pregnant. I dated Bill for a few more weeks and then he just suddenly stopped seeing me, and I never knew the reason. I called and left messages but he didn't return my calls.

But he did leave a little gift behind: he gave me herpes. The first man I'd ever had sex with outside of my husband and now I have a venereal disease that I can never get rid of, and have to tell ever other man about from now on. I'm disgusted, outraged and heartbroken. It's hard for me to believe that a man could be like this. When I was a teenager, men were gentlemen, and nobody worried about venereal diseases. I said to myself, "well stupid, welcome to the new world; you sure were naive." – Mabel, administrative assistant, born 1940, Tacoma, WA.

A Serial Killer comes to town

In 1981, at San Francisco's General Hospital, people with a strange disease began to arrive. Most of them were young gay men, many with a rare type of pneumonia, or the purple skin lesions of Karposi's Sarcoma, a rare cancer-like tumor. It was the beginning of the AIDS epidemic.

More than a million people died of AIDS in 1996. According to the World Health Organization, about twenty million adults worldwide are infected with the HIV virus. It is now epidemic in Asia and Africa.

In 1986 Rock Hudson, with Doris Day at his side, was the first celebrity to publicly announce he had AIDS. Another celebrity, tennis great Arthur Ashe, also died of AIDS from a blood transfusion.

In 1991 basketball's most admired star, Magic Johnson, announced he was HIV positive. He retired, vowing to become a spokesman in the battle against AIDS. In 1996, still very healthy, he returned to resume playing basketball.

In the summer of 1989 my twenty-nine year old gay son got a very bad flu which laid him up for a couple of weeks, causing him to miss work. That was the beginning of a series of illnesses— gastrointestinal trouble, an eye infection, cold sore outbreaks, night sweats, a persistent cough, the flu twice— and on and on. He was constantly sick for several months before I was finally able to persuade him to see a doctor because he didn't believe in the medical profession. I think he was really scared to find out. He got tested for the HIV virus and of course he was positive. The doctor wanted to start him on AZT right away, but Jerry refused. He came over to the house and told me he was just going to let nature take its course and die when his body gave out. He said he'd seen too many of his friends go through the horror of getting one illness after another, going to the hospital and getting patched up and, a month or so later, get something else, and go through it all again. He said he was convinced there was an afterlife, and he simply wasn't going to go through that agony just so he could stay on earth maybe another couple of more years, while feeling sick the whole time. Six months later he died at home of pneumocystis carinni pneumonia. A nurse came to the house and hooked him up to a morphine drip, and he went into a coma and died in his sleep. It was very peaceful, and exactly the way he wanted. – Karen, mother and homemaker, born 1937.

With the newer combination drugs to fight AIDS, patients are managing their health and living many years longer than those who were initially infected, when AZT was the only available drug and death soon followed the diagnosis of full-blown AIDS.

To Parent or not to Parent?

Maria Molinari, born at home June 24th, 1936, in Rochester, N.Y.

In 1999 the FDA said it would approve RU-486, a drug that could provide a non-surgical abortion, thus allowing women to procure a private abortion from their doctors without enduring the protests of pro-life advocates. The decision was expected to dramatically increase the number of doctors willing to administer a pill that could trigger an abortion, especially those who had abandoned the surgical practice because of threats by pro-lifers. It would also make it harder for anti-abortionists to target for harassment, or even violence, women who were planning an abortion, because the decision could now be made in her doctor's private office. It was the pro-life movements' worst nightmare. In response, they sent letters to every doctor in the U.S. informing them they would be watched and carefully monitored to see if they would prescribe the drug for abortions.

I was terrified when I went to Planned Parenthood on Saturday morning for my scheduled abortion. My husband and I already had three children, and this one was an accident. I'd been on the pill since our last one, but somehow it failed us. We were devastated when we finally made the decision that we couldn't possibly afford another child, and I'd have to have an abortion. It just wasn't fair to bring a child into the world who was unexpected and unwanted. We were barely able to pay our bills now, and we were anticipating three kids being ready for college in a few more years. It just wasn't possible. But, what made the abortion decision even more painful was that, when we arrived, we were faced with having to walk through a gauntlet of ugly, screaming people holding pictures of dead fetuses and signs saying abortion was murder and God would punish us. I clung to Jack and some women from the clinic escorted us through the mob, but I was shaken to the core. The entire traumatic event was one of the most horrible things I've ever gone through. – Anita, supervisor, purchasing department, born 1964, Eugene, OR.

A phenomenon of the latter part of the century was the sight of fathers in the delivery room. Not only were fathers allowed to witness every part of the delivery, and even go so far as to record it on a video tape, other relatives were often admitted to witness what was once considered a most private event. Deliveries without anesthesia, particularly using the Lamaze Method of conscious relaxation and control of the contractions, became popular.

Poison in the Air

Autoimmune diseases such as sinusitis, arthritis, allergies and hayfever, have become epidemic in the latter part of the century. A new term was coined: "environmentally-sensitive people." Smog and other pollutants were blamed for this outbreak, and no cure was in sight, although drugs could provide some relief. Some women stopped wearing perfume because it offended certain people.

In the forties people who lived in rural areas were exposed to the sight, smell and particles in the air from light planes swooping down and dusting crops with pesticides. No one thought it was a health hazard. Now those who can afford it prefer to buy organic food which uses no pesticides and no artificial ingredients.

This photo was taken in 1924, when I was 3 years old. My grandpa, Leon Roberts, had a farm in Hanover, Maine, and three generations of the family lived there, where we raised animals. My mother had a huge vegetable garden that provided for us, with enough left over for her to take to town and sell. - Mary Billings, Bryant Pond, Maine

When I lived on a farm as a kid mom grew all of our vegetables in the garden. We never heard of vitamins, but we certainly didn't need extra supplements because we got them from our own vegetables which were grown in soil that wasn't depleted of nutrients, and contained no insecticides. We picked the bugs off by hand. People today have no idea how good those freshly-grown vegetables tasted and how much better the flavor was than the chemically-engineered stuff we buy today. We also had all the fresh fruit we wanted from wild strawberries and grapes, and the trees that my dad had planted in the orchard. My mother would spend the summer baking fruit pies and canning the rest.

One thing I didn't like was when mom would pour us a glass of milk that was warm because it had just been taken from the cow; pasteurization was unknown then. We didn't have a refrigerator, and we didn't even have an ice-box because there was no ice other than what we had in the winter. – Vincent Ferigoso, former bread deliveryman, born 1918, Newark, NJ.

A Hole in the Sky

A hole first appeared in the ozone layer above the earth in 1980, and it has doubled in size every four years. The ozone layer is a thin band in the stratosphere that plays a key role in shielding all life forms from dangerous ultraviolet radiation from the sun. Because of this hole, which has been largely caused by mankind's chemicals, ultraviolet rays, which once were blocked from reaching the earth, are now penetrating the earth's surface. The result is a dramatic increase in melanoma, a sometimes fatal skin cancer, and an increase in cataracts. Suntanning, which once lured hundreds of pale white people to the beach in search of a golden-brown body, is now anathema. But some people continue doing it anyway. Beauty before health.

When I was a teenager in the forties, my sisters and I use to climb onto the roof of our house every weekend to get a tan. We spread out our blankets and lay there until we burned. We didn't have any beaches in the part of Montana where I lived, so that was the only way to get rid of the pasty-white look of winter. And we didn't have to use that greasy suntan lotion because there was no need to. There was no hole in the ozone in my day, and lying in the hot sun for several hours was never considered a health hazard. On the contrary, people were told they needed sunshine to stay healthy. – Naomi Rowe, school principal, born 1933, Long Beach, CA.

In the latter half of the century, people became more environmentally conscious, and more disturbed about what pollutants were doing to their health. They began protesting against polluting factories, incinerators, power plants, heating systems, blast furnaces, cars and anything else that contributed to dust, smog, grit and grime. In response Congress passed the Clean Air Act in 1963, which created standards for measuring air quality, and guidelines for reducing pollution. This forced industry, especially oil companies, coal and steel mills, to clean up their act.

Many cities shut down huge incinerators, and public utilities were often required to generate heat by burning low-sulfur oil or natural gas instead of coal. In most cities blast furnaces and other industrial polluters have closed for good. Black smoke no longer covers cities such as Pittsburgh, once the hub of America's industrial heartland. Railroads switched to diesel fuel, and coal-burning furnaces were converted to natural gas.

When I was in the United Kingdom during the war in 1944 pea soup fogs were frequent. In the fifties each fog episode killed hundreds of people, and eventually it was realized that what was killing them were the pollutants trapped in the air mass that produced the dense fogs. When they started cleaning up the pollution, the death rates went down. – Mack Williams, retired forester, born 1925, Toronto, Canada.

The Big "C"

Federal Art Project, New York Between 1936 and 1938.
Courtesy Library of Congress

Although the "war on cancer" was started in the thirties, it hasn't been very effective. Since 1971 the government has poured thirty billion dollars into cancer research, but the program has largely failed because the death rate from cancer remains essentially the same as it was at the time. Lung cancer is the most common cause of cancerous death for both men and women. It tripled between the early 1970s and the early 1990s. Second in line for women: breast, and for men: prostate.

By the end of the century melanoma was the fastest rising cancer and the most common cancer in the age group nineteen to twenty-nine, mainly attributed to sunbathing. Its incidence has doubled in the last twenty years. Fifty years ago melanoma killed one person in every 1500. Today it's eighty-four out of every 1500.

Cracking the Code of Life

In 1953 Francis Crick walked into the Eagle pub in Cambridge, England and announced that "we have found the secret of life." That morning he and James Watson, an ex-physicist and a former ornithology student, had finally figured out the structure of DNA, deoxyribonucleic acid, the "double helix" that carries life's hereditary information on our genes. This discovery, for which they received the Nobel Prize in Medicine, revolutionized the world! The discovery of DNA opened the door to how biology works, and what makes each living organism different from all others. Additionally, DNA has been used extensively in fighting crime, and also in exonerating prisoners who have been wrongly accused, and in settling paternity suits.

Francis Crick and James Watson in 1953

Taking us into the next Century: Gene Therapy and Growing Tissue in a Petri Dish

The mapping and manipulation of genes promises a future in which science will be able to defeat many of our ancient enemies. Tests for the presence of genes that either cause disease, or predispose people to it, are becoming increasingly available. The hope is that disease will become more predictable, and medicine will develop preventive methods, instead of treatment after the fact. But the possibility of misuse of this information by insurance companies, employers, and even potential partners, is frightening. For many people the question they face will be: "Do you want to know if the news is bad?" And, "Do you want your insurance company to know?"

The last great medical discovery of the twentieth century was the isolation by researchers of a master cell that can be directed to grow bone, cartilage, or skin. Called "stem cells," scientists may eventually be able to inject specific types of cells into patients, which would then grow into replacement bone, tendon or muscle. If the technique proves successful, it could be used to replace tissue lost to cancer, osteoporosis, injury, or even dental disease, thus saving our smile.

And the final medical coup of the century: research has begun on "tissue engineering," a procedure designed to grow your own organs in case they should fail! If this eventually succeeds, it will eliminate the agony of thousands of people who are now awaiting the limited number of replacement organs.

As we enter the twenty-first century scientists are mapping the human genome and, in 2003, they declared they had a complete map of homosapiens' genes. A genome is all the DNA in an organism, including its genes. Knowledge about the effects of DNA variations among individuals can lead to revolutionary new ways to diagnose, treat, and someday prevent the thousands of disorders that affect us.

Has Frankenstein Been Unleashed?

In 1997, in an experiment many scientists thought would be impossible, Ian Wilmut, an embryologist at the Roslin Institute in Scotland, announced that he had created a lamb using DNA from a mammary cell of an adult sheep. The embryo from the donor sheep was transferred into a surrogate mother sheep, and a lamb named Dolly was born, genetically identical to the donor sheep.

This first cloning of an adult mammal brought the unthinkable within reach: could science clone a human being? If so, what does it mean to be human? Are we creators like God? Although the idea would be ethically unacceptable, Wilmut said that, in principle, there was no reason the technology couldn't be used to clone living humans. Fearful that scientists were treading on God's domain, Congress quickly passed a bill declaring no federal funding would ever be provided for experiments on cloning homosapiens.

"Little Lamb, who made thee?

Dost thou know who made thee?"

- William Blake, "Songs of Innocence"

Different Strokes for Different Folks

Alternative health care methods have finally gained some recognition, even from practitioners of traditional medicine, and many people are now turning to acupuncturists, chiropractors, naturopaths, vitamin, mineral and herbal therapy, homeopathic medicine, hypnosis, meditation, music therapy, massage, spiritual healers, affirmations and visualization to promote their own healing. Possibly due to the influx of Asians in the U.S., ancient healing practices such as acupuncture have been incorporated into the treatment methods of many traditional doctors.

In the 1990s a third of adult Americans, most of whom consulted medical doctors as well, spent an estimated $13.7 billion a year out of their own pockets on alternative treatments. In 1992, Congress responded to this trend by establishing the Office of Alternative Medicine at the National Institute of Health. Its mission is to facilitate the evaluation of alternative modalities and treatments, support research, and establish an information clearinghouse for the public.

Insurers too, have begun to take notice, and several will now pay for acupuncture, biofeedback and massage, if prescribed by a physician.

In the latter part of the century people became increasingly more health-conscious. Vitamin stores began to flourish as people realized, in spite of the traditional opposition of organized medicine, that they cannot get all the vitamins they need from overprocessed food that has been grown in soil depleted of nutrients and sprayed with pesticides. The medical profession finally acknowledged in the late 1990s that certain vitamins can actually prevent disease. Folic acid was proven to reduce birth defects, and studies with vitamin E showed that it could help reduce coronary disease.

One of my biggest complaints about drugs is simply the difficulty of getting into the damned bottle! I have arthritis in my hands and these childproof lids make it next to impossible to open the darned things. Once I actually took a hammer to a bottle of cold medicine because I'd struggled unsuccessfully for over ten minutes to get it open. And that goes for other stuff that you get at the store that has safety caps and hermetic seals and wrapped in a ream of hard plastic that's even hard for scissors to cut through. I suppose it's necessary but, in my day, nobody ever tried to poison a perfect stranger. I wish these companies could figure out a simpler way to package their goods. – Jim Croux, retired farmer, over 80, Iowa.

Coming Full Circle

The quality of life for older people has improved, aided by such innovations as artificial joints, lens implants and advanced medications. Although coronary disease is still the nation's number one killer, because of medical treatment and certain changes in lifestyle, the death rate from heart attacks has dropped thirty percent in the past three decades.

Many afflictions however, have remained intractable to modern medicine, such as AIDS, arthritis, Alzheimer's, asthma, diabetes (controlled but not cured), cancer (some progress but still no cure), genital herpes, chronic fatigue syndrome, hepatitis C, lupus, muscular dystrophy, multiple sclerosis, and the ubiquitous common cold, all of which are statistically higher now than they were at the beginning of the century. And, as the century draws to a close, asthma and allergies, largely resistant to current treatments, have become epidemic.

When the twentieth century began, infectious diseases were the major killer and, as it comes to an end, such diseases are once again regaining their power. The wonder drugs that saved so many lives for most of the century, were overprescribed and overused, not just by humans, but also by such practices as injecting farm animals with antibiotics, and many drugs are now beginning to lose their potency. Following Darwin's evolutionary principle, germs have learned to adapt to the assault, and many bacterial and viral diseases are now drug-resistant.

In 1969, William Stewart, the United States Surgeon General, testified before Congress that it was time to "close the book on infectious diseases." His prediction was exceedingly premature! Along with the appearance of new diseases such as AIDS, antibiotic-resistant strains of bacteria are appearing worldwide. Because of immigration and international travel, infectious and contagious diseases will likely be the scourge of the twenty-first century. In 1996, Dr. Hiroshi Nakajima, the director of the World Health Organization said: "We are standing on the brink of a global crisis in infectious diseases."

CHAPTER NINE

Science and Technology!:

Hal and His Pals

The 'Apparatus for Treating Air' (U.S. Pat# 808897) granted in 1906, was the first of several patents awarded to Willis Haviland Carrier.

One year before the beginning of the twentieth century, Charles Dowell, the head of the U.S. Patent office, urged in a letter to President Grover Cleveland that "everything has been invented already. Let us close down the patent office." Shortsightedness in the extreme!

The twentieth century was the century of invention, which produced the most dramatic changes in the history of the world, and its major characteristic was the intense, exponential growth of scientific knowledge. Because of accelerating technology, the last one hundred years ushered in more discoveries and inventions than in the entire chronicle of civilization. It was the age of splitting the atom, medical imaging, nuclear reactors, atom and hydrogen bombs, of probing the nature of the galaxies and our own psyche. It brought us the transistor and the silicon chip, plastics, organ transplants and artificial knees, antibiotics and vaccines, radio and television, lasers, satellites, radar, transcontinental flight, computers, wireless communications, the Internet, the World Wide Web, and landings on the moon.

Astronaut Edwin E. Aldwin, Jr. Pilot of the First Lunar landing of Apollo 11 July 20, 1969. Courtesy of NASA.

With now laughably limited thinking, by the 1950s many scientists had decided that everything important that could be discovered, already had been. Yet the most startling discoveries came after that time, and changed the life of mankind in awe-inspiring ways. By the end of the century daily life had changed almost beyond recognition by those born in the first half. From high-speed trains to cars to jet planes, and then the Internet, we now have increased mobility, instantaneous communication around the globe, and electronic eyes and ears. But, although these changes greatly improved our lives, they also brought their own set of miseries: pollution, overcrowding, homeless people wandering the streets, freeways turned into parking lots, and increased crime. The makers of Prozac, an anti-depressant, boasted worldwide sales of $1.5 billion a year. Doctors wrote over a million prescriptions a month in 1997. Not everyone was happy with the technological advances.

The Information Revolution

In 1977, Kenneth Olsen, the president and founder of Digital Equipment Corporation, was convinced that "there is no reason for any individual to have a computer in their home." A good businessman perhaps, but not very good at prognosticating!

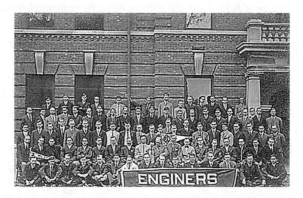

These 1939 Grads Didn't Learn to Spell

With the advent of computers, about two-thirds of the way into the century, the industrial age became transformed into the information age. As a result, there has been more information produced in the past thirty years than in all of previous history! A single edition of the "New York Times" contains more information than the average person would come across during a lifetime in Shakespeare's England. Technology has not only been the single greatest contributor of this transition but it also provided the speed with which that change occurred. You could, for instance, be in Barcelona and want to get your Denver, Colorado credit card approved to buy an antique vase. This involves a journey of about 5,000 miles, but the transaction can be completed in *ten seconds* over computer and phone lines.

Stepping Stones to the Information Age

Although computers revolutionized the transmission of information, many inventions occurred in the first few years of the twentieth century that speeded up the process.

Guglielmo Marconi, an Italian physicist, opened the technological century in 1901 by transmitting the first transatlantic telegraphic messages from Cornwall, England to Newfoundland, Canada. In 1902 the great operatic tenor Enrico Caruso made his first scratchy phonograph recording, and 1903 heralded the first ever recording of an opera: Verdi's 'Ernani.'

Although electricity was discovered in the nineteenth century, it was only in the twentieth that its use began to proliferate, and mankind soon became wholly dependent on its light, ability to run machinery, and even provide us with music in our homes.

I was born in 1932, so home radios hadn't been around very long. When I was a little boy we had a big console radio in the living room. No one had small portable radios then because they were powered by large vacuum tubes. The tubes were always burning out so you had to keep a supply on hand because if one burned out on Friday night, you wouldn't have a radio until 11 o'clock Tuesday morning when the stores opened again, because many of them were closed on Mondays. Most households had only one radio, so you didn't have music to accompany you while you were in the kitchen cooking, or in the basement workshop. We didn't have a record player of course, because records came later, and when they finally arrived they were thick, scratchy vinyl 78rpms and, if you accidentally dropped one, it would break into pieces. When we got the plastic ones after the war you had to be careful not to leave them near a sunny window because they'd warp and melt quite easily.

About 1960 I bought my first transistor radio; a tiny thing you could hold in the palm of your hand that ran on batteries. It was amazing! That meant we could carry it to the beach, and even have a radio in the car. That seems really strange now when I have a Walkman that I use on my morning run, and a portable CD player that I take to the beach.

Another invention I really liked was cassette players. Magnetic tape was invented in 1942, but cassette tapes didn't become popular until the sixties. Then we had the eight-track tapes which were popular for awhile, but for some reason they died out. Music on cassette is good, but it can't match a compact disk for quality, and you don't have to get up to turn them over in the middle of a symphony. – Bob Harrison, electrical engineer, Miami Beach, FL..

Courtesy Library of Congress

Inventions that Transformed the World

It's hard to fathom today that the atom had not even been discovered at the beginning of the century. In 1912 Wilson's cloud-chamber photographs lead to the detection of protons and electrons. That same year Viktor Hess discovered cosmic radiation, and just a year later Neils Bohr formulated his theory of atomic structure. In 1914 Albert Einstein postulated his General Theory of Relativity and the now famous equation: $E=Mc^2$, which gave man the power to unleash unprecedented destruction on his own kind.

The splitting of the atom in 1942 was achieved by Enrico Fermi, a U.S. scientist, and that discovery led to the development of the atomic bomb, which is fraught with danger to civilization. Nuclear warfare was launched with massive destruction on Japan, ending World War II, and demonstrating that man now had the power to destroy himself and the earth.

When I saw the pictures in the newspaper of the ghastly aftermath of dropping the atomic bomb on Hiroshima, I was so shocked at the massive destruction that I shook with fear and horror. Of course we were outraged when the Japanese bombed Pearl Harbor, and knew we had to strike back, but I never imagined it could be with such ferocity! It was worse than Dante's description of hell in the Inferno, and I couldn't help but think "What Has Man

Wrought?" I pray we'll never have to obliterate thousands of innocent people in such a horrendous ball of fire again. – Wayne Echols, retired school superintendent, born 1929, Monterey, CA.

Checking the Map on a Georgia Highway in 1921

Radar, developed by Scottish physicist Sir Robert Watson Watt in 1935, was one of the most significant inventions of the twentieth century. Not least is its enormous contribution to television; early radar displays were generally cathode-ray tubes. It was first developed during World War II as a defensive tool against enemy bombers, when Britain was completely vulnerable to German airraids. British and American pioneers used radar to track and destroy enemy planes, and changed the course of the war. In 1945 a radar fuse detonated the single atom bomb that was dropped over Nagasaki at an altitude of 1,900 feet.

Radar enabled us to fly airplanes at night, and to know the location of other planes. The thousands of planes that take off from American airports every day couldn't function without radar and its spinoffs. Microwaves and other devices were derived from the development of radar, and we're all familiar with the ubiquitous radar speed-traps of the police. Radar-equipped satellites track the world's weather, and without them we wouldn't have our nightly weather report, and we would never have made it to the moon! These satellites also made the Global Positioning System possible, which is a world-wide navigational system run by the U.S. Department of Defense. With a GPS in their car, the directionally-challenged no longer need to get hopelessly lost, or be frustrated by the inability to figure out a map.

Sending Messages the Old-Fashioned Way

The teletype machine came into restricted use in the U.S., Britain and Germany in 1928, and was used mainly by the press, but now it's been replaced by computers. Western Union began sending messages for the general public in the forties, but they were extremely expensive and usually reserved for emergencies.

Western Union Teletype Operating Room   Seattle, WA, 1930

I worked for Canadian National Telegraphs in the fifties as a teletype operator. The press wires were in the back offices, along with a few Morse Code keys that were still being used by some old-timers, mainly sending messages to ships at sea. It was a really exciting job because of course we got to read the telegrams while we were sending them. People today wouldn't like that form of message transmission because it isn't private enough. We were all sworn to confidentiality, but sometimes we'd call another operator over to share a particularly interesting telegram, usually from a movie star, or some other famous person. On the late night shift when there wasn't much business, we'd go to the back room and read the news coming over the wires from the United Press and Associated Press.

Getting a telegram in those days was a big event and sometimes very scary. During the war people were frightened by them because they were afraid they would bring bad news. People would send telegrams to someone who might not have a phone, or they wanted to put the message in writing. The telegraph boy in his black and yellow uniform would come to your house and hand it to you personally; that service was part of what you were paying for. People liked to send them to wish someone a happy birthday or anniversary. Somebody capitalized on that by inventing the 'singing telegram,' or telegrams delivered by someone in a gorilla suit, which were always fun to get. – Melanie Yates, retired teletype operator, born 1934, Ottawa, Canada.

After 150 years of use, in February, 1999, the Morse Code signal "S.O.S." sent by ships at sea that were in distress, was officially replaced with messages sent through a satellite system. Some old-timers took off their caps and bowed their heads in a symbolic gesture of sadness at the departure of a reliable old friend.

Samuel Morse's Telegraph Key. Courtesy: Smithsonian Institute

When I was young the way we found out about the election results was that the local newspaper would get them over the teletype machine and everyone would go downtown and they would project them on a big screen with a transparent slide, and hundreds of people would gather around and watch. No one that I knew had a radio then, so this was the only way to get the news. – Rocco D'Angelo, graphic artist, born 1910, Toronto, Canada.

Going Outside to make a Phone Call

A 1940s Switchboard and Phones

At the beginning of the century only eight-percent of homes had a telephone, and long distance calls were so expensive, people made them only in dire emergencies. A three-minute call to New York City from Denver cost eleven dollars; a huge amount in 1903.

The first enclosed phone booth was installed by the Bell System in 1912. It was wood and glass with folding doors, and was the first public phone where customers dropped in a nickel and the operator said: "Number please?" It was quite a novelty to be able to call from a telephone booth on the street; now people are upset if they can't find one within a few blocks. But we now have pre-paid phone cards, so you don't even need a coin. By the 1970s vandals had destroyed thousands of pay phones and shredded the phone books, and they had become a favorite place to make drug deals and spray-paint your name. AT&T stopped making enclosed booths in 1972 in favor of telephones mounted in a small box attached to a hollow post, with the base embedded in concrete. Customers lost the privacy and quiet of an enclosed booth, and Clark Kent could no longer dash into one to change into his Superman outfit.

'We'll call you every Wednesday evening!"

Until we got a rotary dial phone in 1935 we picked up the phone and asked the operator to get us the number. Usually it was a party-line so there were one or more other families sharing a line with you. In those days relatives often lived close to each other, so your grandparents or great aunt might be on the same line. If someone was talking when you wanted to make a call, you just had to wait your turn unless it was an emergency, and then you could ask the operator to break in. The operator and your neighbors on the party-line could also listen in to your call if they had a mind to, but people were usually too polite to do so in those days; otherwise, this system wouldn't have worked very well.

To call someone on your party-line you used a hand-crank, and each home had its own ring made up of one or more short or long turns of the crank, so every time the phone rang we would all be quiet and listen to the ring to distinguish if it was for us. It sounds very primitive today, but we didn't even have phone books then, and not everybody had a telephone. A long-distance phone call was so rare the whole family would usually gather excitedly around the phone when one came in. Then we would talk very quickly because the calls were enormously expensive.

Converting to touch-tone in the seventies changed the world of communication. Now in seconds I can phone anyone in the world who has a telephone, and I can phone them with my cordless phone while I'm in the backyard sitting by the pool, or use my cellular phone while driving down the freeway. If they're not there, then probably their answering machine will be on, or they may have voice-mail where I can leave a message. Or, I can page them and leave my number on the pocket-size unit they may have hooked to their belt. I can even call home from 30,000 feet in the air, using the phone on the plane. I can send e-mail from a cruise ship out in the Atlantic, and go backpacking in the woods with my cell phone and a Personal Digital Assistant. With caller I.D. I can see the number of whoever is calling me, and decide whether or not I want to bother picking up the phone. Not answering the telephone was something unheard of in the thirties and forties when people would jump out of the shower or interrupt whatever they were doing, even making love to your wife, if the phone should ring. It wasn't polite to ignore a phone call, or not answer the doorbell; it just wasn't done. That seems really strange now.

We also have to deal now with the horror of voice-mail, which I think is a symbol of corporate coldness. You can seldom talk to a human being anymore, but instead you're given a mind-boggling array of choices that make you feel like a rat having to find its way through an endless maze to get a small piece of cheese—If you ever get the cheese at all; a lot of the time you land in "voice mail jail," an endless series of "If you want this, press 1, or 2, or 3, or 4, etc. etc., and finally you're disconnected. It drives me crazy!" – Adrian D'Angelo, photographer, born 1940.

Because of downsizing, companies have often slashed staff to the bone, and the easiest way to answer calls, or not answer them, is to have a machine do it. This has led to a giant surge in the national frustration level.

Number Please?

*In 1934 there were 10 working telephones at Lockheed, the
California aircraft manufacturer. Ten years later, when I worked
in the communications department in 1944, there were 5,871. I'm
in the white blouse and floral skirt, just over the right shoulder
of the supervisor. - Beth Northridge, Placentia, CA*

*When I first started with AT&T thirty-five years ago, operators,
who were always female, had to wear dresses and heels, even though
the customers never saw us. We would always answer by giving our
name, and saying 'How can I help you?' But now we're impersonal
because we don't have the time. You just can't spend time with people
because you only have so many seconds for each call, and it's all
counted automatically so the company can track your performance.
In the old days people would call and maybe ask you about a storm
that was coming up in a city nearby. Now I'm just a disembodied
voice identified with the phone company by a number. That makes it
easier to just disconnect a customer if they're rude to you, and a lot
of people are these days, they just don't have any patience.*

*Thirty-five years ago we use to plug the calls manually into a
"cord board," and each operator only took care of about six local
cities or towns. If you wanted to go beyond that you had to call the
long-distance operator. The end of the world for most operators
came in 1984 when AT&T divested. At that time there were 40,000*

operators, and now there are about 8,000, and there'll be even less in another ten years; just enough to handle the problem calls. With computers and voice synthesizers, the customers can do their own dialing and save some money, and so can the company. – Clarita Morenez, telephone operator, born 1946, Pittsburgh, PA.

Rotary phones were slow and inaccurate because the caller had to wait until the dialer had made a complete stop and then returned to its normal position before you could dial the next digit. In 1963 AT&T introduced the ten-button keyboard, which was a technological revolution and made possible answering machines, voice-mail, checking one's messages from another location, punching in a credit card number to pay for a call, and even Internet connections. Most customers loved the speed of the touch-tone phones, but millions of people are still using use their old rotaries because of habit, or because they don't trust technology.

Mary Gould was the chief operator of the telephone exchange in Englishtown, N.J. in the '30s. Here she's seated at the board in 1939, ready to plug in the next call.

My mother, Mary Gould, was a night operator, and the switchboard office was in the front room of our house, Mom often slept with me when I was a child, and the bedroom had a big bell that clanged when there was a call and kept clanging until Mom ran downstairs to answer it. I memorized all the numbers and still recall many of them: #1 was the firehouse, #2 was Al Young's garage, #3 was the Hamilton's Drugstore coin box. And on it went as far as 199.

There were four party lines with the letters J, R, M and W. Some of the rural lines had as many as eight parties, so there was lots of eavesdropping and sometimes even arguments. The telephone office was also the clearinghouse for community news. If the fire siren sounded, the shutters on the switchboard started falling furiously as folks called in to see where the fire was.

The light in the telephone office burned all night, and people in need felt free to drop in and ask for help. Linemen out troubleshooting would stop by to warm up and have a cup of coffee. Because Mom had a sympathetic ear, lonely hearts found a friend in her, both by telephone and in person. — Sally Smith Lewis, Freehold, NJ.

Cataloging the Numbers

Radio stations were first listed in the Yellow pages in 1923, and television was first listed in 1948. In 1997 there was another first: Pacific Bell, a California telephone company, began distributing Yellow Pages that included a separate section listing Internet and e-mail addresses classified by businesses. The guide is very small but it's a start; the first telephone directory listed only fifty names.

The Boob Tube

Nothing has revolutionized our leisure time more than the advent of television. The tube has been a blessing to seniors and others who'd rather stay at home and watch a movie than go out at night, has entertained people confined to bed, is a great surrogate baby-sitter for busy parents, especially with educational programs like *Sesame Street,* provides relaxation for the weary mind and body after a hard day's work, and has expanded our knowledge-base by bringing news of the world into our living rooms the moment it is happening. The drawback of course is that some kids (and some adults) have become addicted to TV and become couch potatoes, growing increasingly obese as they unconsciously munch on chips, while at the same digesting a menu of mush for the brain.

Another problem is the proliferation of gratuitous violence that influences the minds of impressionable young people. In the National Television Violence Study conducted in 1996, it was found that fifty-seven percent of programs contained violence, and seventy-three percent of it went unpunished. Even children's cartoons are permeated with violence, which is reflected in their speech as toddlers. A backlash finally occurred in 1996 when television producers agreed to a Code similar to those used for motion pictures, so parents could identify programs with too much sex or violence. It was roundly criticized as being too vague to do much good.

We always ate together in our family, and discussed our day over supper, until that stupid tube came into our lives and totally disrupted everything. It was the death of communication. The thing was usually on in the background throughout the meal, and sometimes we actually ate sitting in front of it in semi-worship of the new god. Even when my folks invited friends for dinner, we didn't sit around the table and talk after the meal, as in days of yore, but we retired to the living room to watch the game or the latest sit-com. On summer weekends we didn't discuss whether to go to the beach or the mountains, we simply settled down before the blaring machine and let it entertain us into stupefaction.

On chilly winter nights or rainy weekends, we no longer sat around the dining room table and played games together, instead we argued about which program to watch and, as we gathered on the couch, barely spoke a word to each other, except "pass the chips." It wasn't long before the arguments about what to watch became so intense that mom got her own set and retired to the bedroom to watch it, then Bobby had to have one in his room, and dad watched the game in his basement workshop, so eventually everyone watched the programs they liked, alone. As far as I was concerned, that damned thing wrecked our family life. – Marilyn Wilson, day care operator, born 1937, Vancouver, BC.

At the World's Fair in Flushing, New York in 1939, Franklin Delano Roosevelt was the first president to be televised.TV sets went on sale the next day and RCA began regular broadcasts on a daily basis. Sets costs a whopping $600 which, in today's money, would be about $7,000, not within the budget of most consumers. Because there were very few programs, there was little interest, and not many sets were sold. Programming stopped almost completely after Pearl Harbor was bombed and World War II began, although a few stations continued broadcasting on a limited basis. News of the war was not shown on TV sets, but in movie theaters on projection screens. England resumed broadcasting on June 7, 1946.

That same year the first televised heavyweight fight, Joe Louis vs. Billy Conn, was viewed by a record 140,000 people, mostly at bars which had TV sets. One year later, the Louis-Walcotte fight was viewed by a million people. One of television's critics, Darryl F. Zanuck, head of Twentieth Century Fox, was quoted as saying: "Television won't be able to hold on to any market it captures after the first six months. People will soon get tired of staring at a plywood box every night." By 1947 there were about 44,000 TV sets in the U.S., vs. forty million radios.

The first commercial was for Bulova watches, which simply showed the face of the watch, and made the network a profit of $7.00.

In 1954 the first national coast-to-coast color-cast took place with the broadcast of the "Tournament of Roses Parade" from Pasadena, California, to twenty-one network stations. There were only 200 RCA electronic color sets able to view the show. This is acknowledged as the first day American television officially changed from black-and-white to color. RCA launched color television, with the sale of their CT-100, at $1,000 each. Less than 5,000 sold the first year.

The first issue of the national version of television's Bible, TV Guide, was published on April 3, 1953, with a photo of the baby of TV's most popular stars, Lucy and Desi Arnez, on the cover.

It wasn't long before people tired of constantly getting up and down from the sofa or their easy chairs to change the station, or turn the volume up or down, even though most families parents had the kids do it. Zenith established itself as the leader in the development of the remote control in 1950, but it had a wire running between the TV set and the sofa, a hazard for all. In 1955 Zenith released the wireless remote control, which used a beam of light aimed at one of the sensors on the four corners of the tube. With this labor-saving device, one was even able to mute the sound of the commercials! No longer did people need to drag their tired bods off the couch to change channels; they could now just point and click. "Channel surfing," done mostly by males, became a new hobby, and a new point of contention in the family.

Bits, Bytes and Gigabytes

Two of the greatest inventions of the twentieth century were transistors and the microprocessor, and both were invented in America. In the summer of 1946, a tiny electronic device the size of a pea, called a transistor, was presented to the world during a press conference at the headquarters of Bell Laboratories in New York. This little device, invented by Walter H. Brattain and William Shockley, was one of the century's greatest technological discoveries, underlying all of modern electronics, from supercomputers to talking greeting cards. The transistor, with solid-state electronics, replaced vacuum tubes, and transformed the electronic world. It eventually turned furniture-sized living-room radios into walkmans and boom-boxes that could blow out your hearing, and its direct descendant, the integrated circuit, turned room-sized computers into laptops and hand-held devices. Today the world produces about as many transistors as it does printed characters in all the newspapers, books, magazines, computer and electronic-copier pages combined.

The integrated circuit was invented by a six-foot-six engineer named Jack Kilby, who worked for Texas Instruments. This invention won him the Nobel Prize and launched the digital revolution, transforming the way people lived and worked. Along with transistors, this breakthrough invention in 1958, shrank tons of complex circuitry to the size of a fingernail and enabled the development of microwave ovens, mobile phones, and a host of automated devices, including the garage door opener.

"In my opinion, there are only a handful of people whose works have truly transformed the world and the way we live in it— Henry Ford, Thomas Edison, the Wright Brothers and Jack Kilby."
– Tom Engibous, Chairman, Texas Instruments.

Exactly twenty-five years after the microprocessor was invented, a tiny silicon chip no bigger than a postage stamp, known as the computer's brains, was designed by Frederico Faggin, Marcian Hoff and Stan Mazor, three engineers from Intel Corporation in Silicon Valley, California. They created new industries by etching electronic components onto a single silicon chip the size of a pencil eraser. These inventions opened the way to the exploration of space and made the information age possible.

The transformation of modern society with the invention of the microprocessor has been like an earthquake, shaking up our working and private lives. The computer is the signature technology of the latter half of the twentieth century and, without really being aware of it, our daily lives are dominated by them.

One of the early computers – before the invention of the desktop.

Instead of the harsh ringing of an alarm, I awaken gently in the morning to music floating from my clock radio, triggered by an internal computer. As I prepare to go to the office I use the computer-controlled remote device to click on the TV and get the morning news and weather. Then I pour a cup of hot coffee which is already made because I had preset the coffeemaker's internal computer to start brewing at 7 a.m. After dressing (low tech), I put some oatmeal into the microwave where the computer cooks it to perfection. My toast pops up from a device which has a computer chip telling it to shut off when done. This is quite an improvement from the toaster we had when I was a kid that didn't automatically pop up the toast,, but had to be watched and hand-turned when each side of the bread was done. This resulted in a great deal of burned toast. When breakfast is finished, I put the bowl and cup in the dishwasher, which is now full, and press the button which tells the computer to run through the wash, rinse and dry cycle while I'm gone. Then I brush my teeth with my sonic toothbrush which is also operated by a computer chip.

As I leave the house I use a hand-held remote device with a computer chip to unlock the door of my BMW. Then, settling into the soft, tan leather seats, I turn on the computer-controlled radio with its pre-set stations and get the latest update on the traffic. At an intersection on the way to the freeway, a sensor in a city street tells the computer-regulated traffic light to stop oncoming cars and give me a left-turn green arrow. When I hit the freeway, I set the automatic cruise control and sit back to enjoy the smooth ride in my computer-controlled car. If I'm low on oil, or I forget to put on my seat-belt, a light will inform me. On the way to the office my cell phone beeps, letting me know an important e-mail has arrived, and I can read it on the small display screen on my phone.

Arriving at the office, I check my digital watch to see if I'm on time, and then insert a pre-programmed card into a slot which recognizes me and opens the door. The office heating system is also controlled by a computer to keep the air comfortable. When I arrive at my desk there sits a laptop connected to a high-speed DSL line which I will use to send e-mail to New York, Toronto, and Tokyo, and to access the Internet for information I need for my project. Later I use my modem to fax a customer in Denver. At lunch time I walk to the company cafeteria where real humans prepare salads and sandwiches without the benefit of a computer, but the cost is run up on a computer that automatically calculates my change.

After I leave the office, I stop at the supermarket for some dog food, and a computer scans the bar code and registers the price. Although I don't have enough cash with me, I don't have to write a check because I can pay for it with my bank card, which automatically deletes the amount from my checking account. When I arrive home in the evening, a sensor in the light over the driveway flashes itself on, and I use the computer-controlled remote to open the garage door.

While greeting my excited little dogs, I click on the stereo with another remote device. Next comes the mail, which includes an incredible pile of unsolicited junk. Computers have put my name on endless lists without my consent or awareness. Although the Internet has made my shopping simpler, it has also made it much easier for people to invade my privacy. But there's a greeting card in the mail, because tomorrow's my birthday. I open it and it plays "Happy Birthday to You." This little card contains more computer power than existed in the entire world before 1950.

Dinner is already made because I put it in the oven this morning, and the computer turned it on at the correct time, and cooked it exactly as programmed. But, before eating, I take the dogs for a walk, and enjoy looking at the golden leaves of autumn, totally free for a few moments from the automated world of computers.

But it doesn't last long because, after dinner, I log on to an Internet dating-service, looking for romance in cyberspace. A part of me is still old-fashioned enough to hope someday my knight will come. After logging off, I watch an old Cary Grant movie, longing for the romantic old days of the past. My grandmother would have found my day to be absolutely mind-boggling! – Maybe even frightening! – Valerie, web designer, born 1975, San Jose, CA.

Born in a Garage

In 1939, in a garage behind his Palo Alto, California home, Bill Hewlett formed the Hewlett-Packard Corporation with his friend David Packard, and it became one of the world's most successful electronic companies. This was the beginning of what became known as "Silicon Valley" in the Bay Area of California, the birthplace of computers, and still the major home of the industry.

On February 14, 1946, ENIAC turned on the first general-purpose electronic computer. It filled an entire room and weighed fifty tons. Thanks to transistors and integrated circuits and other technological innovations, computers eventually became so small they could be put in a pocket, and they now contain more processing power than the mainframe machines of just a few decades ago.

In 1975, a nineteen-year-old Harvard drop-out, Bill Gates, and his friend Paul Allen, formed Microsoft Corporation, now based in Redmond, Washington. By 1990 William Gates was the richest man in the entire world.

In 1979 Steve Jobs, age twenty-one, and Steve Wozniak, age twenty-six, worked together in Job's parents garage in Palo Alto and formed the Apple Computer Company in California on April Fool's day. The Apple II was unveiled at the first West Coast Computer Faire. The first Macintosh rolled off the assembly lines in January of 1984, and quickly developed a following of devoted, addicted fans. It became the favorite computer of artists and schoolteachers because of its ease of use and facility with graphics.

In 1981 IBM launched the personal computer, commonly known as the PC. In less than ten years we progressed from main frames and block-long computers to multi-media CD ROM, talking, full-color, stereo-music-playing desktop home computers. And, even smaller portable laptops, iPods and hand-held notebooks. Twenty years ago there was no personal computing industry; today it's the third-largest industry in the world.

I'm a writer, and I've spent a good part of my adult life cutting and pasting little pieces of paper together to weave a story, and then re-typing drafts over and over again every time I wanted to make a single change. When my high-tech girlfriend urged me to make my life easier by getting a computer, I was afraid to do it, but she prevailed, and I bought my first Macintosh in 1985. Once I got the hang of a word processing program I was delighted and amazed! I could move sentences and whole-paragraphs around simply by using "cut" and "paste," and I could change the character's names instantly by using "find and replace," even though the name may appear a hundred times in the manuscript. If I couldn't think of the appropriate word, I'd just go to the computer's thesaurus and select one, without having to interrupt my writing to go to the bookcase and look it up in Roget's Thesaurus. And, most delightful of all—an instant spell checker that even catches it when I type a word in duplicate by mistake. Typing a manuscript the old way now seems like something prehistoric, and I'd never go back to my Neanderthal ways. – Gordon Feingold, freelance writer, born 1941, San Diego, CA .

Another phenomenal achievement of computers occurred in 1997 when, in a stunning showdown between man and machine, the IBM supercomputer "Deep Blue" decisively beat world chess champion Garry Kasparov, the best player on earth. When he saw the outcome of the match, Kasparov became very emotional. Deep Blue didn't.

I'm fifty-seven years old and I used to say 'thank goodness I'm old so I won't have to learn computers.' Then my husband died suddenly and I had to find a job, so I enrolled in some computer classes. I always liked to teach, so I started a business where I taught classes in local hotels on weekends. Without my computer I could never have done it. The first thing I had to do was design some flyers to advertise my class, and I did it on my Macintosh so I didn't have to pay an artist. I also need the computer to track my income for tax purposes, and to keep a database of my students so I can mail flyers to them about future classes. I send the students a confirmation letter when they sign up and give them directions on how to get to the class. Because they live in many different cities I have to have a database of information on getting to my location from wherever they are. This would take an enormous amount of time if I had to do each one on a typewriter. I'm really convinced that it would be impossible to operate my business without a computer because it would just be too much work, and I couldn't afford to hire a staff. – Shirley Aikens, seminar leader, born 1943, San Francisco, CA.

The Connection that Wired the World

In 1988 the word "Internet" began its journey to omnipresence when it appeared for the first time in many large American dailies in front-page stories about a virus threatening most of the nation's large research computers. The word quickly worked its way into television and movies, many dictionaries, and became a topic of conversation in everyday life. The "World Wide Web" made its debut on the Internet in 1991. From the thousands of interconnected threads of the Internet, network designer Tim Berners-Lee wove the Web and created a medium for the masses, enabling a layperson with very little computer knowledge to access millions of entries instantaneously from sources all over the world. Tim Berners-Lee designed it, gave it freely to the world and he, more than anyone else, has fought to keep it open, nonproprietary and free. Because of his vision, everyone with a computer connected to the Internet has a library in their home so vast it would take more than a single lifetime to process all of it. Today over 350 million people all over the world log on to the Internet every day, and it's growing exponentially.

Geek Speak

Computers have changed our language and given us a new vocabulary. After World War II Americans often talked about and dreaded the prospect of the Soviets acquiring the atomic bomb and aiming it at the United States. Terms related to this technology became part of pop culture, with Diners serving Atomic Burgers and Atomic Shakes, and atomic toys displayed on the shelves of every toy store. Today, computers have added other words to our language:

Cyberspace, the Internet, RAM and ROM, hard drives and floppy disks, silicon wafers, integrated circuits, semi-conductors, bits, bytes and gigabytes, motherboards, mainframes, Net surfing, browsers, search engines, the information superhighway, hyper-speed, nanoseconds, CD-ROMS, faxes, modems, viruses, e-mail, laptops, Palm Pilots, computer-literate, hackers, nerds and geeks, to name a few.

When we were planning to move to Colorado, we found several realtors on the Internet who listed property in that state. The one we chose e-mailed us information on the type of properties we were looking for, including photos and addresses, so we could check the map to see if it was in the area we wanted. We took a virtual reality tour on the Internet of the interior and exterior of homes in our price range, and got information on the school district. When we had decided on six homes that met all our qualifications we flew out there and purchased one. This was so much more efficient than contacting a realtor by phone and having her try to describe houses that way, and we saved a lot in long-distance calls. – Diane Harrison, wife and mother, born 1963, Vermont.

Nora Freedman at her desk in 1996

Now that we've got a computer, when my wife and I want to go out on a Saturday night, we go to the Internet and call up a review of the Los Angeles restaurant scene, including the menu and prices, and we can even book our reservation with restaurants that have Web sites. If we want to see a movie after dinner we can check the local movie theaters on the Net to see what's playing, what times it will be showing, what rating a film carries, read the critics' reviews, and even see a preview in full color and sound. We can also buy our tickets in advance through a credit-card debit system, thus avoiding lines when we arrive at the theater. The only thing we can't do is order the popcorn! It's sure made our lives a lot simpler, and we continue to be fascinated by the ease with which we can do these things. – Mark Galliano, health club operator, born 1965, Long Beach, CA.

Working in your Pajamas

With the advent of computers, printers, e-mail, and fax/modems, home offices and 'telecommuting' have become very popular. Not only does it give employees more access to their families, it also gets their cars off the road: no more being stuck in gridlock traffic to and from work. The downside: some people feel very isolated not going to the office and interacting with their peers. People miss people; they want to be seen, and relate with others.

The other day I had to renew a contract with a supplier in Dayton, Ohio. I hadn't noticed our contract had expired, and they wouldn't deliver any more products until the contract was signed. The purchasing manager faxed it to me at my home in San Jose, California, and I signed it and faxed it back. In less than an hour the deal was completed. I still can't help but be amazed at this, because of course with traditional "snail mail" it would have taken at least three days to get it across the country, and then three more days to get it back. We've broken through Mach 2 — the mail barrier. – Kenneth Garrison, purchasing agent, born 1968, Chicago, IL

Typesetting, 1905. Courtesy Library of Congress

When I first started working in an office, if something had to be printed, I would take it down to the local printer who used hot type or typesetting to set it up, and maybe would take a week or two to print a sales brochure. Then came offset printing and things got done a lot faster, but now we have desktop publishing and I design the manuals and brochures right at my desk on my Mac, and print them in full color on my desktop laser printer, and they look really super. If I don't have time to print a large job I just take it down to the local copy store and run it off. All of these changes have taken a lot of the drudgery out of clerical office work.

Another neat thing is that I can wear pants or casual clothes to the office and don't have to trip around in those stupid high heels all day, breaking my back. And—my boss is a woman. – Stephanie Reagan, designer, born 1965, Hollywood, CA.

Cyrano on the Internet

A new type of obsession is affecting some users of the Internet: Net addiction. Compulsive Net-surfers are so enthralled with the on-line world that some spend as much as forty hours a week huddled over their computers, sometimes even losing jobs or marriages because of their absorption. A growing number of people are hooked to the on-line experience to the point where their lives are disintegrating. Kimberly Young, a psychologist at the University of Pittsburgh, thinks it's so prevalent she would like to see "Internet Addiction Disorder," added to the psychiatric diagnostic manual. Many of the cyberjunkies are fans of role-playing adventure games known as MUDS's (multiple-user dungeons), or, they are inhabitants of on-line chat rooms devoted to sex and relationships.

Myst by Ubi Soft Entertainment, one of the most popular games

I'm an engineer who works with computers during the day, and I began going into the den and playing with my computer in the evening too. I think it started partly to get away from the hollering kids and relax my mind. My wife loves to read, so once the kids were in bed she usually got into our bed, curled up with a book and fell asleep. Before I knew it I was getting to bed at two and three and even four a.m., and then going to work sleep-deprived, and had trouble concentrating. But I couldn't seem to stop myself from taking a quick nap on the couch in the evening and then going right back on-line. At first I played a lot of dungeons-and-dragons type games, but then gradually I started wandering off checking out the chat rooms.

One of the fascinations of the Net is that you can re-invent yourself and be anyone you want to be. Nobody can see what you look like, so your description is up to your imagination and the extent of your ego. I have to admit I made myself a lot more interesting in my computer identity than in real life. In the world of cyberspace you're in charge, you're God, and you have total power.

Eventually I connected with a woman in Dallas who was as charmed by my new persona as I was beginning to be myself. Naturally my wife wasn't as fascinated by me as this woman was because she'd lived with me for ten years and knew I snored and was grouchy in the morning, and all those other little habits you try to hide from everyone else. So you can figure the rest...I got myself so involved my wife began to call my computer my mistress, which in a sense it was, and she eventually left me for someone who could relate to her instead of a machine. Now I'm trying to get up the nerve to meet the woman in Dallas in person, and let her see who I really am. I hope she won't be disappointed. – Rick, software designer, born 1968, Silicon Valley, CA.

Cyberspace Hoodlums

One downside of computers is their vulnerability to criminal types who have broken into military, corporate and university computers, and stolen important and top- secret information. Other hooligans have acquired private telephone numbers and used them to rack up thousands of dollars in long-distance calls, or gained access to personal credit card numbers. Commercial use of the Internet has been limited by the inability of technicians to develop a foolproof way to keep so-called "hackers" from capturing passwords and credit information. At the end of the century, "Identity Theft" was fast becoming a major crime.

Viruses, usually developed by immature males who think it's a fun thing to do, have also created havoc by programming them into the Net to spread to thousands of computers. Instructions on how to build bombs or other nefarious devices are also easily available on the Internet for the use of any mentally disturbed person who has access to the Web.

Another computer-related problem is pedophiles who have lured children, mostly young teens, into meeting with them for their own depraved purposes. Child pornography has developed a huge market on the Internet, and many 'chat rooms' feature sexually-explicit photographs.

In spite of these problems, computers have enhanced and improved our lives enormously, and there's no turning back. The blessing of TV was that it gave us an eye into the whole world. Now the Internet and the World Wide Web promise to give us the same, and this time we can interact with it.

*Nicola Tesla Born in 1856 in Austria-Hungary,
died in 1943 in New York City.*

Inventions: A telephone repeater, rotating magnetic field principle, polyphase alternating-current system, induction motor, alternating-current power transmission, Tesla coil transformer, wireless communication, radio, fluorescent lights, and more than 700 other patents. Tesla was a great genius who didn't get the respect he deserved.

A senior citizen is a person who was here before The Pill and the population explosion. We were here before TV, penicillin, polio shots, open-heart surgery and hair transplants. Before frozen food, nylon, Xerox copies, fluorescent lights, credit cards, ball-point pens and Frisbees. ...In our day cigarette smoking was fashionable; grass was for mowing; Coke was a refreshing drink, and pot was something you cooked in. – AARP Chapter 2889, Elmhurst, NY.

CHAPTER TEN

Women:

You've Come a Long Way Baby!

The past 100 years witnessed extraordinary advances for women and produced the most dramatic changes in their status! At the beginning of the twentieth century, half the population was denied the right to vote by the other half, and women were subservient to their husbands or fathers.

Although much still needs to be done, women in developed countries have now overturned their second-class citizenship and hundreds of years of oppression, to participate fully in society. We have won the right to vote, run for public office, own property, have custody of our children, keep our own names after marriage, have credit in our own name, and earn and control our own money. All of this was accomplished during the last century and, during that space of time, many women have gone from being mere chattel, or at best domestic servants, subject to their husbands' whims, to having a voice and making decisions about their lives.

Showing up at the Ballot Box

Suffragists Marching in New York in 1913. Courtesy Library of Congress

In 1904 Susan B. Anthony organized the International Woman's Suffrage Alliance which called for an amendment to the Constitution giving women the right to vote. Anthony's organization was joined by suffragist Lucy Stone and her husband, Henry Blackwell, and The Nineteenth Amendment was finally passed in 1920. Most people who opposed woman's right to vote believed that women were less intelligent and less able to make political decisions than men, and some feared that it would lead to the end of family life.

When I was growing up in the fifties, my mother, who was a homemaker, was very anti-female. She said men were superior beings and women were catty and basically stupid. I thought that was strange because she was one, and that must mean she didn't like herself. But, as I looked around at the women I knew, they really didn't appear to be very bright because all they talked about most of the time was their kids, and what kind of floor wax was best. I had no interest in either of those subjects, and never really aspired to be a mother, which made me almost a monster in those days. At the very least, there was something the matter with me because I didn't have a so-called maternal instinct and a burning desire to have three or four kids running around the house.

Looking around me in 1952 it seemed that men were able to do all the interesting things, and held all the jobs that took some brains, like flying airplanes, producing newspapers, running the government, making the laws, being doctors, lawyers and engineers. There were almost no women doing anything as exciting as that in those days. But it seemed as though it wasn't only men who didn't think women should be doing those things, some women thought that way too. It was almost like they felt threatened that they'd no longer be the "protected" class, with men taking care of them financially if they broke out of their limited role and started doing more challenging things. But often they didn't have the opportunity, even if they had the desire. In my family there was no question that the only one who would be going to college was my brother; sending a girl was considered a waste of money. The more education she had, the less marriageable she was. – Julie Dentrey, attorney, born 1938, Long Island, NY.

Even as late as 1973, author Marabel Morgan's book, "The Total Woman," told us our lives would be sunny and bright if we would simply always remember to defer to our husbands and treat them in the regal manner they so deserved. Most of us believed this during the fifities when our highest goal in life was to be a good wife and mother.

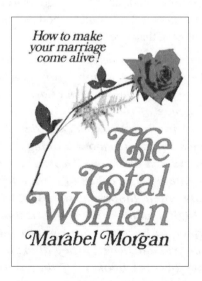

Keep 'em Barefoot and Pregnant

Family Limitation, the first book on birth control, written in 1915 by Margaret Sanger, earned her a jail term. Undaunted, the following year, with the help of her sister Ethel Byrne, she opened the first U.S. birth control clinic in Brooklyn. It was quickly shut down and the two women were tried and imprisoned, spending a month in jail. She was also indicted on charges of inciting violence and promoting obscenity for publishing "The Woman Rebel," a feminist monthly that advocated birth control. Deliberately trying to limit the number of children a woman brought forth was considered obscene in those days. It was one's Biblical duty to "go forth and multiply," no matter the burden that might be placed on the family's finances, or the woman's body.

It was illegal at the time to send material relating to birth control through the U.S. mail. It was not until 1965, more than halfway through the century, that the U.S. Supreme Court said contraceptives were legal for married couples. The unmarried, except for men in the military who were given condoms to prevent V.D., didn't get that right until 1972. Now, of course, one can buy contraceptives in any drugstore, but the Catholic Church to this day forbids the use of any kind of external contraception, even to prevent venereal disease.

In 1931 futurist and historian H.G. Wells said: "When the history of our civilization is written, it will be a biological history, and Margaret Sanger will be its heroine." In 1921 Sanger founded the American Birth Control League, which evolved into Planned Parenthood. In 1923 she organized the first U.S. birth-control conference and she lived to see "The Pill" approved by the Food and Drug Administration in 1960, amidst great controversy. But, at the end of the century, the fight for control of women's bodies has not ended, and may be more controversial now than ever.

In 1955 I wanted to do some charity work so I moved to a slum area in Montreal and opened a home for unwed mothers, with a clothing store for the poor. I was a strict Catholic in those days, and followed all the dogmas of the church to the letter. But, I got very disillusioned living in that economically-deprived neighborhood because there were so many worn-out-looking mothers who had ten, or twelve, or even sixteen children. They were stay-at-home moms, and of course the fathers had a hell of a time trying to support all those kids, usually on a laborer's salary. The children weren't educated beyond high school, and seldom accomplished even that, so they were destined to have low-paying jobs too. The boys would often grow up to be truck drivers, if they didn't become priests, and the girls sometimes became hookers if they didn't get married. It was the fastest way to get out of poverty. In those days there weren't any fast-food joints, so they couldn't get a job slinging hamburgers.

The situation disgusted me and, for the first time, I began to take a serious look at some of the teachings of the Church. Of course there's nothing in the Bible about contraception; that was the Church's idea, probably to increase the number of Catholics decades ago. And naturally the Church isn't going to change its dogma at this late date and bring on the fury of those families who felt compelled to have numerous children in the past. I think a lot of Catholics, like me, make up their own mind now about certain of the teachings of the Church, and aren't as strictly bound by its teachings as we used to be. – Marga Picard, retired administrator, born 1912.

Good Housekeeping, 1949

The Little Pill that Changed History

When the birth control pill was introduced in the U.S. in 1960 it was a major medical achievement that changed the future and rewrote the history of women. It has proved to be the most socially significant medical advance of the century. Eighty-percent of American women have taken The Pill, and it is an important part of women's history. For the first time, women could safely and effectively control childbearing, and that meant they now had sexual freedom.

In the forites Margaret Sanger conceived of a simple pill that would relieve women of years of being pregnant that they were subject to at the time. Sanger herself was one of eleven children, and her mother had also had seven miscarriages. At the age of seventy-one she convinced American biologist Dr. Gregory Pincus, to work on developing a contraceptive. A pill using progesterone was developed with the aid of gynecologist John Rock, a devout Catholic who defied his church. In 1955 it was tested on hundreds of women in Puerto Rico. Although they complained of nausea, headaches, dizziness and stomach pain, this was ignored and Enovid®, produced by Searle, a U.S. pharmaceutical company, began distribution in the U.S. in 1960. It was introduced in the U.K. in 1961, but prescribed only for married women.

Women taking the original ten-milligram-dose pill suffered from a wide variety of side effects, including blood clots and strokes. Male physicians were very sexist at the time and simply dismissed these complains as exaggeration. The modern version of The Pill contains only a fraction of the original dose and side effects are less likely to occur.

I got pregnant in 1952 when I was only seventeen. My boyfriend immediately said it wasn't his, although I'd been dating him exclusively for two years. That kind of thing happened often in those days, the boys just denied it, and it was your word against his. And of course we didn't have DNA testing then to establish paternity. Sometimes if the girl's father threatened a lawsuit, or insisted on marriage, the boy would get some of his friends to say they'd had sex with you too, and then you were stuck because nobody believed girls then, especially ones who were so immoral as to have sex before marriage.

I was panicked because I couldn't tell my folks, my dad would beat the shit out of me, and I knew my mom would cry her eyes out. It would have killed me to carry the baby for nine months and then just hand it over to someone else; I just couldn't face that. And

I couldn't keep the baby because I hadn't even finished high school, and nobody would give me a job if I was an unmarried mother. You didn't go to school pregnant in those days. I think it's really astonishing today how these girls walk around school with huge stomachs and aren't the least bit ashamed of it. In 1952 you didn't want anyone to know you'd even had sex if you weren't married; that in itself was a disgrace and labeled you a tramp.

My boyfriend found out about a woman who performed abortions for $100, so he saved every penny he could get and arranged it for me. Just to do me a favor you understand, even though he claimed he wasn't the baby's father.

The whole thing was absolutely horrible, the worst event of my life. I had to stand on the corner of Fifth and Main Street for about half an hour, and finally a car came by with two men in it. They opened the window and called my name, so I got in. The one in the back pushed me down in the seat, put a blindfold on me, and told me keep my mouth shut. When we finally arrived it was a dilapidated old shack in a run-down part of town and there was garbage everywhere. An old woman with two front teeth missing, who barely spoke English, told me to get up on the kitchen table where she had put a sheet and a towel. I gave her the money and she gave me a little glass of brandy to drink which helped calm me down because I was shaking like a leaf. I'm not even sure what she did to me because I was really out of it. Then the men came back and drove me back to the corner and let me out. That night I was sicker than I'd ever been in my life. I was sure I was going to die, and I wanted to go to the hospital, but I didn't dare tell anybody in the family what was going on. I was afraid if I went to the hospital the doctor would figure out what happened and arrest me.

Thank god women don't have to go through that kind of trauma anymore! – Mary, former teacher, born 1931, Anaheim, CA.

Hanging up Her Apron

A great societal change took place during World Wars I and II with the mass exodus of women out of the home and into the workplace when men were overseas and women were needed in factories to build war munitions. But, when the wars ended, the majority were laid off their jobs, and returned to their traditional role as housewives. Most people, including females, believed a woman's place was in the home.

So Proudly We Serve

U. S. MARINE CORPS
Women's Reserve

I joined the Women Marines in 1955, when I was eighteen, because I wanted to see the world. The whole process was a very scary ordeal, starting with my arrival at Parris Island, South Carolina, for boot camp. The rules were strict, with emphasis on "conduct becoming a lady." One day, after visiting the PX, I was ordered to report to the company commander. His first words were "Private Crocker, do you consider yourself a lady?" "Yes sir," I said, "I do." "Well," he continued, "your conduct today at the PX was not becoming of a lady." He then told me that an NCO had seen me at the PX with my legs crossed, but not at the ankles, which was the Women Marines way. I was wearing "utilities," pants and shirt, and had casually crossed my legs at the knees, as I would have as a civilian.

The CO reminded me that I was not a civilian and said my punishment would be to sing "The Marines Hymn" twenty times while wearing my dress blues and standing at attention in front of a mirror. It's hard to believe today that marines had such petty rules to control the behavior of females. – LaQuita Crocker-McCarthy, Grass Valley, CA.

Doing Dishes in 1934 - Good Housekeeping Magazine

The greatest cultural change of the century in the Western World was the revival of feminism during the late sixties, sparked initially by the publication of Betty Friedan's *The Feminine Mystique,* in 1963. Her book raised women's consciousness about male domination and revealed the emptiness and frustration of many American women with their traditional roles. Friedan gave voice to their discontent, and made them aware of male oppression in government, the Church and the home. Her best-selling book created a desire for self-actualization outside the confines of the household, while raising the ire of many men. In 1966, she co-founded and served as president of the National Organization for Women (NOW), an organization dedicated to equal opportunities for women.

When I read Friedan's book it hit me like a bomb! It was 1969 and I was married with two kids, and worked part-time as a secretary to the V.P. of a construction company. This man, who earned far more than I did, used to send me out for coffee every morning. It only cost a dime, but he never once gave me the money, allowing me to pay for his coffee every day. I didn't dare ask him for it, because confronting your boss just wasn't done in those days.

When I got to work in the morning the first thing I did was dust off his desk, sharpen his pencils, and make sure he had plenty of lined paper for his notes. I even had to buy birthday and anniversary gifts for his wife. That type of thing was all part of being a secretary in those days, and I never thought of challenging it.

At the end of the day I'd make supper for everyone, get the kids ready for bed, do the dishes and clean up the kitchen afterward. Clay watched TV while I was doing this. If he wanted a cup of coffee or something while he was watching it, he'd just call out to me, and I'd have to stop what I was doing and get it for him. In fact, I waited on him hand and foot. On weekends I'd do the wash and clean the house while he went out with the boys. It's hard for me to believe this now but, when he came home he would actually put on a white glove and run his finger over the mantelpiece and other furniture, to make sure I'd dusted it properly. Being reduced to little more than a servant was taken for granted in those days, it was just what a woman did. I was a fifties housewife and my husband was the absolute master. He didn't want me to go out to work because he was afraid I wouldn't always be available to take care of his needs, and that meant every time I needed a dollar for something, I'd have to ask him for it. And he carefully watched every penny I spent, complaining if he thought I was spending too much on groceries.

When I read Friedan's book it was just like blinders were removed from my eyes and I realized I'd been subservient to men my whole life, just like my mother was. And that even included the Church. I had put men on a pedestal, buying into society's concept at the time that men were somehow superior, and women were on earth to serve them.

Because our kids were grown by then I decided it was time for me to get a life of my own. I'd spent enough of it serving my husband and children, and now opportunities were opening for women. In spite of great protest from Clay, I went back to school and then got a job as an editorial assistant at a university. My husband couldn't take my freedom and we decided to get a divorce.

My boss was a female professor who was a feminist. She asked me if I liked coffee in the morning. When I said yes, she said she did too. Then she suggested that she get the coffee for both of us one day, and I get it the next. Equality—I love it! – Carrie Showalter, born 1933, Mountain View, CA.

Betty Friedan

In addition to the "consciousness raising" generated by the women's movement, other factors contributed to the revival of feminism. As the service sector of the economy expanded, unprecedented numbers of married women were being drawn into the job market, and the availability of the birth control pill resulted in smaller families. The inflation of the latter part of the seventies made two incomes an economic necessity, and thrust many women into the workplace. The result was that the majority of women from that time forward would never again be full-time stay-at-home wives and mothers. By 1998 women were earning over forty-percent of medical, law and doctorate degrees and over sixty percent worked outside the home, making up forty-six percent of the labor force. The concept of "male only" professions became outmoded. Women were no longer considered 'transitory workers,' just waiting for marriage or pregnancy to quit their jobs. More opportunities to work, the trend toward smaller families, plus the desire for consumer goods such as a second car and a color television set, helped transform the female labor force from one of primarily single women under twenty-five as it was in 1940, to one of married women and mothers-over -forty by 1960.

Salesman showing vacuum cleaner to housewife in 1940

Mothers working outside the home changed the lives of everyone around them. The consequence was they often held two jobs; one in the workplace, and the other at home. Men who were accustomed to being waited on by their wives, naturally resented now being asked to help cook, clean and look after the children. After all, these were men who had grown up in a home where dad came home after work and mom had dinner ready. After eating, dad retired with his newspaper to the living room, while mom cleaned up the kitchen, gave the kids their bath and put them to bed. His job was done, and he had no plans to continue working once he left the office or the shop.

The children's lives were also changed by mothers going out to work. "Latch-key" kids were created as children came home to an empty house after school, instead of mom ready to greet them with milk and home-baked cookies. Because the neighborhood moms were also at work, there was no one to keep an eye on the kids until the parents got home from work. Younger children were reared by day-care centers. This profound change in our style of living has had enormous consequences for society.

Taking off their Girdles and Burning their Bras

I graduated from San Francisco State University in 1970 with a B.A. in Psychology, Magna Cum Laude. To my dismay, every job I applied for just wanted to know if I could type. My degree meant nothing. Meanwhile, guys at places where I worked were being trained for management without a degree. When I would complain about this, the bosses just smiled at me in a patronizing way but did nothing. There wasn't any formal complaint system for discrimination at that time, so there wasn't anything I could do about it. That motivated me to get a master's degree in psych, and this time I did get a job in my field. – Paula Garfield, born 1948, San Francisco, CA.

The Women's Movement was the stepchild of the civil right's movement, which culminated in the passing of the 1964 Civil Rights Act. It seemed like a vibrational field had been created by the civil rights movement and was followed by several groups who began seeking rights. Student power, Students for a Democratic Society (SDS), resistance   to the Vietnam war and   draft-resistance activities were on the rise. So-called "consciousness-raising" groups for women began to spring up around the country, and courses on women's studies were introduced at universities. The focus was directed at building a "Women's culture" to challenge the patriarchy of the past.

They're Man-Hating Dykes

The first new feminist organization was the National Organization for Women (NOW), founded in 1966 by Betty Friedan. Initially gay women were often the organizers of local NOW groups and predominated (by about four to one) in the small groups. Lesbians were seeking the right to openly love whomever they wanted, and a vocal group articulated lesbianism as the essential feminist idea. NOW initially rejected sexual preference as a legitimate feminist concern, although lesbians continued to join NOW in large numbers. A struggle ensued over this for several years because the straight women were afraid feminism was going to be labeled "anti-male" instead of pro-woman, which fueled the animosity towards the movement from some men, and some housewives who were threatened by the loss of protection from men.

In 1975 NOW passed a "National Plan of Action" which included elimination of laws on private sexual behavior and discriminating on the basis of sexual preference. In 1977 all feminist and most women's organizations acknowledged this as an important part of the feminist agenda. A small number of heterosexual-identified women actually decided they preferred women to men, and became romantically involved with them, sometimes for life. These were dubbed "political lesbians."

Vicki Meagher, Customer services field person...Photo by Bill Baritea.

At NOW's 1966 founding convention it passed a broad statement of purpose which articulated a general philosophy of equality and justice under law. The following year it passed a Bill of Rights for women to be presented to candidates and parties in the 1968 elections. The first six planks were quickly passed. They were: enforcement of sex discrimination laws; paid maternity leave; tax deductions for child care; establishment of public, readily available, child care facilities; equal and unsegregated education; equal job training opportunities, housing and family allowances for women in poverty.

Proposals to support reproductive control were controversial; they passed, but several members quit as a result. By the time NOW organized the first national feminist march down New York City's Fifth Avenue on August 26, 1970, reproductive freedom and the right to an abortion, were now seen by all feminist organizations as an intrinsic part of the feminist agenda.

As a result of the feminists' activities the Equal Employment Opportunity Commission changed many of its originally prejudicial attitudes toward women. Numerous lawsuits were filed under the sex provision of Title VII of the 1964 Civil Rights Act. Complaints were filed against several hundred colleges and universities, as well as many businesses, charging sex discrimination. Articles on feminism appeared in virtually every news medium, and a host of new laws were passed prohibiting sex discrimination in a variety of areas. The Equal Rights Amendment passed Congress in 1972, as did Title IX of the Educational Equity Act. The Supreme Court legalized most abortions in 1973 and radically rewrote Constitutional law on women by 1976. The Pregnancy Discrimination Act was passed in 1978 so employers could no longer fire a woman simply because she was pregnant.

*Mrs. Doughman's family and friends enjoy her baking. Here
she's putting a family favorite - cheesecake - into her electric over.
Timer will tell when it's baked.*

The Supreme Court reinterpreted the basic premise against which laws affecting women were to be judged, from one of protection, to one of equal opportunity. Despite the sexism some women still encounter, because of the work done by the women's liberation movement, they have developed new skills and confidence, and defied conventional, limited concepts of femininity. The movement brought about a re-examination of society's traditional "masculine" and "feminine" roles, which helped liberate both women and men from constricting cultural definitions.

Although women have won the right to work outside the home, there is still a fundamental assumption that the principal social unit is the two-parent family, only one of whom is the primary wage earner, usually the man. There is still a basic division of labor in which men are expected to be the "breadwinners" and women are expected to focus their energies on the family, although he may help her with "her" housework. Women still do not have full "equal pay for equal work" although the concept is no longer arguable. Because women are often in lower-skilled jobs, such as assembly lines, waitress or teacher's aide, feminists have pioneered a new concept, that of comparable worth for jobs of equal skill and expertise. By 1987 more than forty states had taken steps to implement this policy.

The Hot Button Issue of the Century

The women's liberation movement accomplished many profound and lasting changes in society. Because feminists regard the right to an abortion as vital to women's self-determination, they have played a key role in decriminalizing abortion, and subsequently working to keep it legal despite continuous efforts, sometimes even involving the murder of doctors, to prohibit it.

The "Joy" of Rape

It's astonishing to realize that, until the feminist movement, it was legal for a man to rape his wife. It was considered her wifely duty to submit to his sexual demands whenever and however he wanted, whether she wanted to or not. It was not until the late seventies that coercing one's wife to have sex was no longer legal.

Feminist efforts to reverse the law's traditionally punitive stance toward victims of rape have been quite successful. Most states now prohibit evidence regarding a woman's past sexual history to be admitted in cases of rape, and no longer require proof of resistance.

Words such as "domestic violence" were not a part of the common vocabulary until the late 1970s. If the police were called to the home they generally chastised the woman and told her to try harder to be a good wife, and not upset her husband. Now many police departments have adopted new policies for investigating rape and domestic violence.

A 1950's movie, "Frenzy," produced by Alfred Hitchcock, contained this scene:

Two English gentlemen are sitting in a pub discussing a serial murderer who has been killing women by strangling them with his necktie. The barmaid overhears the conversation and interjects "I hear he rapes them first." As she walks away the two men smirk at each other as one says, "As they say, for every cloud there's a silver lining."

It shocks one's sensibilities today to think that such incredible sexism was permitted, reinforcing an old fantasy (held by some men) that women actually enjoyed being forced into sex against their will.

I moved to Oakland, California in 1966 with my new husband, Roy, and we both got jobs right away. I worked as a secretary and he got a job at a furniture store as a carpet salesman. We were married only about six months when he started verbally abusing me, and one night he suddenly slapped my face and punched my arm during a disagreement. I was stunned! I'd never been hit by anyone before and I just wasn't going to tolerate it. The next morning I went to the police department to file a complaint. The cop at the desk smiled at me and said, "Now why would a man want to hit a pretty young girl like you?" The clear implication being that I had done something to provoke it. I told him I didn't know why, but I wanted it stopped, and what could he do. He told me if I filed a complaint they would go to Roy's work and arrest him and he might spend a couple of days in jail if I didn't post bond. I thought about that for a moment and realized if he was arrested he'd be fired immediately, and then I'd be the sole support, and he'd probably have a hard time getting another job. I told the cop to forget it, and left.

That evening I told Roy I'd been to the police, and said if he ever hit me again I'd leave him. The next time was about a month later. Distressed as I was to break up my new marriage, and fearful of the thought of living alone in a strange city where I had no friends, I went after work to find a place to live. There was a cute, little house not far from my office for only $85 a month. But, when I tried to rent it, the landlord said he wouldn't rent to a female because I wouldn't be able to take care of things. "Like what?" I said, "put out the garbage, and mow the lawn? Of course I'm capable of doing those things." After much hassling, he finally relented and let me rent it. There were no "anti-discrimination in housing" laws then.

The next day I got off work early, talked a guy at the office into helping me haul some furniture in his truck, and left Roy a note. Now it was Roy's turn to be stunned, and I hope it taught him a life-long lesson. Then I went to the pound and got myself a sweet-natured white terrier for a companion, and Sugar and I lived peacefully together. — Anita Williams, born 1944, Northern CA.

Before 1967 a married woman in America could not purchase a home in her own name. A single woman would usually be denied financing for a home loan.

No Place for a Lady

Fifty years ago there were almost no female lawyers, judges, office managers, company presidents, architects, psychologists, airline pilots, police officers, politicians, lawyers or doctors (and most people, especially men, would not go to the few that were practicing). By the end of the century, women had made incredible progress, but still had not achieved financial equality with men. In the U.S. they still earn only seventy-two cents for each dollar that men earn. Women hold less than five-percent of senior management positions, and less than ten percent of our nation's senators and governors are female.

I worked as a secretary for General Electric in Long Beach in the late fifties and early sixties. I was always smart and a fast learner, so one day I went into the boss' office and told him I'd like to be trained to be an office manager. He looked at me with a smirk on his face. 'We don't promote women to management,' he said firmly, and simply dismissed me. That was it, there was no appeal process; there was no point complaining to the personnel department because they'd support him, and the union wouldn't back me on it either, so I was stuck in my low-paying job. It's hard to believe today that a boss can tell a woman she can't be promoted simply because she's female. They still do it of course, but now its done surreptitiously. – Margaret McFerran, retired AT&T manager, born 1933, Louisville, KY.

In 1976 the U.S. Air Force Academy admitted fifteen women, ending the all-male tradition at U.S. military academies. But it wasn't until 1996 that women broke through the last bastion of all-male public education when the U.S. Supreme Court overwhelmingly declared that they could not be excluded from the Virginia Military Institute. Strict military-style institutions, renowned for training men to be leaders, were the only remaining state colleges that limited classes to the male gender.

Subtle Sexism

Women have more freedom of opportunity now than they have ever had throughout history. In the first half of the century, by the time a girl reached maturity at eighteen, she was expected to marry, stay at home, raise a family and be economically dependent on her husband. The first question a prospective mother-in-law generally asked about the woman her son had chosen to marry was: "Is she a good cook?"

June Mulcaby baking in 1964

In the past, if a woman wasn't married by the time she was twenty-five, she was considered an "old maid." If she decided not to marry, or if no man asked to marry her, she could become a teacher, nurse, secretary, clerk or waitress. She was often refused admission into college, and so-called "male" jobs were flatly denied her.

Before the Women's Movement, as a lesbian and an attractive woman, I was constantly being asked that tired old question: "How come a pretty girl like you isn't married?" I used to just smile sweetly and say "I haven't met the right man yet." To stop the constant scrutiny, because I could lose my job in those days if I were found out, I made an arrangement with a gay man to get married because he was having the same problem I was trying to keep up a front. We exchanged wedding rings, had photos of our "mate" on our office desks and went to each other's company parties. When the office staff would discuss what they'd done over the weekend, I'd talk about what I'd done with my female partner, but I substituted Carl's name. That protected both of us from inquiring minds, but then the question I often got was "How come you two haven't had children yet?" My stock answer: "The good Lord hasn't blessed me with them yet." Nothing they could say about that—it was up to God. – Gladys Ross, born 1947, Toronto, Canada.

Harriet DeCellles in 1950 supported 4 children as a waitress

Open Sexism on the Job

In 1906 night-shift work for women was internationally forbidden. Until the 1960s airline stewardesses could be fired if they got married. In the first half of the century schoolteachers were fired if they got married. Teaching was considered too much of a distraction because she should be devoting herself to home, husband and children. Males of course, made this decision, because administrators and principals were almost always men. Women were considered suitable for teaching grammar school, and sometimes even high school, but professorships at colleges were reserved for men.

In the fifties a female student was not allowed to walk across most college campuses wearing pants; it was considered unfeminine. Few co-ed schools had athletic programs for women, and the first women's athletic scholarship wasn't offered until 1975. In men's sports, there were few female reporters, and the ones that were, were not allowed to cover sports in the press box, nor to enter locker rooms.

Back in the fifties I always felt awkward going to meetings with my husband, who was a chiropractor. When we were introduced to another couple the men always shook hands, but I stood there with nothing to do but look demure since women were not expected to shake hands, it was considered too assertive an act for a female. And we woman were always called "girls." I thought it was odd that middle-aged men were never called "boys," but a woman of any age was still considered a girl. It was demeaning, and I think it was designed to keep us child-like and inferior. Once I was in a furniture company talking to the salesman, and he said he'd get "one of his girls" to type up the contract. I looked behind him and saw three women in a little booth sitting at typewriters, each of whom had to be over forty. I knew if they were males, he would never have referred to them as "his boys."

My neighbor recently saw a female cardiologist for her heart condition, but later was transferred to a male doctor. When she told me about it she called the female doctor a girl, but the male of course was referred to as a man. "Gosh," I said, "do they have girls as doctors these days? I wonder if there are boy doctors too?" She looked as me as though I were crazy.

Of course in those days I was addressed by everyone I met as Mrs. Robert Goodson; I didn't even get to have my own first name after we married. I really liked it when the women's movement began using "Ms." instead of Miss or Mrs. After all, men didn't have to reveal on every correspondence whether they were married or not, so why should women have to be designated by their marital status?

And, speaking of designations, until the women's movement, every reference to humans in general, in books, theater or newspapers, was always to "he" or "him". Women were just assumed to be included in that. Many men thought we were being picky when we started to object, but I wonder how guys would feel if every reference were to "she." How about: "We hold these truths to be self-evident, that all woman are created equal." Hey guys — don't be so sensitive, that includes you too. – Grace Martin, hotel supervisor, born 1936, Hollywood, CA.

In 1904 a New York policeman arrested a woman for smoking in public but, during World War II it became acceptable for women to smoke, and most movies featured stars such as Ingrid Bergman, Lauren Bacall, Joan Crawford, and Betty Davis constantly smoking. In the seventies Virginia Slims™ cigarettes began advertising "You've Come a Long Way, Baby," showing photos of women in the early part of the century sneaking a smoke behind their husband's back. The right to impair your health is now an equal opportunity.

Kim DeCelles in 1975

When I got a divorce in 1969 I had to prove mental cruelty. After five years of marriage my husband and I had agreed we were mismatched and had made a mistake. Fortunately, we didn't have any kids, and we didn't have any property, so the agreement to divorce was very amicable, and it should have been simple. Instead, I had to charge him with mental cruelty, and had to talk two of my girlfriends into testifying that he had been verbally abusive, would stay out overnight without bothering to let me know where he was, and a bunch of other trumped-up nonsense. I hated to perjure myself, and I didn't want to defame him that way in a court of law and have it made a public record, but that's what we had to do to get divorced. This seems incredible now.

In 1980 I got a divorce from my second husband. Actually, it wasn't a divorce because we lived in California where it's now called "Dissolution of Marriage." I drew up the papers myself and went to court with them. We had signed an agreement of property division, and once again, there were no children involved. The judge merely asked me if there was any hope of reconciliation, to which I replied no, and he replied "Dissolution granted." That made a painful process far less painful. Now Congress is talking about making divorce difficult again, but I don't see how you can force people to stay together who don't want to. The sensible thing to do would be to make getting married more difficult instead. – Maria Constances, born 1933, Albuquerque, NM.

Community property laws in several states also made divorce simpler and avoided countless settlement battles. The changes brought about largely by the women's movement, also included the end of automatic alimony to wives. Feminists thought alimony kept women dependent and, since most were now earning their own income, it was no longer needed. But statistics showed that many women who had children were thrown into poverty when the primary breadwinner left. Most had been housewives for years, and had no marketable skills. Child-support remained in place, but was frequently not paid.

In the past, custody of the children of divorce was automatically awarded to the mother. After the seventies, judges began awarding joint custody, and the kids began to shuttle back and forth between mom's house and dad's.

Good Housekeeping Ad, 1943

After getting divorced in the sixties, I was in for a shock when I tried to re-establish my life as a single person. I wanted to rent a small three-room cottage but the landlord refused to rent to me because he didn't think a female was capable of taking care of a house by herself, so I had to get an apartment. Then I went to Sears to establish credit in my own name and buy some furniture. They refused to give it to me, claiming that, since I had no credit record, they couldn't establish my ability to pay. In those days all the credit had to be in your husband's name, so there was nothing in my maiden name, and companies didn't think women made enough money to be trusted with a credit card. These weren't Visa or Mastercards, there was no such thing then, they were just department-store cards for furniture and clothing. The irony was that my husband was totally irresponsible when it came to money, and I had always paid all the bills and made sure I did it on time. He got the benefit of my frugality and responsible habits because we had a perfect credit record when we divorced, but that didn't do me any good; it was all his. It wasn't until the women's movement of the seventies that Congress passed a law making it illegal to deny women credit in their own name. – Merlinda Schrader, bookstore owner, born 1940, Louisiana.

Lost Identity

In the past the society pages of newspapers always related social events as held by, for example: "Mr. and Mrs. Robert McBride." After the resurgence of feminism, women began objecting to losing their entire identity to the male after marriage, and insisted on being called "Mrs. Nancy McBride." Some women chose to keep their own last name after marriage, often hyphenating it into a double-name.

When I married David back in the fifties, I was really proud to be called "Mrs. David Logan." I remember I used to write that name in my journal over and over before we were married, and I could hardly wait to be called 'Mrs.' because married women had more status then. In fact, if you weren't married by the time you were twenty-four people thought there was something wrong with you, and you thought so yourself. Nobody wanted to be an old maid. Men were the superior sex, so if you wanted to be somebody you had to be married to one. And the more important he was, the more important you were, because that's where your identity came from.

After marriage I seldom used my first name when introducing myself in public, I was Mrs. David Logan, and that's how I addressed all my mail. And you know, it never really dawned on me until the " seventies when I read "The Feminine Mystique" that I had lost my total identity with that name. I didn't have my last name anymore, and I didn't have my first name either. I wasn't a person in my own right—I was David's wife. When I finally woke up to how I'd been so willing to give myself up, I was mad. — Call me Meredith."

This very formal postcard of two serious-looking ladies, was sent by a wife to her husband in Arlington, Virginia, on May 30, 1920. Her name is unknown because she doesn't use it, but simply calls herself "wife." The back of the card reads: "Dear Husband: This is a photo of my sister, Mrs. Collinge, and myself. It is very good of my sister but not so good of me. Love, wife."

A Woman's Place is in the House (of Congress)

The growing influence of women in Washington was evident in President Clinton's Cabinet. In his first term he nominated Ruth Bader Ginsberg to be the U.S. Supreme Court's second female judge. He also appointed Jocelyn Elders to be Surgeon General, Hazel O'Leary as Energy Secretary, Donna Shalala as Secretary of Health and Human Services, Carol Browner as head of the Environmental Protection Agency (EPA), and Janet Reno as the Attorney General of the United States. In his second term he appointed Alexis Herman as Secretary of Labor, and she was the highest-ranking black woman in the administration. Clinton's personal doctor is also a woman: Dr. Connie Mariano.

Until the late 1970s the State Department generally consigned women to clerical and administrative jobs. If they got married, they were expected to resign from these positions on the belief that they couldn't successfully handle the duties of both a housewife and an outside job. A class-action suit challenged that view in 1976 and charged that the State Department's rigid testing system unfairly screened out women before they could get hired, and that its pay, promotion and awards policies discouraged women from advancing in their careers once they got in the door. That lawsuit helped transform the climate for women at the State Department, where they now make up nearly half of new recruits and about one-third of the 720 senior diplomats in Washington and at U.S. embassies around the world. Of the thirty-two officers who had regular contact with the secretary of state, nine were women.

In 1996 Madeleine Albright, Ph.D., an expert on international affairs, was nominated by President Clinton to replace Warren Christopher, and became the nation's first female secretary of state. This was the highest political position a woman had achieved in the U.S. Government. Albright has been a teacher at Georgetown University, an ambassador to the United Nations, and national security advisor to President Jimmy Carter.

In March, 1997, President Clinton nominated Major General Claudia J. Kennedy to be the Army's first female three-star general. In April he selected former representative Lindy Boggs, an eighty-one-year-old Democrat from Louisiana, and a leader in women's rights legislation during her eighteen years in the House, to be the first female U.S. ambassador to the Vatican.

In 1997 a large marble statue of three suffragette women, which was completed in 1921, but was stored in the Capitol basement in Washington, finally made its way to the Rotunda, alongside the statues of prominent men. The thirteen-ton slab honors Lucretia Mott, Elizabeth Cady Stanton and Susan B. Anthony, all three looking somewhat stern. Perhaps they were tired of waiting for recognition.

Women found their voice in the twentieth century. No longer silent and passive, no longer subservient to men, no longer confined to kitchens and bedrooms, women are and can be in any profession they choose, thanks in great part to some of the women mentioned here.

NATIONAL ARCHIVES

Sally K. Ride, Ph.D. Former NASA Astronaut. Photo Courtesy of NASA.

CHAPTER ELEVEN

Getting There:

from Horse and Buggy
to Outer Space

*This picture of my father, Edwin, sitting in the center, wrapped
in a blanket because of the cold, was taken in 1906 when
he was a year old. He was with his grandparents in front
of their house in Aitkin, Minnesota. – Helen Wendt Smith*

*When I was a child in the twenties I loved to listen to the clippity-clop
of the horses' hooves as they trotted down the street. We kids played
on the street because there were hardly any cars. We used to just have
dirt roads, but when they paved them over they put rubber shoes
instead of metal on the horses' feet because that made it easier for*

them to walk on the hard concrete. There were horse troughs full of water every half mile or so, which had one side for the horses and one side for humans. It was mostly filled with rainwater. There was usually an old tin cup hanging on a post that everyone in town used to drink from. That would be unimaginable today! – *Lorna McKenzie, mother and grandmother, born 1917, Canton, OH.*

When the twentieth century opened, traffic in New York City was total gridlock. There were no traffic lights or stop signs at corners, and horses and carriages fought their way down the streets through chaos and bedlam. The huge influx of immigrants pouring into the city overwhelmed the ability of local streets to contain the number of wagons, horses and pedestrians trying to move from one place to another. One had to step carefully while walking down the street to avoid the numerous piles of horse droppings. Although there were already subways in cities such as Boston and London, on March 24th, 1900, ground was broken for the New York subway. The building of this massive transportation system was awesome, and disrupted citizens and businesses for several years. It was built mainly by Italian immigrants, many of whom lost their lives in the process.

Automobiles Take Over Cities

In 1900, there were less than ten miles of concrete roads in the entire country and, four years later, there were only eighteen miles of asphalt road. But, not many roads were needed because there were only 8,000 cars in the entire United States. New York State law required that you give a week's notice before taking a trip. That year, President William McKinley became the first U.S. president to ride in an automobile. It was a dangerous thing to do because it frightened the horses, but he didn't have to worry about being stuck in a traffic jam. A year later New York passed the first state law requiring registration for automobiles, collecting a total of $954 in fees. Connecticut became the first state to enact uniform, statewide motor vehicle laws and the speed limit was set at 6.5 miles per hour.

In 1902 Henry Ford, with capital of only $100,000, founded the Ford Motor Company, which produced the first Model T in America in 1908, and launched the first century of coast-to-coast transportation. Ford pioneered the assembly line in his factory, and started mass-production of automobiles. As the Model T sputtered along, people stood at the side of dirt roads and scoffed: "That'll never work. It's noisy, it uses fuel that explodes, and only a Charles Atlas could turn the crank to get it started. And besides that, it's no good outside the city because there aren't any paved roads, and how is it going to refuel when it runs out of gasoline?"

Fifteen million Model T's were eventually sold, and our lifestyle was forever changed. America put the horse to pasture. Ford's low-priced car made it possible for the general public to own cars, taking ownership out of the exclusive hands of the rich. People were no longer isolated by distance, and journeys that used to take several weeks by horse and buggy, were now reduced to days. When the automobile first appeared, hardly anyone had traveled more than twenty miles from where they were born. In general, only "old settlers" and Civil War veterans, of which there were few remaining, had first-hand knowledge of the world beyond their own neighborhood. The automobile opened up the world and was one of the most significant inventions of the century.

The steering wheel was first used on the Packard Model C in 1900. Before that time, automobiles were steered by tillers, much like boats. The 1901 curved-dash Oldsmobile was the first car equipped with a speedometer. Because the original cars had to be cranked by hand to get them started, you could break an arm if you weren't paying attention. Charles Keltering eliminated this problem in 1911 when he developed the first practical self-starter.

This picture was taken by photographers from the Standard Oil Company for promotional purposes. It shows me at 2-1/2 years old with my father and a salesman. In those days when you got gas you also got your windshield cleaned, oil checked and gas pumped, without asking. - Larry Lundholm, Florence, Washington

Until the 1960s automobiles had running boards which a person could jump on and go for a ride on the side of the car, and they had small side-windows which helped deflect the wind. These were removed in the seventies in an effort to give cars a more streamlined modern look, but many women didn't like the change because the side windows prevented the wind from flowing into the driver's seat and messing up their hair.

My father drove a seven-passenger 1917 Chandler touring car during World War I. It took ten hours to go 160 miles to my dad's farm in Iowa. In those years if you could drive fifty miles without getting a flat tire, you were really lucky. Of course if you did get one, you changed it yourself; there were no service stations along the two-lane highway. My first car was a 1923 Model T Ford, which I bought for $150 in 1930. In 1941, I earned $3,000 a year, and I bought a brand-new Pontiac for $1,100 and drove it from Cleveland to Boston in one day. That sounds like a lot of money, but today people often spend more than a third of their yearly pay to buy a new car. – Donald Roan, retired butcher, born 1912, Iowa.

This station was actually built inside a tree on the outskirts of Ukiah, California. It was built from the butt of a huge redwood that was said to have been 1,500 years old! The log used to build the station was 18 feet long and 17 feet in diameter. There was enough wood removed from the inside of the log to build 15 houses. The

station's rest rooms were made from hollowed-out sections of smaller redwoods. Bing Crosby stopped here once and so did Clark Gable and Carole Lombard, on their honeymoon trip. My first job was at this station in the 1940s—keeping the soda case filled and passing out postcards to the thousands of tourists every summer. – Ronald Ford, Redwood Valley, CA.

As automobiles caught on, roads began to be paved to accommodate the new vehicles and keep people from being covered with dust when they arrived at church. The first mile of concrete pavement was laid in Detroit in 1908 for the astronomical sum of $13,534, and the first modern long-distance road was the Pennsylvania Turnpike, which opened in 1940. As the years went by, cities finally realized life would be a lot safer if they had stop signs, and the first electric traffic signal was installed in Cleveland, Ohio on August 5th, 1914. It consisted of a red and green light, and a warning buzzer to alert drivers when the lights were about to change. Gulf Oil opened the first drive-in gas station in 1913 in Pittsburgh and, six years later, Oregon was the first to realize you could put a tax on gasoline. By the 1920s service stations began to spring up in heavily- trafficked areas where these new-fangled inventions could be refueled for longer journeys.

When I was a kid you didn't have to waste time trying to find the car keys in the morning because they were in the ignition in the car. The car doors weren't locked and neither were the doors to the house. In fact, you got into trouble if you accidentally locked the doors because nobody ever carried a key. – Carl Keller printer, born 1932, Boston, MA.

Car radios, developed by Motorola, came along in 1929, and were installed as an option after purchase. In 1956 Chrysler offered the first in-dash record player as an option, and they offered the first in-dash stereo cassette tape player/recorder in 1971. The first windshield wiper was designed by Prince Henry of Prussia, who fitted it to the windshield of his Benz automobile when he drove from Hamburg to London in July, 1911. One drawback: it had to be operated by hand, a considerable distraction to the driver. Automatic wipers were developed in America in 1916. Air-conditioning was first offered as an option by Nash in 1939.

This Rio Flying Cloud Sports Coupe was a wedding present in 1933.
After the groom's death it was put in storage for almost 25 years, then
was purchased in 1990 by Opal and Wes Tarr, who completely restored it.
Their daughter and son-in-law used it for their son's wedding and
will use it again for their second son's wedding.

When I bought my first car, a big Pontiac, in 1938, none of the modern conveniences had been invented, but of course I didn't miss them. It had a heater but one usually arrived at their destination before the heat kicked in. There was no radio, and therefore no antenna, There were no turn-signals, so you had to roll down the window and stick your arm out to indicate which way you wanted to turn. But in those days we always kept the windows open in the summer because there wasn't any air-conditioning. It was a gear-shift of course, because automatic drive hadn't been invented yet, so one had to become adept at changing gears in traffic. But, since there was very little traffic, that wasn't much of a problem. – Jonathan Wilson, retired dentist, born 1921, Grand Rapids, MI.

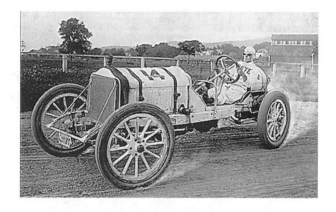

As cars proliferated, the government stepped in and formed The Department of Motor Vehicles in 1937 to write and enforce rules on how people were going to drive them. Drivers were eventually required to purchase a permit to drive a car, and to pass a little test to demonstrate they really knew how to drive one safely. Laws against drunk driving were established, but were enforced with little more than a slap on the wrist until "Mothers Against Drunk Driving" was formed in the seventies, and the courts got serious about the carnage caused by drinking drivers. Speed limits were established at thirty-five miles per hour in 1942 and, in 1972, the government imposed a national speed limit of fifty-five miles-per-hour. Seat-belts were available as an option until 1962 when Wisconsin passed the first law requiring all cars sold there to have the belts installed.

When I was a teenager my boyfriend taught me how to drive in his 1926 Ford. I didn't have to get a temporary permit because he didn't even need to have a driver's license. We couldn't drive at night because it was too dark and there weren't any highway lights. In fact there really wasn't a highway, it was just a paved two-lane road with no dividing line down the middle. Of course the car had a clutch and a choke and it was really difficult to learn how to change gears without stalling the thing. I sure was glad when automatic transmissions came out and all I had to do was put it in Drive. – Marcy Buluran, retired educator, born 1910, Detroit, MI.

The amount of computing power in cars these days is truly amazing. Computers control combustion, timing, engine and transmission controls. The entire car is measured and monitored so that most new cars today have more computing power than the original Apollo that went to the moon! The drawback, however, is that it's becoming increasingly more difficult for mechanics to fix them.

On the Road Again

By the end of the century the nation was totally dependent on automobiles as a means of transportation. In large cities such as Los Angeles and Boston, commuters could spend a couple of hours or more on the road, getting to and from work, greatly increasing the stress level, and alienating families.

In Toronto where I was born, before the sixties almost everyone took public transportation to work, and we were generally no more than twenty minutes from our job. Streetcars and buses were almost instantly available, which they certainly had to be during the winter or you could freeze to death if you had to wait too long. Now I live in Sunnyvale in Northern California where the majority of people drive to work solo, so the freeways are jammed, and it can take over an hour just to go thirty miles.

On Sundays when I was a kid the whole family would often just go for a drive so we could see the leaves turning in the Fall, or the buds opening in the Spring. The highways in Ontario were always surrounded by a profusion of trees, so driving was a delightful and aesthetic experience. Sometimes we drove down the Queen Elizabeth Highway, which was a two lane road, and went to Niagara Falls to be awed by one of nature's most incredible spectacles. I never tired of looking at that. Sometimes mom would make us a picnic lunch and we'd sit out on the grass somewhere and just enjoy the scenery.

We often dropped in on our relatives if they happened to be home and not taking their own Sunday drive. We kids would be sent to the neighborhood grocery store for a few pints of ice cream while the housewife made iced tea or lemonade for the adults. We'd eat the ice cream while looking at my uncle's comic book collection, and the adults would sit out on the porch talking about weather, politics, and when, if ever, the Depression would end. Today, unless you live in the country, it would be unthinkable to go for a Sunday afternoon drive. Even on weekends the freeways are clogged with people going to the malls, and doing their other business.   – Bill Oaker, writer, born 1936

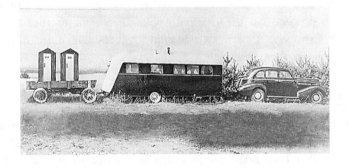

In 1952 I bought a brand new Buick. It was about a block long and had those big fins at the back. I was so proud of that car, but it sure was a gas guzzler. I used to drive into a station and ask the guy for fifty cents worth of gas because that's all I could afford, but that would get me around town for a week. Of course we didn't have "self-serve" stations then or I would have gotten my own gas and saved myself the embarrassment of asking for only fifty cents' worth.

I graduated from my Buick to the obligatory station wagon when the kids were young.. These seem to have been replaced now by mini-vans and Sports Utility Vehicles, with child protective seats built-in. After the oil crisis of the seventies people started preferring compacts and even mini-compacts to save on gas, but that crisis is forgotten now. I'll always remember that classy, roomy Buick. Your first car is something like your first love—hard to forget. – Rebecca Borden, editor, born 1933, Chicago, IL.

In this photo I'm sitting on my 1958 Chevy, sporting a Beatles' haircut, which the girls seemed to like, but my dad said "Stamp it out before it multiplies!" I'm also wearing Beatle boots, which were popular at the time, and I had four different styles. I paid $5 for admission to a Beatles' concert that year. –Bob Gouveia, Burlington, MA

I Hear that Lonesome Whistle Blow

Although trains were the primary mode of transportation in the nineteenth century, run by steam or electricity, the diesel engine was first used on German trains as early as 1912. During the 1950s diesel engines became common and the age of steam was over. But electric trains still run because they have proved themselves under all kinds of working conditions, such as the Swiss Alps. They don't pollute the air and need fewer people to run them.

We wore our Sunday best in the forties an fifties whenever we rode "The City of Portland." People who traveled by streamliner journeyed in comparative luxury. The dining room had elegant accommodations and fine service. We slept in Pullman cars, and the porter would wake us up a half-hour before we arrived at our destination. - Elaine Livingston, La Grande, Oregon.

My father was a railroad executive and we always traveled by train. The Pullman cars were first-class, and the porter made the seats up into beds at night. Upper berths folded down from the ceiling. My parents took the lower berth while my brother and I got the upper. It was an interesting exercise to get dressed and undressed lying horizontally in the limited confines of those beds. But the rhythmic click of the wheels over the rail joints was a wonderful way to fall asleep.

It was fun to peer around the side of the car from the open platform of the observation car at the end of the train. I could see the engine and cars ahead as the train rounded a curve. But those steam engines threw out cinders that stung and forced me to close my eyes. I solved that problem by going to Woolworth's and buying a pair of aviator goggles. – Robert Fisk, Houston, TX.

Luxury dining in a train

Fly Me to the Moon

At Kitty Hawk, North Carolina, on December 17, 1903, two small-town businessmen invented a technology that would define the twentieth century. The golden age of flight began when Wilbur and Orville Wright flew the first sustained power-driven airplane, which they patented as a "flying machine." The craft soared to an altitude of ten feet, traveled 120 feet, and landed twelve seconds after takeoff. This ingenious invention revolutionized how commerce was conducted and how wars were fought, and may have been the centuries most important invention. The first non-stop transcontinental flight took off from New York on May 2nd, 1923, and landed in San Francisco twenty-seven hours later. Imagine the misery of being cramped into a tiny cockpit, and trying to stay awake for more than a day and night!

In 1927 Charles Lindbergh became the first person to cross the Atlantic by flying nonstop, solo, from New York to Paris. When he landed the "Spirit of St. Louis" at Le Bourget airport, only automobile headlights illuminated the field because it had no electric lights. Lindbergh was hailed as an American hero and given the largest ticker-tape parade in New York that has ever been held, before or since. The era of global flight had truly begun.

On October 14, 1947, Air Force test pilot Chuck Yeager made history by breaking through the sound barrier: Mach 1. Yeager flew at 700 mph, slightly faster than the air could carry the shriek of his own speeding plane. Some scientists feared the invisible wall would smash to bits any plane that tried to pierce it, and one pilot had already died attempting the same feat. While the aircraft shook, bounced and buckled, on the California desert below, the craft's sonic boom thundered into human ears for the first time. The space age was launched, and the familiar drone of propeller planes was replaced by the roar of jets.

I took this picture in 1934 in Mt. Vernon, New York. The trolley was frozen to the tracks and couldn't move. I used to take this trolley to high school, and later to work. – Astrid Swanson, Caledonia, N.Y.

From Propellers to Jet Engines

More than any other single technology, the jet engine revolutionized air travel around the world. Unlike the old propeller-driven planes that were powered by piston engines, jet planes could fly at tremendous speeds, thus cutting down travel time. Jet-equipped airplanes also could climb faster and fly higher. There were, however, major concerns because airline executives were aware that, although jet engines were simpler than the old piston engines, they also had high operating temperatures that required very expensive metal alloy components that ultimately would affect an aircraft's longevity and reliability. Moreover, jet engines used far greater amounts of fuel. The initially low takeoff speed also required longer runways. All of this added up to increased costs. As a result, U.S. passenger air-carriers didn't support the building of jet airliners in the immediate postwar years, and adopted a "wait-and-see" approach before embarking on this costly path.

When I was an American Airlines stewardess from 1946 to 1949, everyone went first class! I felt my passengers were my guests, and it was my job to help them feel comfortable and safe. It was fun hard work, women's work – no men need apply. Applicants had to be ages twenty-one to twenty-six, between 5'2 and 5'6 and couldn't weigh more than 135 pounds. Our hair had to be worn short and off the collar; makeup had to be natural (no blue eyeshadow!) and we couldn't wear eyeglasses. They didn't have contact lenses in those

days so, if you needed glasses, you couldn't be a stewardess. Ostentatious jewelry was also prohibited. The professional look was completed with a navy-blue tailored uniform and a stewardess' cap.

When we finished the airline's stewardess school, each graduate received a Bulova watch. An advertising slogan at the time was: "American Airlines runs on Bulova Watch Time."

Passengers were treated like royalty. I addressed each person by name during the flight. I hung up their coats and gave each lady a hatbox. Our training included feeding babies and changing diapers. Our filet mignon and chicken cordon bleu dinners were served on Syracuse china with real silverware and cloth napkins, and the dinner tray was placed on a pillow in the passenger's lap. Liquor was never served.

Many people were fearful of flying in those early years of passenger flights so, before I was employed, only nurses were hired to be stewardesses, hoping to ease passenger fears. When nurses were called to action during World War II, the requirement changed to just a four-year degree. Later, it was changed to two years of college. At the time my salary was $135 a month. – Lorraine Marik, Riverside, ILL.

AIRFARE IN 1949

New York To:

Miami	$ 50
Los Angeles	$ 99
Cleveland	$ 20
Paris	$ 493 (roundtrip)
Calcutta	$1,177 (roundtrip)

The worst tragedy in flight history happened in January, 1986 when the space shuttle Challenger blew up in mid-air shortly after blasting off from Cape Canaveral. The entire crew of seven was killed instantly, including two women, one of whom, Christa MacAuliffe, was a schoolteacher who was the first layperson to fly in space. The incident shocked the world, and was one of the saddest days in American history.

I'll never forget that terrible day in January when the Challenger blew up! I just sat down to breakfast and turned on CNN so I could watch the take-off. This time I was really excited about a shuttle blasting off because for the first time it carried two women, one an astronaut and the other a lay-person. It was truly an historic moment, which had never happened before, and has never been repeated. Part of the tragedy was that thousands of schoolchildren were also watching, knowing a teacher was on board. And then suddenly—WHAM—the cloud of white smoke—the fire—the shock of disbelief—the yell that escaped from my mouth. It was horrifying and absolutely unbelievable. All seven men and women annihilated in a single instant! I must have seen that moment over and over a hundred times in the ensuing days, and it's burned forever in my memory. I had nightmares for weeks after that. – Carla Shiffman, Illustrator, children's books, born 1961, Indianapolis, IN.

During the mid '20s my dad was the ranking man on one of the emergency vehicles operated by the Consolidated Gas Company In New York City. Painted brilliant red, with shiny brass rails in the back, they resembled fire trucks but had no sirens or flashing lights. Instead, there was a brass gong on the side that was operated by pulling a rope. The three-man crew responded to emergencies such as gas leaks, explosions, fires, and floods caused by broken water mains. – Edward Dziowgo, O'Neill, NB.

The grandest and most heroic event, not only of the twentieth century, but in the entire history of civilization, took place on July 10th, 1969 when Apollo 11 landed on the moon's surface. Neil Armstrong put a foot onto the moon and made his famous statement: *"This is one small step for a man, one giant step for mankind."* This remarkable flight, launched from Cape

Canaveral, Florida, signified man finally escaping his environment, and was the most breathtaking event of the century. President Kennedy, who started the space race, was not here to share the glory; he had been assassinated six years earlier.

There are memorable occurrences in everyone's life, but I believe what will stand out for most Americans are the two major events of this century: the assassination of President Kennedy, and Neil Armstrong landing on the moon. I'll never forget where I was when both of these events happened because I was so stunned, and probably had my mouth hanging open both times when I watched them on TV. In each case people began yelling, and even crying, even though one was a disaster, and the other a celebration. Watching that astronaut step outside of his spacecraft and put a foot on our moon was absolutely mind-boggling! When I was born in 1925 just traveling from one city to another was a big event because hardly anyone had a car. If you weren't close to a railroad line you had to take a horse and buggy to get there, and now, in my lifetime, a man is actually walking around on the moon, and leaving the American flag there! It's truly amazing! – Paul Langer, retired insurance salesman, Santa Fe, NM.

Disappearing Traditions

<u>Burma-Shave</u>
signs along the highway

These signs

We gladly

Dedicate

To men who've had

No date of late

Burma-Shave

Henry The Eighth

Sure has trouble

Short on wives

Long on stubble!!

Burma Shave

A whiskery kiss

For the one

You adore

May not make her mad

But her face will be sore

Burma-Shave

To kiss

A mug

That's like a cactus

Takes more nerve

Than it does practice

Burma-Shave

CHAPTER TWELVE

A Potpourri of Changes

A 1920s Accounting Class

Most people who were alive when the twentieth century opened, didn't get to celebrate their fiftieth birthday; the average life span was only forty-seven years. Life was fairly primitive in 1900, you couldn't take a bath unless you lived in one of the fourteen percent of homes in the U.S. that had a tub, and only eight percent of homes had a telephone.

People worked for what would be considered starvation wages, even compared to the cost of living at the time. The average wage in the U.S. was twenty-two cents an hour, and the average worker, almost always a male, made between $200 and $400 per year! A professional, such as a dentist or accountant, could expect to earn between $2,000 and $2,500 per year. Most people, particularly women, had never graduated from high school, and one in ten U.S. adults couldn't read or write.

Crime: From Criminal Organizations to Kids with UZI's

One of the most significant changes after the 1960s was the increase in crime. When the twentieth century began, there were only 230 reported murders in the entire United States! This was soon to change.

Al Capone

Early in the century, organized crime began rearing its hideous head in certain large American cities. One of the most violent and bloodthirsty criminal organizations of the twenties, the Sicilian Mafia, was headed in Chicago by Neapolitan-born crime lord Al Capone, known as "Scarface Al." Among his many felonies, he was reputed to have ordered the "St. Valentine's Day Massacre," where six members of a rival gang, and an observer, were lined up against a wall and summarily murdered with a volley of over 100 shots from machine guns.

Bonnie Parker and Clyde Barrow were a notorious couple who went on a shooting spree across Texas, killing at least twelve people. They eventually were gunned down by Texas deputies while they were speeding down the highway. Hollywood later glorified them in a movie starring Warren Beatty and Faye Dunaway.

When I was a housewife in the fifties, home alone with my three little kids, salesmen would often come knocking on my door, selling things like hair brushes, encyclopedias and vacuum cleaners. They were uninvited and unannounced, yet I always opened the door to them. If I were interested in their product, I would even invite them to come in and give me a demonstration, and it never occurred to me that they might rob or rape me. Sometimes they were hucksters, peddling wares that soon broke down, or expensive items that I really didn't need, but got talked into because of low monthly-payment schemes or special discounts. But for the most part they were honest, hard-working enterprising men who had to live on commissions earned with a smooth line of talk and a pleasant personality. I often welcomed their calls because I was starved for the companionship of an adult, and they seemed to know that sharing some local gossip helped persuade women to buy their product. Today I never open my door for someone I don't know, especially a male. At night I never even answer the door unless I know someone's coming over. – Maria Parades, social worker, born 1936, Los Lunas, NM.

Some Infamous Crimes of the Century:

In 1924 Nathan Leopold & Richard Loeb were sentenced to life imprisonment for the kidnap and slaying of fourteen-year-old Bobby Franks, the son of a wealthy Chicago family. Hydrochloric acid was poured over his face, and his body was stuffed into a drainpipe. At the time this was considered the crime of the century, horrifying the world. It seemed unthinkable that the two friends, who were highly intelligent and from an influential family, could possibly have killed the boy. Although Frank's parents received a note demanding $10,000 in return for the boy, by then he was already dead. Leopold and Loeb confessed they had murdered him just to see what it would be like to kill someone. Dubbed "the thrill killers" by the press, people were stunned to learn that they murdered an innocent boy out of curiosity. In 1936 Richard Loeb was stabbed to death by another prisoner. Nathan Leopold served thirty-four years and moved to Puerto Rico upon release.

Leopold and Loeb Arrested

One of the most publicized and repellent crimes of the thirties was the kidnapping of revered national hero Charles Lindbergh's first-born twenty-month-old son, who was snatched from his bedroom. New Jersey police, joined by several other law enforcement agencies, set up the most intensive search party since Booth shot Lincoln. A ransom of $50,000 was paid, but the baby's body was finally found with a leg and hand missing, clubbed to death. The convicted kidnapper, Bruno Richard Hauptmann, was executed in 1936. In response to this horrific crime, Congress passed the "Lindbergh Law," which made kidnapping across state lines a federal offense.

The "Scottsboro Incident" in 1931 was a landmark case in the history of U.S. criminal law. In the second year of the Depression some hoboes, both men and women, jumped on a freight train in Chattanooga, Tennessee. A fight broke out between young white and black hoboes, and the whites were thrown off the train by the blacks. In revenge they reported to the stationmaster that the blacks had raped two white girls who were on the train. A posse seized the blacks from the train and arrested them. Eight of the nine, who came to be known as "The Scottboro Boys," were sentenced to death, and the ninth to life imprisonment. The Supreme Court reversed the convictions on the grounds that the defendants didn't have adequate representation by council and ordered a new trial. Although one of the women involved testified at the second trial that no rape had occurred, all of the men were re-convicted. After several appeals and reversals, charges were dropped for four of them. Two others got life in prison, one got 75 years, and one twenty.

A famous case of the fifties was that of Dr. Sam Sheppard, a Cleveland osteopath who was convicted in 1954 of second-degree murder for killing his pregnant wife, Marilyn. He was acquitted in a second trial in 1966, and died at the age of forty-six in 1970. For several years his son, Sam Reese Shepard, sought a civil trial to clear his father's name and prove that he was wrongfully convicted at the first trial. His attorney contended that blood at the crime scene linked the murder to the family's handyman, who was now in prison for another crime. The jury however, didn't agree, and upheld the conviction.

One summer evening in 1972, my two girlfriends and I went to a swanky restaurant in San Francisco for dinner. We parked our car at Coit Tower and then walked down a tree-lined pathway lighted by lamplights, to the restaurant. When we left about 10 p.m. a young man came from a side street and started walking up the stairway with us. He was nicely dressed in a blue velvet jacket and seemed very personable. (This was long before the days of gangs). We chatted while climbing the stairs and he said he was a firefighter who lived in one of the houses on the hillside. Then he got ahead of us and, as we rounded the corner, me walking in front, I was suddenly looking at a gun, which he stuck in my stomach. As is very common when people confront something totally foreign and unexpected, my first reaction was that it was a joke, and this was a toy gun. I quickly realized that was a fantasy when the man said: "Give me all of your money, and I mean all of it, and I mean right now." We rapidly complied. Then he told us to get going. The scariest part was turning our back on him as we ascended the stairs, fearful that he might shoot us. Half way up the stairway we met another young man on his way down. For a brief moment I thought I should tell him not to go down there because of the robber, but something told me to just keep walking. As we passed this man, I saw that he had a gun too, hidden underneath a baseball cap he was carrying in front of him. I guess he was the accomplice to warn the first guy if somebody was coming down.

When we got to the car, my girlfriends both started to cry, but I actually felt lucky because the man hadn't taken our car keys, which would have made it very difficult to get the fifty miles back to San Jose. He hadn't taken our purses, or our credit cards, so we still had our I.D. In the worst scenario, he could even have captured one of us and taken us off and raped or killed us.

We drove to a police station and reported it. What really got me about that was the cop said "Was he gay?" "How the hell would we know?" Margaret replied sardonically: "We didn't ask him what his sexual orientation was." Although there is a large gay population in San Francisco, there is almost zero crime in that community.

After that I became extremely cautious whenever I was out in the streets at night. —Bernadette Dorien, 50-something, born San Jose, CA.

Helter Skelter

The most horrific murder spree of the century took place on August 9, 1969. Actress Sharon Tate, wife of director Roman Polanski, was keeping company in her Beverly Hills home with Abigail Folger, the coffee heiress, Folger's boyfriend Voytek Frykowski, and hair stylist Jay Sebring. Sharon was eight month's pregnant.

Around 12:30 a.m. Tim Ireland, who was supervising a camp-out less than a mile away, heard a chilling scream:"Oh, God, no, please don't! Oh, God, no, don't, don't…"

Winifred Chapman, Sharon Tate's housekeeper, came to the main gate of the house a little after 8 A.M. and called the police. When the cops arrived they found a Rambler in the driveway with a young man slumped on the passenger side, drenched in blood. There on the beautifully manicured lawn lay two bodies. Someone had battered the man in his head and face, while savagely puncturing the rest of his body with dozens of wounds. The other body was that of a young woman lying in a her nightgown, with multiple stab wounds.

On the lower half of the front door the word "PIG" was scrawled in blood. A young blond woman, very pregnant, was lying dead on the floor, smeared with blood, a rope around her neck that extended over a rafter in the ceiling. The other end of the rope was around the neck of a man lying nearby, also drenched in blood.

Charles Manson. Courtesy Los Angeles Times

Later that Saturday night, Leno and Rosemary LaBianca and Susan Struthers, wealthy grocery-store owners, who lived in the Los Feliz area of Los Angeles, were found dead by Rosemary's son. When he entered the house he saw Leno in his pajamas, lying with a blood-drenched pillow over his head and the cord of a lamp tied tightly around his neck. His hands had been tied behind him with a leather thong. A carving fork protruded from his stomach and the word "WAR" had been carved in his flesh. In the master bedroom, they found his wife Rosemary lying on the floor, her nightgown up over her head. She too had a pillowcase over her head and a lamp cord tied tightly around her neck.

In three places in the house, there was writing which appeared to be in the victims' blood: on the living room wall, "DEATH TO PIGS;" on another wall in the living room, the single word "RISE;" and on the refrigerator door, "HEALTHER SKELTER," misspelled.

Charles Manson, leader of a hippie commune, was convicted of first degree murder, along with three others, Tex Watson, Susan Atkins and Leslie Van Houten, and they were sentenced to death. Later the California Supreme Court declared the death penalty unconstitutional and they were given life in prison, where they still are. Lynette "Squeaky" Fromme took over the leadership of the "Manson family" and tried to assassinate President Ford in 1975. She is in a Federal prison in Florida.

The Symbionese Liberation Army

On April 15, 1974, at the Hibernia Bank in San Francisco four white women and a black man walked in with guns drawn and yelled, "It's a hold-up! Down on the floor! On your faces, you motherfuckers!" Nineteen-year-old Patricia Campbell Hearst, who had been missing for over two months, was photographed wielding a submachine gun.

Hearst, born in San Francisco on February 20, 1954, was the granddaughter of William Randolph Hearst, the newspaper magnate. She was kidnapped February 4, 1974 from her Berkeley, California apartment by a tiny leftist group called the Symbionese Liberation Army

Hearst Posing for an SLA picture

By her account, Patty was kept blindfolded for two months in a closet at the group's headquarters, unable even to use the bathroom in privacy. The apparent leader, Donald DeFreeze, called himself Field Marshall Cinque Mtume. He wanted to start a revolution of the underprivileged, and he realized that Hearst's visibility as a social figure would showcase his cause, so he used several coercive methods to turn her into an angry revolutionary. Later communications from her revealed that she had changed her name to "Tania," and was committed to the goals of the SLA. In September 1975, she was arrested in an apartment with other SLA members.

In her trial in 1976, Hearst claimed she had been locked blindfolded in a closet and physically and sexually abused, which caused her to become a convert to the SLA. This defense did not succeed and she was convicted of bank robbery. Her sentence was commuted after twenty-two months by President Jimmy Carter. Hearst was released from prison on February 1, 1979.

The Football Hero's Last Play

The double homicide of thirty-five year-old Nicole Brown Simpson, former wife of O.J. Simpson, and twenty-five year-old Ronald Lyle Goldman, a waiter, occurred in the Brentwood community of Los Angeles on Sunday night, June 12th, 1994. The murder trial of the suspect, retired football legend O.J. Simpson, went on for nine months. and mesmerized the country. Eleven lawyers represented him and twenty-five people worked around the clock for the Los Angeles' prosecutors' office. It was the longest trial ever held in California, costing over twenty million dollars. There were 150 witnesses called to give evidence before a jury that was sequestered at the Hotel Intercontinental in downtown Los Angeles, from January until October.

The tragic deaths of Nicole Brown Simpson and Ronald Goldman became somewhat backstage, as the man on trial for their murders commanded center stage in his fight to prove bigotry and racism were the real issues on trial. In the end he was found not guilty by a jury of eleven blacks and one white. A later civil trial found him guilty. He claims he is now busy "looking for the real killer."

Murder on Christmas Eve

Winding up a century of brutal murders, on Christmas night, 1996, the homicide of six-year-old Jon Benét Ramsey, a beautiful and talented child, stunned America. This murder, which took place in a wealthy Boulder, Colorado home while the child was sleeping, reactivated every parent's worst nightmare. The public's shock at the murder soon began to share equal time with its growing dismay at the Boulder police's investigation, a dismay fed by a steady stream of leaks from the Boulder County District Attorney's office about the inept investigation being conducted. Even Jon Benét's ten-year old brother was suspect, but nothing was ever proven and this high-profile murder case remains unsolved.

For their part, the Ramseys launched a sophisticated and expensive public relations campaign, including staging various interviews and news conferences in their on-going parry with Boulder authorities. They also published a book, *The Death of Innocence,* (that exonerates them and their son, Burke, while advancing various speculations regarding the killer), and promotes their web site that offers a $100,000 reward for "information that will lead to the arrest and conviction of Jon Benét's killer."

Although these were extreme cases, everyday crime was far more rampant at the end of the century than it was at the beginning, and touched every community and every socio-economic level. But the nature of the crimes and the perpetrators have greatly changed, and their age has been greatly reduced. In the last half of the century criminal family organizations were outnumbered by street gangs who spent much of their time trying to eliminate members of other gangs. In one decade, between 1960 and 1969, crimes of violence in the U.S. increased fifty-seven percent.

Locked up

The Century's Worst Terrorist Attack

On the morning of April 19, 1995, just after parents dropped their children off at a day care at the Murrah Federal Building in downtown Oklahoma City, a massive bomb inside a rental truck exploded, blowing half of the nine-story building into oblivion. 168 people were killed.

Timothy McVeigh was charged with the bombing, and his ex-Army buddy, Terry Nichols, was charged with conspiracy. McVeigh was executed on June 11, 2001 and Nichols was sentenced to life in prison.

In Buffalo when I was a kid an Italian baker who had a little grocery store a few blocks from our house would come by in a horse and enclosed wagon once a week and deliver the bread. If nobody was at home, he would simply leave it on the windowsill, and no one ever took it. Stealing a neighbor's loaf of bread was unthinkable in those days. A few week's ago I moved into a new neighborhood. I had an old rattan chair that I decided to leave out on the front porch. It was gone in the morning. – Roberta Berg, cake decorator, born 1926.

The New Face of Criminals: Children

The first juvenile court was established in Chicago at the turn of the century, and was intended to deal with little miscreants who might throw a rock through a schoolroom window or steal candy from the corner grocery store. By the end of the nineties juvenile crime had exploded and now involved incredible brutality, enormous destruction of property, rape, and even gratuitous murder. Tragically, in nearly half the cases of violent crimes against twelve to nineteen-year-olds, the offender is another juvenile. This generation has available something that no other generation of young people has ever had: easy access to guns. What has changed dramatically in the last two decades is that some children today no longer slug it out with fisticuffs, but instead settle their disputes or perceived slights by pulling out a gun. In 1994 eight out of ten minors who committed murder used a gun.

When I was a kid in the twenties I bought some candy at the corner grocery store and Mr. Baglieri mistakenly gave me an extra nickel in change. I didn't realize it until I got home and then I debated whether to walk all the way back to the store and return it. I sure could use five cents because that bought a lot in those days, but I also knew that stealing was a sin, and I didn't want to cheat Mr. Baglieri. When I brought the money back he was so appreciative of my honesty that he gave me a free piece of candy, and I knew I did the right thing. – Phil Hammer, notary public, born 1921, Toronto, Canada.

Many children today have two working parents, and they live in a world of much greater threats to their well-being than the children of the first half of the century. In the forties and fifties, nuclear war was an ever-present threat, but a very distant one in the everyday life of a schoolchild. Today the threat to a child's security is more direct and may come in the form of violence from one's own peers. Before 1970 no child would have brought a gun to school, because no child thought they had to protect themselves from their fellow students. Concern about being a victim of crime, has limited kids' access to one of the key ingredients of healthy growth: unrestricted free play with their peers. Neighborhood children no longer play together out on the street under the watchful eye of other parents because neither the children nor the parents trust anyone else.

One of the driving factors in the increase in crime is the increase in drug usage. Widespread use of so-called recreational drugs has contributed to numerous crimes, and street gangs have heavily involved themselves in the buying and selling of illicit drugs. Gangs, who often advertise themselves with graffiti sprayed on every available building, sometimes wear body armor and carry semi-automatic weapons, often outgunning the police.

When I went to school in Kansas City in the forties they showed us the movie "Reefer Madness," about a guy hooked to marijuana. There were dire warnings that one hit of weed would turn you automatically into a junkie that couldn't control your urgings, and therefore would naturally lead to a life of crime to pay for your habit, and you'd die young. It was really frightening to the unsophisticated high school students of my generation, and we believed every word of it. Besides that, there weren't any drugs available anyway, except cigarettes and alcohol, and nobody said much about them. Now kids get the simplistic message from Nancy Reagan: "just say no." But they're saying yes instead. – Nick Evans, *restaurant owner, born 1929, Pittsburg, PA.*

One of the most horrifying crimes of the last year of the century was the Columbine killings. Laughing as they shot, two armed students clad in long black coats fired shotguns at their fellow students at Littleton High School in Colorado, killing thirteen people, including one teacher, and wounding twenty others. The boys, said to be members of the "Trench Coat Mafia," then shot themselves. Police later found thirty explosives that had been planted around the school. It was the most horrific outbreak of violence ever witnessed in America's schools.

I think part of the problem with kids these days is that many parents don't discipline them anymore. Some parents say they can't because of child abuse laws that make hitting your kids a crime. But there are other ways to discipline kids—like taking away privileges.

The other evening I was in a little neighborhood restaurant having dinner by myself and reading the paper. It was a cold, rainy night and there was only one other couple in the place sitting across from me; two mothers with their two young children, each about five years old. While the mothers enjoyed an after-dinner drink, the two kids ran wild throughout the restaurant, jumping up and down on the seats, yelling and chasing each other, and their mothers paid absolutely no attention to this noisy display. Finally, one kid crawled under my tablecloth and popped her head up grinning at me. By this time I was out of patience and said as loud and adamantly as I could: 'Is this a restaurant or a playground?' After that outburst the mothers decided it was time to make their little darlings settle down. - Kim DeCelles, Long Beach, CA.

I remember when I was a kid discipline was no problem in our house, even though there were seven children. One reason was that mom and dad always put up a united front and never contradicted each other, so playing one off the other wouldn't work. One stern look of disapproval from my father was enough to shrivel your spine and stop whatever misbehavior you were engaged in. Talking back was something totally unknown because you'd probably get the switch for it, so we didn't do it. And we didn't walk out when our parents were trying to tell us something, slamming the door behind us and mumbling something nefarious under our breath. If we did we'd just be hauled back in and have to sit in a chair for a few hours until dad was through lecturing us. Or maybe we'd be sent to our room for the night without any supper. 'Father Knows Best' and the fourth commandment: 'Honor Thy Father and Mother,' were considered laws in the early part of the century. Famous threatening words were "Just wait until your father gets home." Parents were respected in those days, but now I think a lot of kids have lost respect for their parents because they've failed to give them guidelines or set boundaries. – Frank Hanford, hospital worker, born 1938, San Jose, CA.

Children collecting scrap metal for the war effort in 1943

My family and I moved out to the country about twenty years ago to get away from the crime, traffic and stress of St. Louis. Last year we decided to take a trip back to the little town where I grew up, and one of the first things I wanted to do was visit the old Catholic church I had worshipped in as a little girl, and frequently trembled inside the confessional. On a sunny afternoon I drove over to the church and was stunned when I found the doors were locked! Churches weren't supposed to have locked doors; they were safe havens, sanctuaries where one could go and commune with their God at any time of the day. It's a symbol of our perilous times I guess; after all, even in the country we now lock our door when we go out or go to bed. In fact, we even have a peephole on the front door so we can see who's there. When I was a child, we opened our door to everyone who knocked, but now I never open the door when I'm home alone. Life, sadly, has become far too dangerous, and there's nowhere to get away from it. – Emily Crilly, quiltmaker, born 1940.

On a more hopeful note, in 1999 the Justice Department reported a continuing decline in violent crime. The Bureau of Justice Statistics said the national rate for robbery, rape, assault and other crimes fell by an overall 12.4 percent between 1994 and 1995. Juvenile felony arrests dropped seventeen percent from 1993 to 1999.

When I was 14 years old I was very introverted and loved to read. On Sundays I would take a book with me and go to a ravine I'd discovered in back of Casa Loma in Toronto. I enjoyed strolling by myself down the path through the woods, just listening to the chirping of the birds, and watching the sunlight stream through the trees, and maybe see a little chipmunk or squirrel run by. When I got to the little wooden bridge that crossed over the stream, I'd sit on the edge and let my feet dangle into the cool water, while I read my book. It was so peaceful there, I always felt close to the creative power of the universe, and it was really an inspiration. Sometimes people would stroll by, but it was very rare because this ravine was rather isolated. If a man came by walking alone, we would usually just exchange a greeting, and he would be on his way. No one ever bothered me there. Today the idea of an adolescent girl walking alone in the woods is preposterous; the sad fact is there's a good chance she wouldn't make it out alive. — Marta D'Angelo, writer, born 1936.

Will Work for Food

The gap between the poor and the wealthy continues to widen, and the head-spinning array of endless consumer goods is offset by the sight of homeless people begging in the streets, sometimes quite aggressively. Homelessness has become a hallmark and a plague of the last few decades, with hundreds of dirty, disheveled men in the inner cities wandering around aimlessly, or slumped on the sidewalk, begging for a handout. Shopping carts are commandeered from grocery stores and filled with junk collected while meandering the streets. Sometimes two or three of them are strung together, clattering noisily as they are dragged down the street, then often abandoned, cluttering our neighborhoods. Forgotten by someone who can no longer remember where he left it, or why he collected it. Many of these men (and an occasional woman) are psychotic, drug addicts and alcoholics. Before the sixties, when psychotropic drugs became available, these mentally-ill people would be given a bed and three meals a day in an institution, instead of shouting and flailing on the street in response to inner voices.

I used to love to drive into San Francisco with my girlfriends and go to the opera, but I never go there at night anymore. The parking lot where I used to leave my car was hit several times by crooks breaking into the cars, and a few cars were even stolen, so that's not safe. The last time we were there, when we were walking down Market street we were accosted three different times by homeless drunks who rudely and aggressively demanded money from us. One of them followed us down the street for a whole block cursing at us. It just isn't worth the hassle. – Maureen Banson, age 51, educator, Alameda, CA.

There are many reasons for the increase in homelessness; some of it was caused by the closing of our large mental institutions and putting people into half-way houses who were unwilling or unable to take their anti-psychotic medication; some of it was because the inflation of the late seventies made low-cost living, (such as a fifty-cent-a-night flop-house, or a seventy-dollar-a week apartment,) no longer possible. Some is simply due to the stress of living, with which certain individuals are unable to cope, and a very small part of it is due to another phenomena of the latter part of the century: loss of a job which resulted in loss of health insurance, and a continuing downward spiral.

In the old days a hobo would occasionally show up at our door asking for a sandwich or a cup of coffee, always in exchange for doing some work around the place. We didn't fear these men because they were usually harmless, and they weren't aggressive, but often very polite and self-effacing. They were considered unconventional types who didn't fit into traditional society and wanted their freedom. In some ways they were even envied because they lived this carefree life, maybe riding the rails and going from place to place. It had a certain romance to it. – Sandra Lowry, homemaker, born 1929, Oakland, CA.

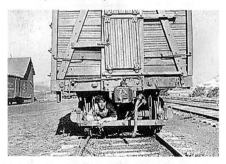

A hobo rides the rails

DISAPPEARING TRADITIONS

Going My Way?

Hitchhiking had always been a part of the American landscape until the seventies when the rise in crime made it too dangerous. During the Depression the roads were filled with people hitchhiking to other towns looking for work and, since few people had a car, they were usually given a ride. During the war years gas was rationed, and people helped each other by giving them a lift. Soldiers often hitchhiked home or back to the base, and it was considered a patriotic duty to pick them up. The hippie phenomenon of the sixties saw hundreds of colorfully clad young people, often carrying backpacks and even guitars, hitchhiking everywhere with signs reading 'Berkeley or Bust," "New York or Texas" or, for the more adventurous: "South America." Telegraph Avenue in Oakland and Berkeley was always full of college students hitching a ride to the University of California, and people readily accommodated them. Some hitchhikers were heading the call of beatnik Jack Kerouac's *On The Road*, and going out to see America instead of starting the drudgery of a full-time job. Sometimes part of the fun of a long drive was being entertained by a hippie who would tell far-out tales of his adventures as a free spirit.

Back in the '30s, I lived in the country with mom, grandma and my three siblings. We often hitchhiked to town because our car

didn't run most of the time. Eventually, mom and I hitchhiked from Ohio to Washington, D.C., and then all the way to California. When we went to D.C. we had only $1 per day, and we stayed at the YWCA for .25¢ each. We had only $37 when we went to California, and we slept on the ground with the blankets we carried with us. Once in Los Angeles, we splurged and stayed in a cabin for .75¢ a night. – Leila Williams, Zanesville, OH.

As crime on the road began to rise, many states passed laws against hitchhiking, but they were difficult to enforce. Some young people even welcomed staying overnight in jail because it gave them a free place to sleep. But, by the middle of the seventies, rapes, and even murder of hitchhikers, had escalated around the country.

Fifteen-year-old Mary Vincent's tragic ordeal began when fifty-one-year-old Lawrence Singleton picked her up on Sept. 30, 1978, hitchhiking on a California highway. She was later found in a daze with her forearms chopped off as she wandered along a highway near Modesto. After this horrifying story hit the news, few dared risk hitchhiking anymore, especially females.

During the summer of 1952 my brother hitchhiked from Toronto to Monterey, California to visit my parents for Christmas. Then he took off for San Antonio, Texas to see the Concept-Therapy Ranch. He stayed there a week and then hitchhiked all the way to Alaska, and then back home to Canada. He was only seventeen years old, and it was a wonderful experience for him because it was the only time he ever got to see the country. When he left he had only twenty-five dollars on him, and when he got home three months later he had ten dollars. People who picked him up often bought him meals and even let him stay overnight on their couch, or in the garage. He was jailed overnight in Albuquerque for hitchhiking, but other than that he had no trouble, and he found shelter and meals at places like the Salvation Army whenever someone didn't offer it to him.

Last month I had to take my car in for repairs and leave it there for five hours, so I decided to walk the mile home instead of waiting. It was extremely hot and I started to wilt and regretted my decision. So, when a woman stopped her car at a red light, I stuck my head into her open window, explained my problem, and asked her if she'd give me a ride the remaining ten blocks. She refused, rolled up her window and took off. It was in Hartford in the middle of the day, and here I was a gray-haired, middle-class white woman in a little sundress, and she was afraid to give me a lift. How the world has changed! – Marta D'Angelo, born 1936, Toronto, Canada.

An Old Icon Goes High Tech

Card catalogs in most libraries are no more. The three-by-five-inch cards, threaded on a metal rod so they wouldn't be stolen, and attached to slim, long wooden drawers stacked in endless rows, were replaced by computer databases. By 1980 the Library of Congress Catalog contained over sixty million cards, and the New York Public Library, the most heavily used catalog in the world, filed its cards in 8,973 oak drawers. Both libraries are now online so now, instead of rifling through cards in drawers, patrons can sit down in front of a computer monitor and type in their requests, either by author, title or subject, and get an instant response.

The Last of the Five-and-Dimes

In 1997 the venerable Woolworth Corporation announced that it was closing the last of its variety stores, shutting the door on a 117-year-old American tradition. More than 400 stores in the U.S. are closing, and the regulars will no longer be able to sit at the lunch counter and order a tuna sandwich with a bag of chips and a pickle, usually served with a smile by an old-time waitress. Competition from Walgreens, Target, and other discount stores finally proved too much for the grand old lady who once sold everything from aquariums to wool.

The Shade of Stately Elms is Almost Gone

In almost every American city, streets lined with majestic Elm trees, which provided shade from the summer sun as people went for a walk or sat on the front porch, gradually began dying from Dutch Elm disease, and have almost completely disappeared.

R.I.P. Montgomery Ward

Ward closed its many doors all over the nation, in December, 2002, after being in business since 1872. "This company has been my second family. I think everyone feels the same way about this," said Janet Monroe, an employee. Some of the employees at the store's closing sale worked for Montgomery Ward for more than 20 years.

Ward was originally the brainchild of a salesman named Aaron Montgomery Ward who traveled throughout rural areas passing out copies of a single sheet of paper listing 163 items that one could order through the mail. This was the original mail-order catalog. A 1946 exhibit in the Grolier Club, a New York book lovers' group, placed a Montgomery Ward's catalog alongside a Webster's dictionary in a display of what it called the 100 most influential American books.

Ward's Catalog. Christmas, 1980

During its first few decades Wards existed only as a mail-order business and was the first merchant to offer a "money-back satisfaction guarantee." The first brick-and-mortar store opened in 1926 (thirteen years after the death of its founder). For over a century it was a major retailer that competed with Sears and J.C. Penney for the average American shopper.

The popular Christmas song "Rudolph the Red-Nosed Reindeer" was originally a poem that a Montgomery Wards advertising copywriter named Robert L. May created as part of a holiday campaign. Illustrated copies of the poem were distributed to children in every Wards store while they were waiting in line to see Santa Claus. A few years later the poem was set to music and is now a favorite holiday song.

The Debit Man no Longer Visits Us

Back in the thirties you didn't get a computer-generated monthly or twice-yearly bill for your insurance policy; the debit man came to your house each week to collect payment, which often consisted of just dimes and quarters. Insurance could be paid for in fifty-two installments a year, and was personally collected each week. The insurance agents made their rounds carrying an enormous ledger book into which they noted the receipt of every penny, while the homeowner watched. Life insurance was popularized by the legwork of these dependable debit men who were welcome visitors, usually bringing news of the neighborhood, and of the country, to the housewife. They came to know their customers well and often became a friend of the family and confidant to their clients. They usually were invited for tea or coffee at every policyholder's table, which was the official meeting place for the weekly insurance transactions.

In 1936 my mother took out a policy with Metropolitan Life Insurance, which she paid off over the next thirty years. I can still picture our debit man walking the streets of my hometown of Carlstadt, New Jersey. What I recall most about the friendly gentleman was that he was always impeccably dressed in black pants, a white shirt, tie and jacket. He wore a derby hat in the winter and straw "boater" in the summer. These hats have now gone the way of spats, detachable collars and collar buttons.

The actual piece of paper on which the policy was written was huge, decorated with gilt edges and eagles, and written in Old English script. The cost for this beauty was twenty-five cents per week for thirty years. When I cashed in the policy after my mother's death, I felt a special era had finally come to a close; an era when the friendly, dependable debit man was welcomed each week into homes all across the land. – Marshall Holtz, Jr., Vero Beach, FL.

Keeping Warm Around the Backyard Fire Pit

When I think about the "good old days," one of the things I miss most is the sweet smell of leaves burning. Every Saturday during the Fall my dad and brother would gather up the leaves from the big old Oak tree in our back yard and put them in a barrel. At dusk all the kids came and stood around the fire watching the leaves burn while mom was cooking supper. There was no concern then about air pollution because we didn't have enough people, or enough cars, to create a lot of it.

Another thing I miss is getting firecrackers on the fourth of July, which was always a big holiday in my youth. Although my folks were very conservative when it came to the safety of their kids, they seemingly thought nothing of providing my brother and me with firecrackers so we could join in terrorizing the neighborhood kids by sneaking up behind them and dropping a lit one. But, they were too dangerous, and now they're gone in most places. —Mary Jackson, realtor, born 1932, Warm Springs, CA.

A Light That Still Remains

Since the last half of the twentieth century, City Lights Bookstore, standing proudly at the corner of Broadway and Columbus, next door to the famous Vesuvius Coffee House, has been at the heart of San Francisco's literary culture. Its poet founder and owner, Lawrence Ferlinghetti, now in his eighties, with a beret, white beard, and a silver stud in his earlobe, purchased the property for a million dollars in 1999 to ensure it would continue its iconoclastic tradition when he was no longer there. During the fifties, City Lights Bookstore, in the North Beach area of San Francisco, was the home of the Beatnik literati, where poet Allen Ginsberg first read his seminal poem "Howl," which was later confiscated by U.S. Customs. The bookstore was raided by federal authorities three times for selling material deemed obscene: "Howl," Lenore Kandel's erotic *The Love Book* and, in 1969, the sexually explicit "Zap Comix." Defended by the ACLU, charges were dropped in all three cases, and City Lights became internationally famous as a bastion of free speech, and the domicile of intellectual and cultural books. A sign once warned patrons: "If you get caught stealing books, the police will not be called, but you will be publicly shamed."

As a literary meeting place, it was home to the Beats: Jack Kerouac and Ginsberg, Snyder and Cassady, Kenneth Rexroth and Henri Lenoir, the bohemian who founded Vesuvios and lived upstairs. And there was Murao, the bartender next door who became the first employee and, for many years, was as closely associated with City Lights as Ferlinghetti. In later years, North Beach gave way to Italian restaurants, strip joints and porno stores, but City Lights still remains as the cutting edge of politics, poetry and the radical written word.

Going or Gone

3-D movies / 45 rpm records / 8-track tapes / all-men's clubs / "Baby on Board" signs in car windows / beatniks / Betamax VCR / Betty Furness / big bands / blue chip stamps / black and white TV sets / blue flash bulbs / bouffant hairdos / broads, which was replaced by "chicks" and, in the nineties, by "babes" / Brown Derbies / Calvin and Hobbes' comics/carbon paper / cartoons before movies / "Cheers"/ cigarettes and liquor advertised in magazines and on TV / circus side shows featuring "freaks of nature" / coffee shops that had juke boxes on the tables / corsets / crinolines / cuspidors / drugstore fountains / "Dynasty"/ the Edsel / fedoras / fire escapes / garters for men's socks / Gary Larson cartoons / Geiger counters / gray flannel suits / green stamps / hard contact lenses / hippies / home-made pies/Lincoln logs /

instant photo machines in department stores (3 for a dollar) / ladies hats with veils /"M*A*S*H" / Mass in Latin / mending socks / mimeograph machines / miniskirts / Monopoly / New Coke / newsreels in theaters / the nightly Western on TV / one-speed bikes / the nuclear family / outdoor clotheslines / Pac Man / paper dolls / paperboys on bicycles / penmanship classes / pencil-thin eyebrows / plastic flowers / reel-to-reel tape recorders / roller-skate keys / record players / shorthand / signs that said: "No Colored Allowed" / slow dancing / slide rules / Slinky / Smirfs / soda fountains / soda-pop machines that dispensed glass bottles / "Star-Trek"/ Studebakers / telephone numbers that started with a word prefix / tablecloths made of oilcloth / telegrams / Tinkertoys / vinyl records / wedding-night virgins / white gloves / Ziegfield follies / zoot suits.

Disappearing Phrases:

Don't take any wooden nickels.

Far-out man.

Fiddlesticks

He put me through the wringer

He's a hep cat

Heavens to Betsy!

Hey man, what's happening?

Holy moley!

Hubba-hubba!

I'm in like Flynn

It's the cat's pajamas

I've fallen and I can't get up!

Iron Curtain

It's a doozy

It's copacetic

It's hunky-dory

It's the cat's meow

It's your nickel

Jeepers creepers

No wife of mine is ever going to work.

Oh my stars!

She's a spinster or an old maid

She's knee-high to a grasshopper

That's groovy

There's more than Carter has liver pills

Well, I'll be a monkey's uncle

Where's the beef?

Who loves you baby?

You look like the wreck of the Hesperus.

You won't amount to a hill of beans.

Good Old Days?

Some folks talk of the "good old days"
When Grandma was a lass;
They tell us things were better then,
And they're sad to see them pass.
Well, I made jelly, canned the corn,
Spent hours at the churn;
Fed the hired hands, baked the pies,
And at weedin' took my turn.
I carried out the chamber pots,
Plucked feathers for my bed;
Scrubbed all the clothes upon a board,
Stoked fires and made the bread.
I fed the ducks and chickens,
Picked berries in the bog.
My only entertainment was
Sears Roebuck's catalog.
I made the scrapple, kraut and soap,
And all the children's togs.
Then, if I had some time to spare,
I helped at butcherin' hogs.
I raised a pack of droolin' kids,
Was doctor, farmhand, wife.
There was no respite from the chores—
It was a gruelin' life.
The children walked three miles through snow,
Before they reached the school.
I often went to bring them home
Upon our old gray mule.
I baked and scoured from morn till night.
And to make my day complete
I hopped into an icy bed
With hot bricks at my feet.
I milked our old cow twice a day
And often chopped some wood,
If these were the "good old days",
I'm glad they're gone for good!
—Author unknown

In 1932 President Herbert Hoover promised his constituents "a chicken in every pot." In 1992, at his inaugural address, President Clinton promised the voters "a computer in every classroom." These two very diverse statements depict the progress that has been made in the last century, and the last millennium. At the beginning the emphasis was on taking care of our physical needs, but at the end the focus was on advancing our intellectual objectives.

What a Century it has Been!

Kilroy Was Here

PHOTOGRAPHIC CREDITS

Cover: Family at Meal Time: CPL/Popperfoto, ©Retrofile.com
Anti-War Demonstrators: ©Steve Meltzer, p. 74
D'Angelo School of Charm, ©D'Angelo Studios, p.65
Deep Throat: AP Wide World Photos/Universal Studios, p.52
Family Listening to Radio: H. Armstrong Roberts, ©Retrofile.com, p.25
Housewife Serving Dinner: Photographer: 2002 Black Box, ©Retrofile.com, p.43
Housewife Removing Clothes from Line: H. Armstrong Roberts ©Retrofile.com, p.279
Man with Husband's Lib Sign: ©Steve Meltzer, p.41
Nude Model, ©D'Angelo Studios, p.49
Western Union Office: ©Judith A. Walters, p.257
Checking the Map: H. Armstrong Roberts, ©Retrofile.com, p.256
Woman Holding Ration Book: C.P. Cushing, ©Retrofile.com, p.33
Olive Oyl and Popeye, ©King Features Syndicate All Rights Reserved, p.238
Shmoos, ©Capp Enterprises, Inc. 2005, All Rights Reserved, p.80

Hulton Archives/Getty Images and Foodpix:
Hippy Hippy Shake: Ian Tyas, ©Ian Typas, p.73
Housewife with pie: Paula Friedland, ©Paula Friendland, p.19
Overly Friendly Boss: Lambert/Contributor, ©Lambert/Contributor, p.218

Several photographs, which were published with permission of the owners, were also published in REMINISCE Magazine, "The Magazine That Brings Back The Good Times." P.O. Box 991, Greendale, WI 53129-0991.
To subscribe call (800) 344-6913, or send an E-mail to: subscriberservices@reimanpub.com.

BIBLIOGRAPHY

Alcott, Louisa May *Little Women,* Random House, 1987

Alger, Horatio Jr. *Brave and Bold,* Penguin Group, 2000

Alger, Horatio Jr. *Do and Dare,* Penguin Group, 2000

Bailey, Arthur Scott, *Tale of Brownie Beaver,* Ross & Perry, Inc., (2002)

Berne, Eric, *Games People Play,* Ballantine Books, 1996

Bradbury, Ray *Farenheit 415,* Random House, 1953

Brown, Helen Gurley, *Sex and the Single Girl,* National Book Network

Comfort, Alex, *The Joy of Sex,* Crown Publishers, 1972

Dostoyevsky, *Crime and Punishment,* Bantam Classics, 1984

Freud, Sigmund, *An Introduction to Psychoanalysis,* Horace Liveright,
    N.Y., 1920

Freud, Sigmund, *The Future of an Illusion,* Penguin, N.Y., 1927

Freud, Sigmund, *The Interpretation of Dreams,* Penguin, N.Y., 1900

Friedan, Betty, The Feminine Mystique, W.W. Norton, 2001

Hite, Shere, *The Hite Report,* Seven Stories Press, 1976

Hope, Laura Lee , *The Bobbsey Twins,* Grosset & Dunlap, 1989

Jung, Carl, *The Theory of Psychoanalysis,* Modern Library, 1993

Kandel, Lenore, *The Love Book,* Superstition Street Press, 2004

Kerouac, Jack, *On the Road,* Penguin Books, 1991

Kinsey, Alfred, *The Kinsey Reports,* 1948 and 1953

Lawrence, *D.H., Lady Chatterley's Lover,* Grove Press, 1928

Losyk, Bob, *Managing a Changing Work Force,* Workplace
    Trends Pub. 1996

Masters & Johnson, *Human Sexual Response* Little, Brown, N.Y. 1966

McMahon, Ed, *For Laughing Out Loud,* McMahon Communications

Miller, Henry, *Tropic of Cancer,* Grove Press, 1961

Mitford, Jessica, *The American Way of Death,* Vintage Press, 2000

Moody, Dr. Raymond, *Life After Life,* HarperCollins Books, 2001

Post, Emily, *Etiquette.* Funk & Wagnells, N.Y., 1922

Ramsey, John, *The Death of Innocence,* Thomas Nelson Pubs., 2000

Sanger, Margaret, *Family Limitation,* M.H. Sanger, 1914

Silverstein, Charles, et al. *Joy of Gay Sex,* HarperCollins, 2003

Skinner, B.F., *Beyond Freedom and Dignity,* Hackett Pub. Co., 1971

Sophocles' *Oedipus Rex,* Harcourt, Inc., 1949